Abstracts of the
TESTAMENTARY PROCEEDINGS
of the
PREROGATIVE COURT OF MARYLAND

Volume IV: 1677–1682, 1702–1704

Libers: 9A (372–524), 9B, 10, 11, 12A, 12B

by
V. L. Skinner, Jr.

CLEARFIELD

Printed for
Clearfield Company, Inc. by
Genealogical Publishing Co., Inc.
Baltimore, Maryland
2006

International Standard Book Number: 0-8063-5299-X

Made in the United States of America

INTRODUCTION

Purpose of the Prerogative Court.

The Prerogative Court was the central point for probate for Provincial Maryland. It was mirrored after the Prerogative Court of Canterbury. There was a judge as well as clerk(s) of the court. Initially, all probate was brought directly to the Prerogative Court, located in the Provincial Capital. As the Province became more populous, all documents were still to be filed with the Prerogative Court; however, administration of probate was delegated to the various county courts. Even so, there are documents only in the Prerogative Court and not in the appropriate county, and vice versa.

Documents filed in the Prerogative Court.

The following documents were filed in the Prerogative Court: administration bond, will, inventory, administration accounts, and final balances. The testamentary proceedings contain the administration bond and the docket for the court. If the administrator is lax in filing documents, then a summons is also recorded.

Equity Court

The Prerogative Court was also the court for equity cases--resolution of disputes over the settlement and distribution of an estate. The case was brought before the judge and could take several years to resolve. Often depositions were taken and recorded in the minutes.

Notes on the Abstraction.

1. The left hand column contains the liber/folio number. The folio numbers are presented just as they appear in the actual document, e.g., 32a, 78½.

2. The right hand column contains the abstraction text.

3. Various libers specify a particular session for the Prerogative Court, e.g., 1678; or, September Court 1742. This information is presented as "Court Session:" followed by the

appropriate session. Should no session have been specified, then the phrase "no date" is used.

4. An ellipsis (...) is used to indicate a continuation of the previous information, but no relevant genealogical information is present.

5. The following symbols are used in the abstraction:
  ? difficult to read.
  # pounds of tobacco.
  ! [sic].

Abbreviations.

The following abbreviations have been used throughout this abstraction:

AA - Anne Arundel Co.
ACC - Accomac Co.
BA - Baltimore Co.
CE - Cecil Co.
CH - Charles Co.
CR - Caroline Co.
CV - Calvert Co.
dbn - de bonis non
DE - Delaware
DO - Dorchester Co.
ENG - England
FR - Frederick Co.
g - gentleman
HA - Harford Co.
IRE - Ireland
KE - Kent Co. MD
KEDE - Kent Co. DE
LaC - letters ad
  colligendum (for
  temporary
  collection &
  preservation of
  assets)

LoA - letters of
  administration
MA - Massachusetts
MD - Maryland
MO - Montgomery Co.
NE - New England
NY - New York
NYC - New York City
p - planter
PA - Pennsylvania
PG - Prince George's
  Co.
PoA - power of
  attorney
QA - Queen Anne's Co.
SM - St. Mary's Co.
SMC - St. Mary's City
SO - Somerset Co.
TA - Talbot Co.
VA - Virginia
WA - Washington Co.
WO - Worcester Co.

This is a continuation of the series, covering 1677 to 1682. It also includes some inventories and accounts from 1702 to 1704.

9A:372   19 October. Rachaell Stimson (AA)
relict & executrix of Neale Clarke (AA)
exhibited accounts. Col. William
Burges to take oath, since she lies
visited with great sickness.

Elisabeth Jones (CV) relict & executrix
of William Crosse (CV) exhibited his
will. Maj. Henry Jowles to prove said
will. Said Jones was granted
administration.

9A:373   Appraisers: Ninian Beale, James Moore.
Said Jowles to administer oath.

Sarah Clarke (CV) widow & executrix of
Thomas Clarke (CV) exhibited that she
desired William Travers (g, CV) to take
her oath of her accounts, because she is
unable to travel to the Office due to
indisposedness of body. Said Travers is
now lying under great sickness & is
bereft of his senses.

9A:374   Said Clarke took the oath & exhibited
accounts.

Sarah Godson (CH) relict & executrix of
Henry Barnes (CH) exhibited inventory.

Richard Beard, Jr. (AA) sole remaining
executor of Daniell Taylor (AA)
exhibited accounts.

Rebecca Adison relict & executrix of
Thomas Dent (SM)

9A:375   was granted continuance, until her
husband John Addison returns.

20 October. Col. William Ball (BA,
late of VA) administrator of his son
Richard Ball (BA) exhibited inventory of
Robert Wilson (BA) taken by said Richard
Ball. Also exhibited were accounts
proved on 28 November 1676.

William Hatton (g, SM) executor of
Richard Hatton (SM) exhibited accounts.

9A:376   Joseph Weekes (g, KE) exhibited will of
Disborough Bennet (g, KE), proved.

Joseph Weekes (g, KE) exhibited will of
Stephen Whetstone (KE), proved.

Joseph Weekes (g, KE) exhibited:
- Isaac Winchester & Thomas Osborne
  appraisers of estate of Disborough
  Bennet (KE) were sworn on 6 August
  1677.

9A:377 ...
- Mary Blangey widow of Disborough
  Bennet was sworn same day.
- Valentine Southerne & Walter Kerby
  appraisers of estate of Thomas
  Baxter (KE) were sworn 3 July 1676.
- Thomas Osborne & Isaac Winchester
  appraisers of estate of Edward
  Coppedge (KE) were sworn on 6 April
  1676.
- John Winchester appraiser of estate
  of Arthur Ginne (KI) was sworn on 1
  July 1676.

It was exhibited that Richard Ball (BA)
had:
- sworn James Phillips (BA)
  administrator of James Cogill on 14
  March 1676.
- bond on said estate with securities:
  Thomas Long, said Ball.
- sworn Elisabeth Dorman as executrix.

9A:378 Said Cogill refused to execute said
will, since the debts exceed the
credits. Date: 28 February 1676. Said
will was declared void. James Phillips
(BA) administrator of James Cogill (BA)
exhibited inventory.

9A:379 The bond (taken by Richard Ball (g, BA,
dec'd)) of Cornelius Howard (AA)
administrator of John Grange (BA) was
exhibited. Sureties: Charles Steevens,
John Foster. Cornelius Howard exhibited
inventory.

Jackelina Harris (CV) relict & executrix
of James Moore exhibited accounts.

22 October. Sarah Bishop (TA) relict &
executrix of Benjamin Hancock (TA)
exhibited accounts.

9A:380 Henry Exon (CV) executor of nuncupative
will of Thomas Cosford (CV) exhibited
accounts.

Henry Exon (CV) administrator of Thomas
Arnold (CV) exhibited accounts.

Robert Fisher (CV) administrator of his
brother Henry Fisher (CV) exhibited
inventory & accounts.

Joseph Weekes & John Hinson (KE)
executors of John Rodoway (TA) exhibited
inventory
9A:381 & accounts.

On 20 October instant, Jackelina Harris
(CV) relict & executrix of James Moore
(CV) was granted discharge.

Mary Goffe wife of Stephen Goffe
administratrix of Lt. Col. John Jarboe
is unable to travel to the Office,
having been long sick, & was granted
continuance.

Richard Edelin (g, SM) executor of
Samuell Cressey (CH) administrator of
Daniell Russell (SM) as principle
creditor & administrator of John Waas
(SM) was summoned to render accounts on
said estates.
9A:382 Said Edelin was dismissed from
administration.

James Rumzey (CV) executor of Henry
Trulocke (CV) exhibited his will. Maj.
Henry Jowles to prove said will. Said
Rumsey was granted administration.
9A:383 Appraisers: John Witham, Thomas Aldwell.
Said Jowles to administer oath.

On 22 October instant, Hannah Martin
(TA) widow of Robert Martin (TA)
exhibited that she was granted
administration, but declined to take the
oath as it is contrary to principles of
her Religion. She also exhibited that
the orphans have received their
respective portions. She is now
summoned to account for the estate & to
swear to its accuracy, which she cannot.

Judge excused said Hannah.

9A:384 24 October. Joseph Weekes & John Hinson (KE) executors of John Rodaway (TA) were granted discharge.

Cornelius Comagies (KE) on behalf of self & Henry Hosier & John Bowles executors of Walter Spencer (KE) exhibited accounts. Discharge was granted.

The Commissioners of CV exhibited accounts of Mary Taylor widow of Jasper Allen (CV).

9A:385 Maj. Henry Jowles (CV) exhibited will of Thomas Barbery (CV), proved. Susanna Barbery widow was sworn on 15 October instant. Appraisers Daniell Goldstone & Samuell Goozey sworn same day.

Robert Taylor (CV) administrator of Conniers Barbier (CV) exhibited accounts.

Simon Wootton (CV) who married Susanna relict & administratrix of Richard Wadsworth (CV)
9A:386 exhibited accounts.

Samuell Vines (CV) executor of Cornelius Jones (CV) exhibited accounts.

25 October. John Browning (CE) administrator of Capt. John Gilbert (CE) exhibited accounts.

George Parker (Cliffts, CV) administrator of Lownes Eason (CV)
9A:387 exhibited accounts.

Capt. Samuell Bourne (CV) administrator of Leavin Johnson (CV) exhibited accounts.

William Kent (CV) administrator of Richard Williams (CV) exhibited accounts.

Capt. John Cobreath (CV) administrator of Richard Evans (CV) exhibited accounts.

9A:388 William Russell (AA) administrator of
Thomas Chandler (AA) exhibited accounts.

William Peerce (CE) administrator of
George Wilson (CE) exhibited accounts.

26 October. Thomas Hawker (CE) executor
of John Powell (CE) exhibited accounts.

9A:389 James Wheeler (CH) who married Elisabeth
relict & executrix of Thomas Corker (CH)
administrator of Clement Theobald (CH)
exhibited inventory & accounts of said
Theobald.

Charles Harrington (CV) who married Mary
relict & executrix of James Stockley
(CV) exhibited inventory & accounts.

27 October. Margaret Gittings (CV)
widow & executrix of John Gittings (CV)
exhibited accounts.

9A:390 Richard Fenwick (CV) administrator of
his brother Cuthbert Fenwick (CV)
exhibited accounts. Discharge was
granted.

Henry Hooper (g, DO) exhibited bond of
Richard Meakings administrator of George
Bacon (DO) & inventory.

9A:391 Susanna Barbery (CV) widow & executrix
of Thomas Barbery (CV) exhibited
inventory.

Capt. John Coode (SM) administrator of
Thomas Ceely (g, SM) exhibited accounts.
Executor is now in ENG.

On 25 October instant, William Parker
(Hunting Creek, CV) administrator of
Thomas Preston (CV) exhibited that he
cannot show further accounts. Estate
was dismissed.

Hannah Johnson (KE)
9A:392 widow of Jacob Johnson was granted
administration on his estate.
Appraisers: William Bateman, Thomas

Boone. Henry Hosier (g) to administer oath.

Mary Kenniday (KE) widow of James Kenniday (KE) was granted administration on his estate.

9A:393 Appraisers: William Bateman, Thomas Boone. Henry Hosier (g) to administer oath.

On 26 October instant, John Howell (CE) son & one of executors of Thomas Howell (CE) exhibited accounts, drawn by Capt. Jonathon Sibrey who married the relict. Said John & his brother

9A:394 Nathaniell (other executor) are under 21. Said Sibrey was summoned to exhibited accounts & to deliver 2/3rds of estate to the 2 orphans. Relict of said Thomas is now dec'd. Said John is also executor of John Vanheck (CE) & accounts for him have been kept by said Sibrey.

9A:395 Anne Cole (SM) relict & administratrix of John Medley (SM) was granted continuance. Said Anne as administratrix of John Medley executor of his brother George Medley (SM) was also granted continuance.

29 October. Sarah Evans (CV) widow of Guy White (CV) was granted continuance, because she is now in childbed & newly delivered.

Joane Jones (DO) widow of William Jones (DO) was granted administration on his estate.

9A:396 Sureties: John Offley (g), Andrew Insley. Appraisers: James Maudgley, Richard Tubbman. Henry Hooper (g) to administer oath.

30 October. William Bateman (KE) exhibited that William Stanley (KE) died intestate & Mary the widow was granted administration, with sureties said Bateman & Stephen Whetstone. Said Mary is since dec'd, & said Whetstone is also dec'd. Said Stanley left 2 orphans whose portion their mother committed to

9A:397 said Bateman & Whetstone shortly after she married Christopher Andrews who is also dec'd (after said Mary). Said Christopher made a will. Said Bateman was granted administration on estate of said Stanley, on behalf of the orphans. Appraisers: Thomas Boone, Robert Neeves. Samuell Tovy (g) to administer oath.

9A:398 ultimate October. Mary Haley (SM) relict & administratrix of Edward Connery (SM) exhibited accounts.

Thomas Foulkes (DO) for his wife Sarah Foulkes widow of Thomas Fisher (DO) was granted administration. Appraisers: John Turner, Henry Steevens. Henry Trippe (g) to administer oath.

9A:399 Katharine Lewis (SM) widow of John Lewis (SM) was granted administration on his estate. Security: Henry Carew. Appraisers: Walter Hall (g), Leonard Greene.

Mary Spry (SM) relict & administratrix of John Hales (SM) exhibited that Robert Large one of her sureties has whole management of the estate & refused to render accounts.

9A:400 Said Mary was granted continuance.

William Elmes for his wife Jane Elmes (CE) relict & executrix of John Crouche (CE) exhibited that said Jane is afflicted with great sickness. Edward Inglish to audit her account & to take oath.

9A:401 1 November. James Frizby (g, CE) for Richard Woollman (g, TA) exhibited his commission to take depositions of Joseph Billitrey (TA) & James Doude (TA), regarding the will of Thomas Reade (TA). Said Woollman examined both, but they refused to take the oath. They said William Mountague (neighbor, TA) could testify better. William Coursey (g, TA) to take deposition of said Mountague.

3 November. Elisabeth Royall (SM)
executrix of Francis Barnell (SM)
exhibited accounts.

9A:402 Thomas Griffin (SM) administrator of
Peter Eure (SM) exhibited inventory.

Joseph Hopkins (g, CE) exhibited:
- Will of William Tison (KE), proved.
- John White executor of said Tison
  was sworn 4 August 1677.
- Isaac Harness & Ebenezar Blackistone
  appraisers of said Tison sworn same
  day.
- John Dixon & Robert Neeves
  appraisers of William Hewet (CE)
  sworn 20 April 1677.

9A:403 ...
- John Dixon & Isaac Harness
  appraisers of Roger Thorpe (CE)
  sworn 20 April 1677.

Hester Ennis (alias Hester Sprigg, CV)
widow & administratrix of William Ennis
(CV) exhibited inventory.

8 November. Roger Brooke (g, CV)
executor of Philip Harwood (CV)
exhibited accounts. Discharge was
granted.

On 6 November, Joseph Hopkins (g, CE)
exhibited will of Edward Skydmore (AA),
proved.

9A:404 Henry Howard (AA) exhibited his
renunciation of executorship, for self &
William Bateman (KE) overseers of said
Edward Skydmore (CE). Date: 20 October
1677. Witnesses: John Swiny, Robert
Davis. Alice Skydmore widow was granted
administration. Capt. Richard Hill (g)
to take bond.

9A:405 Appraisers (CE): Ebenezar Blackiston,
Isaac Harness. Edward Inglish (g) to
administer oath. Appraisers (AA): Henry
Lewis, John Ricks. Said Hill to
administer oath.

Hester Ennis (CV) widow & administratrix
of William Ennis (CV) was granted
continuance.

Andrew Jones (SO) surviving executor of his uncle James Jones (SO) exhibited that said James made a will, constituting the widow (Andrew's aunt) & said Andrew as executors.

9A:406 Said widow is since dec'd. William Steevens (g) to prove said will. Said Andrew was granted administration. Appraisers: James Dushile, Roger Woollford. Said Steevens to administer oath.

12 November. John Halfehead (CV) exhibited that Nicholas Clemens (CV) was a lodger or sojourner in his house & made a nuncupative will in presence of Joseph Edloe & Jasper Howley,

9A:407 who deposed in court. Said Halfehead was granted administration. Appraisers: said Edloe, said Howley.

Joseph Edloe (CV) executor of William Kaine (SM) exhibited accounts. Discharge was granted.

9A:408 Kenelme Chezeldyne (Attorney General, SM) executor of John Jones (one of attorneys of Provincial Court, SM) exhibited his will, proved before Thomas Notley (Deputy Lt. Governor). Said Chezeldyne was granted administration. Appraisers: Henry Phippes, Robert Graham. William Hatton (g, executor's neighbor) to administer oath.

9A:409 Elisabeth Dash (SM) relict & executrix of John Mackart (SM) exhibited accounts.

14 November. Francis Hopewell (CV) administrator of his brother-in-law John Booth (SM) exhibited accounts.

Sarah Clawe (SM) widow & executrix of William Clawe (St. Jerome's, SM)

9A:410 executor of John Reynolds (St. Jerome's, SM) exhibited accounts for estate of said Reynolds.

15 November. Rebecca Davies (SM) relict & administratrix of John Beale (SM) exhibited accounts. Discharge was granted.

Court Session: 1677

Thomas Jeff (AA) exhibited petition
stating that his father Thomas Jeff (AA)
died 2 years ago & left petitioner with
2 young siblings (brother & sister), one
about 6, the other about 8

9A:411 & that Capt. Hill took them & other
chattel away & bound them out.
Petitioner (being 21) requests LoA.
Said Jeff was granted administration.
Appraisers: Henry Ridgely, William
Mitchell. Dr. Henry Lewis (g) to
administer oath.

The widow Thomas (TA) relict of John
Woolcot (KE) exhibited

9A:412 his will, specifying shares of his land
to the orphans. The personal estate is
inconsiderable. Capt. Philemon Lloyd
to prove said will.

The widow Webb (TA) widow of Richard
Webb (TA) exhibited his will. Said
widow will not swear to execute said
will, that his estate consists chiefly
in land & little personal estate. To
preserve the orphans' share of the real
estate,

9A:413 Capt. Philemon Lloyd (g) to prove said
will.

20 November. William Steevens (g,
Pocomoke River, SO) exhibited will of
James Jones, proved.

22 November. Elisabeth Dash (SM) relict
& executrix of John Mackart (SM)

9A:414 was granted discharge.

24 November. William Bateman (ke)
administrator of William Stanley (KE)
unadministered by his relict Mary
Andrews (KE) exhibited that Christopher
Andrews (latter husband of said Mary,
KE) made a will & is now dec'd. Said
Christopher constituted said Mary as
executrix, but will was never proved.
Samuell Tovy (g) to prove said will, for
benefit of orphans of said Stanley,
Andrews' legatees, & preservation of
small estate said Christopher their
father left them. Said Bateman was
granted administration.

9A:415 Appraisers: Richard Lowder, Thomas Boone. Said Tovy to administer oath.

On 9 October, Katharine Browne (KE) relict & executrix of Arthur Wright (KE) sent his will by Miles Miller (one of witnesses). Said Michaell Miller proved the will.

9A:416 3 December. Margaret Ambrose (CH) sent, via Thomas Notley, Esq. (now Governor), notice regarding the death of her husband Richard Ambrose (merchant, late of Carolina). John Wheeler (of Carolina) deposed that Richard Ambrose (formerly of CH) died on 11 October past in Carolina. Date: 29 November 1677.

9A:417 Said Margaret was granted administration on his estate. Appraisers: John Newton, William Jenkins. Maj. Benjamin Rozer (CH) to administer oath.

Col. William Burgesse (AA) exhibited will of Thomas Roper (AA), proved. Mary Roper executrix was granted administration.

9A:418 Mary Roper widow & executrix exhibited inventory.

Mary Blangey (KE) relict & executrix of Disborough Bennet (g, KE) exhibited inventory.

4 December. John White (CE) exhibited will of William Tyson (KE). Said White is sole executor & was granted administration.

Andrew Jones (SO) exhibited that his uncle James Jones made a will

9A:419 & constituted his wife Sarah Jones sole executrix. Said Sarah died 14 days after her husband. Said Andrew was granted administration on both estates, & exhibited inventories.

9A:420 Lewis Blangey (KE) who married Mary widow & executrix of Disborough Bennet (g, KE) exhibited that said Mary cannot travel as far as the Office to account for estate of Tobias Wells (KE), whose estate was administered by said Bennet.

Court Session: 1677

William Lawrence (g) to take oath.

Capt. Edmund Cantwell (DE) petitioned to exhibit accounts of Daniell Mackary (CE) before Commissioners of CE.

9A:421   Mary Nicholson (SO) widow of James Nicholson (SO) exhibited inventory. Said Mary was granted administration on 2 June last.

Thomas Walker (SO) administrator of William Morgan (SO) exhibited inventory & accounts.

5 December. Anne Jones (Cliffts, CV) widow & administratrix of Merridith Jones (CV) exhibited accounts.

Thomas Allanson (CH) executor of Edward Roberts (CH) exhibited inventory.

9A:422   Thomas Alcox & Edward Rookewood (CH) executors of David Towell (CH) exhibited inventory.

6 December. Edward Man (g, TA) exhibited that Mary Roe widow & administratrix of Edward Roe administrator of Robert Hale (TA) never received any goods. Date: 30 November last.

Nathan Smith (AA) administrator of Thomas Howard (AA) exhibited inventory.

9A:423   William Meare (AA) administrator of Francis Hill exhibited inventory.

Katharine Revell (SO) exhibited the verbal will of Sarah Jones (SO), devising all or a major portion of her estate to said Katharine. William Steevens (g, Pocomoke) to prove said will.

7 December. Garret Vansweringen (alderman of SMC, SM)
9A:424   was granted administration on estate of Mr. John Deery, who died with no relations in Province, as principle creditor.

Court Session: 1677

9A:425 Capt. John Allen (CH) was granted administration on estate of Christopher Dobson (merchant, SM) as greatest creditor. Surety: George Godfrey.

9A:426 John Erickson for his mother Elisabeth Erickson (KE) widow & administratrix of John Erickson (KE) exhibited that said Elisabeth is ancient, sickly, & not in capacity to travel to Office this winter. Said John exhibited accounts. William Lawrence (g) to take oath of said Elisabeth.

Capt. Jonathon Sibrey (high sheriff, CE) was granted continuance in order to produce accounts of estate of Capt. Thomas Howell (CE) & of John Vanheck (CE) per John & Nathaniell Howell (CE) executors of their father & said Vanheck.

9A:427 Thomas Gilbert (DO) exhibited that William Worgin (inn holder, DO) made a verbal will in the presence of John Taylor (DO), Grace Taylor (DO), and Phillip Sutton (DO), constituting said Gilbert as executor. Administration had been granted to John Brooke (g, DO). Sheriff (DO) to summon witnesses.

9A:428 Michael Rochford (merchant, SM) was granted administration on estate of Patrick Lewis (SM), who died single, unmarried, & childless & having no relations in the Province nearer than said Rochford, as principle creditor. Administration was granted to Stephen Murty (inn holder, SM) & said Murty was chief creditor to said Patrick as administrator of John Balley (merchant). Said Rochford to summon said Murty.

9A:429 John Edmundson for widow Earle (TA) widow of Thomas Earle (TA) exhibited his will, but constituted no one as executor. Said widow was granted administration. Capt. George Cooley to administer oath.

Court Session: 1677

Michaell Rochford (merchant, SM)
exhibited the summons to Stephen Murty
(SM), regarding estate of Patrick Lewis
(SM).

9A:430 8 December. Col. Baker Brooke, Esq.
(CV) exhibited will of Thomas Sherridine
(CV), proved.

Col. Baker Brooke, Esq. (CV) exhibited
will of John Sewall (CV), proved.

Dr. John Stanesby (BA) who married Mary
daughter & executrix of Johanna Spry
exhibited accounts.

9A:431 Dr. John Stanesby (BA) executor of
Caesar Prince (BA) exhibited accounts.

Dr. Henry Lewis (g, AA) exhibited oath
of appraisers of estate of Thomas Jones
(AA): Robert Tiler & William Jones sworn
18 October last. John Gray (AA)
executor of Thomas Jones (AA) exhibited
inventory.

9A:432 Capt. Richard Hill (AA) exhibited
accounts of Susanna Gwinne executrix &
widow of William Neale (AA). Date: 21
October 1677.

John Waterton (g, BA) exhibited accounts
of James Philips & William Hollis
9A:433 (BA) administrators of Thomas Wingfield
(BA).

Dr. Henry Lewis (AA) petitioned for
discharge on estate of Nathaniell &
Thomas Stinchcombe, as he was
administrator of Thomas Turner (AA)
executor of said Thomazin Stinchcombe
widow & executrix of said Nathaniell
Stinchcombe, & discharge on estate of
said Thomas Turner. He also petitioned
for discharge from executor of estate of
William Slade (AA); his fellow executor
John Ricks is lately dec'd, & the
petitioned is seized with great
sickness. Said Lewis petitioned that
Commissioners of AA take his security
for the estate due the respective
orphans. Said Lewis never

9A:434 "intermeddled" with Slade's estate because said Ricks married one of Slade's orphans. Upon receipt of discharge of Paul Dorrell on estate of Thomas Turner, said Lewis will be granted discharge.

9A:435 11 December. Katharine Lewis (West St. Mary's, SM) widow & administratrix of John Lewis (SM) exhibited inventory.

Jane Bread (CH) relict & executrix of Dr. Thomas Matthews (CH) was granted discharge.

Mary Ware relict & administratrix of Thomas Pope (CH) vs. Philip Lynes (CH).
9A:436 Said Lynes appeared, but said Mary was absent. Continuance.

Garret Vansweringen (alderman of SMC, SM) exhibited his security on estate of John Deery:
9A:437 John Barnes & Daniell Clocker. William Aisquith (g) to take said bond. Said Vansweringen was granted administration, & said Aisquith to administer oath.
9A:438 Date: 11 December 1677.

12 December.
9A:439 Appraisers (estate of said Deery): John Blomfield, Thomas Innes. John Barnes or Richard Chillman to administer oath.

15 December. John Barnes (SMC, SM) & Richard Chillman (SMC, SM) exhibited oath of said appraisers sworn on 12 December last.

9A:440 Zachary Wade (g, CH) exhibited will of David Towell (SM), proved. Thomas Alcock & Edward Rookewood executors sworn on 22 November. Appraisers Roger Dickenson & John Munn sworn same day.

Zachary Wade (g, CH) exhibited will of Edward Roberts
9A:441 (CH), proved. Thomas Allison executor sworn on 22 November. Appraisers Thomas Alcock & William Boyden sworn same day.

John Halfehead (CV) administrator of Nicholas Clemens (CV) exhibited inventory.

9A:442 18 December. Capt. Thomas Claget (CV) was granted administration on estate of Thomas Oliver (CV), who died single, unmarried, childless, & without kin. His estate is inconsiderable. Appraisers: William Hill, John Loveday. William Travers (g) to administer oath.

9A:443 22 December. James Rumzey (CV) who married Anne relict & executrix of John Bigger (CV) exhibited accounts.

29 December. John Doxey (St. Innago's Hundred, SM) administrator of Richard Chapman (SM) exhibited accounts.

2 January. John Deermot procurator for Martha O'Kaine (SM) widow of Rickart O'Kaine (SM) was granted administration on his estate. Appraisers: Samuell Mattocks, Thomas Jourdain. Capt. John Coode to administer oath.

9A:444 9 January. Elisabeth Royall (SM) executrix of Francis Barnwell (SM) was granted discharge.

9A:445 11 January. Jane widow of John Halfehead (Bay Side, SM) exhibited that her husband died as a result of being struck by a falling tree. Said Jane was granted administration. Security: Nicholas Guyther William Guyther (St. Jerome's). Appraisers: Nicholas Guyther, Thomas Courtney. Gerit Vansweringen (alderman of SMC) to administer oath.

12 January. Thomas Griffin (St. Jerome's, SM) administrator of Peter Eure (SM)
9A:446 was granted discharge.

21 January. Henry Bradle executor of Thomas Sewell (DO) exhibited his will, written by John Yates. Yates' testimony was accepted without his oath, since an oath is contrary to his principle of

Religion. Bartholomew Ennalls (DO) had
taken the oath of Mary Drake (other
witness). Said Bradle was granted
administration. Appraisers: Michaell
Basey, James Peeterkin. Said Ennalls to
administer oath.

9A:447 Bartholomew Ennalls (g, DO) was granted
administration on estate of John
Holyfield (DO), who died a bachelor, no
relations visible in the Province, as
principle creditor. Said estate is
inconsiderable. Appraisers: Daniell
Jones, John Kirke. Henry Bradle to
administer oath.

22 January. Capt. John Cobreth (CV) &
John Hunt (CV) exhibited that Thomas
Paget (CV)

9A:448 made a will, constituting his wife
Elisabeth as executrix & said Cobreath &
hunt as guardians. Said Elisabeth is
since dec'd. Said Cobreath & Hunt were
granted administration, on behalf of
orphans. Capt. Samuell Bourne or
Robert Heighe to take bond. Appraisers:
Marke Clare, William Kent. Said Heighe
to administer oath.

9A:449 Sheriff (CE) to summon Edward English
(CE) to show cause by administration of
estate of Roger Thorpe (merchant, CE)
should not be revoked & granted to
George Parker attorney of Ralph Forth
(leather seller, London) as principle
creditor.

25 January. Justinian Gerard (g, SM)
was granted administration on estate of
Stephen Gupton (SM), who died a widower
& left one

9A:450 child William Gupton (under age), on
behalf of said orphan. Capt. Gerard
Slye to take bond.

9A:451 26 January. Morgan Jones (St. Jerome's,
SM) administrator of John Harrington
(SM) & of John Davies (SM), exhibited
the receipt of Owen Guyther for
Elisabeth Davies his wife's portion paid
said Morgan (who married relict of said
John) out of estate of her father

Davies. Witnesses: William Guyther,
John Martingall. Discharge was granted
on estate of John Harrington & of John
Davies.

9A:452 28 January. Morgan Jones exhibited
accounts of George Charlesworth.
Discharge was granted.

4 February. Henry Taylor who married
Katharine relict of George Bartlet (St.
George's Hundred, SM) exhibited that
said Katharine has been sick for a long
time. Said Katharine was granted
administration on 17 December 1675.
Said Henry married her within 6 months
after the decease of said George, &
there have been no demands or creditors.
Discharge was granted.

9A:453 Further, there are no children's
portions to pay.

William Dare (merchant, CE)
administrator of John Parker petitioned
that John Parker delivered to Thomas
Carleton (Attorney of Provincial Court,
dec'd) 2 bills to keep for said Parker:
John Richardson (Choptank), John
Nuthall. Said Parker died, & then said
Carleton. Arthur Carleton is
administrator of his brother's estate, &
he took possession of said bills &
refuses to deliver them.

9A:454 Said Carleton is ordered to deliver the
bills to said Dare.

Robert Ridgely on behalf of widow &
executrix of Thomas Sunderbee (mariner,
Bristoll)

9A:455 petitioned for search for will,
inventory, & accounts. None existed as
given by Harris administrator in right
of widow & executrix of said Sunderbee.

5 February. Elinor Hammond relict &
administratrix of Abraham Newman
exhibited inventory & accounts. Said
Hammond is infirm.

9A:456 6 February. Thomas Wynne (SM) on behalf
of heirs of Edward Roberts (CH)
petitioned that said Edward made a will

& LoA were already granted, & said
Thomas desires LoA to be sent to heirs
of said Edward in ENG.

7 February. Thomas Gilbert (DO) vs.
John Brooke (chirurgeon, DO)
administrator of William Worgin. Case
dismissed, & said Gilbert to pay court
costs.

9A:457   8 February. Thomas Bland procurator for
Lancellot Todd (AA) exhibited that said
Lancellot's brother John Todd is dec'd,
childless. Said Lancellot was granted
administration. However, he is weak &
unable to travel so far as the Office.
Richard Hill (g, AA) to take bond.
Appraisers: Andrew Norwood, Thomas
Bland. Said Hill to administer oath.

9A:458   Robert Cole who married Anne relict &
administratrix of John Medley (Newtowne,
SM) was granted continuance, as the
weather was so extremely hard that she
was not able to appear before the
Office.

9 February. Kenelme Mackloughlin (CH)
exhibited the will of his
daughter-in-law Elisabeth Lindsey (CH).
One witness has died (since the death of
the dec'd) & the other has removed to
VA. Edeth Woodward can prove the will,
although she is not a witness & is
sickly & unable to travel so far as the
Office. Henry Adams (g, CH) to prove
the will.

9A:459   Said Kenelme is to endeavor to procure
the oath of the surviving witness in VA.

John Wood (CH) administrator of Philip
Browne (CH) exhibited accounts.
Discharge was granted.

12 February. Maj. Henry Jowles (g, CV)
exhibited will of William Crosse (CV),
proved.

9A:460   Elisabeth Jones executrix of her husband
said Crosse & appraisers Ninian Beale &
James Moore were sworn on 29 December
last. Said Jones exhibited inventory.

9A:461 Maj. Samuell Lane (AA) exhibited oath of Nathan Smith (AA) administrator of estate of Thomas Howard (AA) & oath of appraisers Thomas Morgan & Henry Bennet, all sworn on 22 September last.

Maj. Samuell Lane (AA) exhibited oath of William Meares (AA) administrator of Francis Hill (AA) & of appraisers George Lingan & Richard Bedworth, all sworn on 14 October last.

9A:462 Capt. Samuell Bourne (CV) exhibited oath of appraisers of estate of Thomas Morris (CV): Joseph Baker & William Williams, sworn on 26 September last. Martha Dauzey (CV) relict & administratrix of Thomas Morris exhibited inventory.

13 February. Henry Trippe (g, DO) exhibited oath of Sarah Foulkes (DO) relict & administratrix of Thomas Fisher (DO). Thomas Foulkes her new husband tendered no security for her administration. John Stephens (one of the appraisers) would not take the oath.

9A:463 Capt. Richard Hill (AA) exhibited the bond & oath of Lancellot Todd (AA) administrator of George Langley (AA) unadministered by Richard Fetherstone (fugitive) on 15 December last. Sureties: Cornelius Howard, Samuell Howard. Appraisers said Samuell & Abraham Child were sworn same day. Said Todd exhibited inventory.

9A:464 Capt. Richard Hill (AA) exhibited bond of John North & his wife Elisabeth North administratrix of Thomas Toyson (AA). Sureties: Samuell Howard, Jacob Lusbye. Said Elisabeth was sworn on 15 October last. Appraisers Jacob Harness & Jacob Lusbye were sworn same day. Said Elisabeth exhibited inventory.

9A:465 Capt. Gerard Slye (high sheriff, SM) exhibited oath of Justinian Gerard (SM) administrator of Stephen Gupton (SM).

Maj. Benjamin Rozer (CH) exhibited oath of Margaret Ambrose (CH) administratrix of her husband Richard Ambrose (Carolina), sworn on 1st instant. Sureties: John Cassocke, Robert Worrell. Appraisers John Newton & Richard Jenkinson

9A:466 were sworn on 3 December last.

William Steevens (g, Pocomoke, SO) exhibited bond of Andrew Jones (SO) administrator of his uncle James Jones (SO) & administrator of his aunt Sarah Jones (SO). Sureties: Thomas Walker, David Browne.

William Steevens (g, Pocomoke Mannor, SO) exhibited will of Nicholas Rice (SO) on behalf of executors Richard Crocket & John Evans.

9A:467 Said Steevens to prove will by witnesses Thomas Daniell & Thomas Wilson. Said Crocket & Evans were granted administration. Appraisers: David Browne, James Dushile. Said Steevens to administer oath.

Mary Rickes (AA) widow & executrix of John Rickes (AA) exhibited his will. Capt. Richard Hill (g, AA) to prove said will. Said Mary was granted administration. Appraisers: William Jones, John Peasly.

9A:468 Said Hill to administer oath.

Susanna Harness (AA) widow & executrix of William Harness (AA) exhibited his will. Capt. Richard Hill (AA) to prove, by witnesses Nathaniell Heathcote & John Welsh.

9A:469 Said Susanna was granted administration. Appraisers: Nicholas Gassaway, James Saunders. Said Hill to administer oath.

Johanna King (CH) widow & executrix of Thomas King (CH) exhibited his will. Maj. Benjamin Rozer (CH) to prove said will. Said Johanna is unable to travel this winter season as far as the Office.

9A:470 Said Johanna was granted administration. Appraisers: John Wheeler, Robert Robins. Said Rozer to administer oath.

Love Daniell (Pointe-looke-out, SM) widow & executrix of Constantine Daniell (Pointe-looke-out, SM) exhibited his will, proved by Robert Mason & Jacob Lookerman.

9A:471 Said Love was granted administration. Appraisers: Constant Keefe, Thomas Potter. Col. William Calvert (Provincial Secretary) to administer oath.

14 February. Col. Vincent Lowe (high sheriff, TA) exhibited oaths of Richard Collins & his wife Sarah Collins

9A:472 (late Sarah Hambleton) relict & executrix of William Hambleton (TA). Mentions: said Lowe & Capt. Philemon Lloyd were named overseers, younger sons of the dec'd. Appraisers: John Newman, Hugh Sherwood.

Col. Vincent Lowe (high sheriff, TA) exhibited will of James Oliver (TA), proved.

9A:473 Col. Vincent Lowe (high sheriff, TA) exhibited oath of appraisers of estate of James Oliver (TA): Hugh Sherwood & Edward Elliot.

Col. Vincent Lowe (high sheriff, TA) exhibited will of Thomas Campher (TA), proved. Anne Campher executrix was granted administration.

Col. Vincent Lowe (high sheriff, TA) exhibited will of William Godwin (TA), in favor of the orphans.

9A:474 Capt. Samuell Bourne & Robert Heighe (gentlemen, CV) exhibited bond of Capt. John Cobreath (CV) & John Hunt (CV) administrators of Thomas Paget (CV); his executrix is also dec'd. Appraisers Marke Clare & William Kent were sworn 6 February last.

9A:475 Said Paget's inventory was exhibited.

Mary Manning (CH) relict & executrix of John Blackfan (CH) exhibited inventory.

Inventory of William Jones (DO) was exhibited.

9A:476 Philip Lynes procurator for Elisabeth Beck (CH) widow of Richard Beck was granted administration on his estate. Appraisers: Charles Hey, Robert Castleton. Maj. Benjamin Rozer to administer oath.

Thomas Snell (merchant, TA, late of Boston NE) was granted administration on estate of John Cornish (merchant, TA), who died a bachelor soon after his arrival, with no relations in the Province
9A:477 but a brother in Boston, for the benefit of said brother Richard Cornish. Sureties: George Robins, John Edmundson.
9A:478 Appraisers: Thomas Alexander, John Stanley. Edward Man (g) to administer oath.

Elisabeth Beck (CH) administratrix of her husband Richard Beck (CH) administrator of his brother Lewis Beck (CH) was granted discharge on said Lewis' estate.

9A:479 Mary Warde (TA) widow & executrix of Matthew Warde (g, TA) was granted continuance.

Maj. Henry Jowles (CV) exhibited will of Henry Truelock (CV), proved. Appraisers John Witham & Thomas Aldwell were sworn 9th instant.
9A:480 James Rumzey (g, CV) executor of Henry Truelock exhibited inventory.

Henry Hosier (g, KE) exhibited that John David (one of appraisers of estate of William Davies (KE)) is dec'd. Cornelius Comagies is administrator. New appraisers: William Deane, Robert Neeves.

9A:481 Hensier Hosier (g) exhibited that his neighbor widow Finch (KE) desired that William Deane be appointed to appraise her husband's estate. The other appraiser Samuell Tovy is hindered by sickness & lameness. Maj. James Ringgold to administer oath.

Court Session: 1677

15 February. George Cowley (g, TA)
exhibited will of Robert Woolverton
(TA), proved. Capt. George Cowley (TA)
exhibited
9A:482 oath of appraisers: Robert Nappe &
Clement Sayles. Nathaniell Teagle (TA)
executor of Robert Woolverton (TA)
exhibited inventory.

William Coursey (g, TA) exhibited
nuncupative will of Thomas Reade (TA),
taken by deposition of William
Mountague.

Capt. John Coode (SM) exhibited
9A:483 oath of widow O'Kaine as administratrix
of Rickart O'Kaine, sworn on 10
February. Appraisers Samuell Maddox &
Thomas Jourdain were sworn same day.

Lt. Col. Thomas Taylor & Col. William
Burgesse (AA) sureties for Edward
Inglish (merchant, CE) administrator of
John Allen (merchant, CE) petitioned for
said Inglish to be summoned
9A:484 to render accounts on said Allen's
estate.

Sarah Illingsworth (TA) executrix of
Robert Turner (TA) exhibited his will.
Capt. George Cowley to prove, by the
witnesses Roger Nettleship & WIlliam
Kirkum.

9A:485 Sarah Foulkes (DO) wife of Thomas
Foulkes (DO) is the relict of Thomas
Fisher (DO). Her bond was given to
Henry Trippe (g). Said Sarah & Thomas
have been hindered by sickness to find
security & John Steevens (one of the
appraisers) would not swear.
Appraisers: John Brooke, Henry Turner.

9A:486 Garret Vansweringen (SMC) vs. Edward
Dermot (SM). Concerns estate of John
Deery (inn holder, SM). Capt. Gerard
Slye (high sheriff, SM) exhibited that
he found Edward Deermott at Court at SM.

9A:487 16 February. Capt. Thomas Claget (CV)
administrator of Thomas Oliver (CV)
exhibited inventory & accounts.

Court Session: 1677

Inventory of Alexander Magruder (CV) was
exhibited by his executrix.

Col. Vincent Lowe (high sheriff, TA)
petitioned for administration on estate
of William Cannons (merchant, TA), who
died with no relations in the Province
but a wife in ENG,
9A:488 on behalf of said widow. Appraisers:
Thomas Alexander, John Stanley. Edward
Man (g) to administer oath. Since said
Lowe would not post a bond,
administration was denied.

9A:489 Col Vincent Lowe procurator for Anne
Godwin (TA) widow of William Godwin (TA)
exhibited his will, constituting said
Anne as sole executrix. She is unable
to travel this winter as far as the
Office. Said Lowe to prove said will.
Said Anne was granted administration.
Appraisers: James Murphey, John Heaver.
Said Lowe to administer oath.

9A:490 Col. Vincent Lowe procurator for
Alexander Larrimore (TA) exhibited the
will of Nicholas Lorkie (TA),
constituting his wife Mary as sole
executrix. Said will was proved & said
Mary was granted administration for
herself & the orphans (under age). Said
Mary is since dec'd.
9A:491 Said Larrimore was granted
administration, on behalf of the
orphans. Appraisers: Richard Gold,
Ralph Nickson Said Lowe to administer
oath.

18 February. William Lawrence (g, KE)
exhibited oath of Elisabeth Erickson,
sworn on 16 January 1677,
9A:492 on estate of her husband John Erickson
(KE). Said Elisabeth exhibited
accounts.

Henry Coursey (TA) exhibited proof of
will of Matthew Warde (g, TA) & oath of
Mary widow & executrix & oath of
appraisers Thomas Hinson & Richard
Jones, all sworn on 27 October last.

9A:493 Sarah Browne (KE) widow of Edward Browne
(KE) was granted administration on his
estate. Appraisers: Thomas Evans, John
Winchester. Maj. Joseph Wickes to
administer oath.

9A:494 Joanna Mason (KE) widow of Richard Mason
(who died about 2 months ago) exhibited
PoA to William Harris (Chester River,
KE) for administration on his estate, as
greatest creditor.

9A:495 Date: 22 November 1677. Witnesses:
Henry Hosier, Sr., Henry Hosier, Jr.
Said Harris was granted administration,
on behalf of the widow. Appraisers:
Henry Hosier, Jr., Michaell Miller.
Henry Hosier, Sr. to administer oath.

9A:496 Samuell Tovy (g, KE) was granted
administration on estate of William
Norman (chirurgeon, KE), who died a
bachelor at the house of said Tovy, no
relations in the Province, as principle
creditor. His estate is inconsiderable.
Appraisers: William Bateman, Thomas
Boone. Maj. James Ringgold to
administer oath.

9A:497 Michaell Miller procurator for Samuell
Tovy (g, KE) was granted administration
on estate of John Wright (KE), who died
a bachelor at said Tovy's house, no
relations in the Province, as principle
creditor. Appraisers: William Bateman,
Thomas Boone. Maj. James Ringgold to
administer oath.

9A:498 Anne Hood (KE) widow of Robert Hood (KE)
exhibited his will. Maj. James
Ringgold to prove said will. Said Anne
executrix was granted administration.
Appraisers: William Bateman, Thomas
Boone. Said Ringgold to administer
oath.

9A:499 Maj. James Ringgold (KE) exhibited
accounts of Mary Moore (KE) relict of
Stephen Whetstone (KE), & her oath.
Date: 16 November last. Discharge was
granted.

19 February. George Parker procurator for Dr. Henry Lewis (AA) sole surviving executor of William Slade (AA) exhibited that the Commissioners of AA Court neglected to take security of widow Ricks (AA) for the portions of the rest of the orphans of her father Slade in her possession.

9A:500 She is the widow of John Ricks (other executor) & has now remarried James Orrurke.

9A:501 Margaret Ambrose (CH) widow & administratrix of Richard Ambrose (Carolina) exhibited inventory.

21 February. Francis Spencer (CV) & his wife Mary relict & executrix of John Anderson (CV) exhibited accounts.

9A:502 ...

9A:503 22 February. Jane Ebden (BA) widow of William Ebden (BA) was granted administration on his estate. Appraisers: Richard Simon, Thomas Richardson. John Waterton (g) to administer oath.

Miles Gibson (g, BA) administrator of Abraham Clarke (BA)

9A:504 unadministered by Sarah (widow, since dec'd) exhibited accounts.

23 February. Robert Morris for his now wife Katharine Morris (CE) relict & administratrix of Peter Johnson (CE) exhibited inventory & accounts. Discharge was granted.

William Watts (SM) administrator of Thomas Cager (SM)

9A:505 was granted discharge.

Thomas Gerard (g, SM) administrator of his uncle Marmaduke Snow (SM) exhibited receipts from: Thomas Lomax & Joshua Doyne, Thomas Notley, Esq., Matthew Paine,

9A:506 Dr. John Peerce. Discharge was granted.

26 February. George Parker (g, CV) vs. Edward Inglish (merchant, CE) administrator of Roger Thorpe. Sheriff (CE) to summon said Inglish

9A:507 to show cause why administration should not be revoked & granted to said Parker as attorney for Ralph Forth (merchant, London).

28 February. John Coventon (SO) was granted administration on estate of his brother-in-law David Williams (SO) & his wife Jane. Said Jane is sister of the whole blood to said Coventon. No relations for either, other than said Coventon. Appraisers: Levin Denard, Edward Gibbs. Capt. Thomas Walker (high sheriff, SO) to administer oath.

9A:508 Michaell Miller procurator for widow Hood (KE) administrator of Robert Hood (KE) exhibited that William Bateman (one of appraisers) has taken lame of his limbs. New appraisers: William Harris, Thomas Boone. Maj. James Ringgold to administer oath.

9A:509 Joane Davies (KE) widow of John Davies (KE) was granted administration on his estate. Appraisers: William Harris, Thomas Boone. Cornelius Comagies to administer oath.

9A:510 **1 March.** Henry Adams (g, CH) exhibited will of Elisabeth Lindsey (CH), proved by Edeth Woodward. Kenelme Mackloughlin (CH) exhibited certificate from Andrew Gilson (Stafford Co. VA), citing deposition of Richard Right. Mentions: John Helmes (other witness).

9A:511 Said Mackloughlin was granted administration on estate of his daughter-in-law.

6 March. John Cousins (Patuxent River, CV) administrator of John Ramzey, Sr. (CV) exhibited accounts.

9A:512 Michaell Miller procurator for Peternella Oldfield (CE) relict & executrix of Capt. John Carr (CE) exhibited accounts. Augustine Herrman to audit & take oath.

9 March. William Westbury (BA) who
married Margaret eldest daughter &
heiress of Thomas O'Daniell (BA)
petitioned that:

9A:513 her father died about 9 years ago,
leaving a widow & 3 daughters. The
widow soon married James Denton who took
goods & chattel, but never administered
the estate. Said Enton has defrauded
the petitioner & her sisters. Also,
John Lee (BA, countryman of dec'd) has
chattel of the petitioner.

9A:514 The petitioner lived with said Denton as
a servant. Said Margaret was granted
administration on estate of her father,

9A:515 on behalf of herself & rest of orphans.
Appraisers: Thomas Richardson, Arthur
Taylor. John Waterton (g) to administer
oath. Sheriff (BA) to summon said
Denton to release chattel.

9A:516 Thomas Richardson procurator for John
Owen (BA) was granted administration on
estate of Richard Winley (BA), who died
a widower, with no relation in the
Province except one son John Winley
(under age 9), as principle creditor, on
behalf of said orphan. Appraisers:
Richard Simm, John Bird. John Waterton
(g) to administer oath.

9A:517 Robert Cole (SM) who married Anne relict
& administratrix of John Medley (SM)
exhibited accounts.

11 March. Emanuell Ratcliffe (St.
George's Hundred, SM) exhibited that
Thomas Black (age 4, SM) is dec'd, &
said Emanuell's wife Anne is widow of
William Black (dec'd, father of said
Thomas), & said Anne is still living.
Since his marriage with said Anne &
before said Thomas' death, John Mackye
(SM, countryman of said William) gave
chattel to said Thomas.

9A:518 Said Emanuell exhibited that there is no
child of said William younger than said
Thomas, & therefore no heir, unless
"chattel" can ascend to his mother.
Said Emanuell was granted administration

on estate of said Thomas.

13 March. John Coventon (SO) exhibited
that Levin Denard & Edward Gibbs
(appraisers of estate of David & Jane
Williams) would not take oath. New
appraisers: Cornelius Johnson, Henry
Hayman.

9A:519 Anne Assetter (SM) widow &
administratrix of William Assetter (SM)
was granted continuance.

Jane Maddox (SM, Jane Elliott is written
above this entry) relict &
administratrix of John Halfehead (SM)
exhibited inventory.

17 March. No letters of discharge can
be granted to Anne Assetter relict &
administratrix of William Assetter (SM)
until

9A:520 his son & heir exhibits libel against
the inventory.

18 March. Joane Waughop (SM) widow &
executrix of John Waughop (SM) exhibited
his will, proved by John Watson &
William Brewerton. Said Joane was
granted administration.

9A:521 20 March. Susannah Ainsworth (SM) widow
& executrix of George Ainsworth (SM)
exhibited his will, proved by Francis
Miles & Robert Ellys. Said Susannah was
granted administration. Appraisers:
said Miles, said Ellys.

22 March. John Waterton (g, BA)
exhibited will of Margaret Therrill
(BA), proved,

9A:522 proved by Robert Benjar on 3 January
1677. Appraisers John Arden & John
Boaring were sworn on 18 February 1677.

John Waterton exhibited accounts of
Katharine Benjar (BA)

9A:523 widow of John Chadwell.

Capt. Philemon Lloyd (TA) exhibited
will of John Woolcott (TA, former
resident of KE), proved.

Court Session: 1677

9A:524

Capt. Philemon Lloyd (TA) exhibited will of Richard Webb (TA), proved by John Wootters & William Hill. Said witnesses would not take oath, as is contrary to their principle in Religion. Judge ruled that the will is null & void, until the orphans can cause the will to be proved. Lands will descend to use of the firstborn & younger sons must consequently suffer.

Court Session: 1702-1704

9B:1 Inventory of Mr. Samuell White (AA). Servants mentioned: John Mounford, Daniell (boy), William Roberts.
9B:2 <does not exist>
9B:3 ...
9B:4 List of debts: Mr. Charles Ridgely, John Gartherill (?), Jos. Hawkins, Richard Garrett, Mr. John Gresham. Amount: £175.12.6. Date: 30 January 1703. Appraisers: Thomas Reynolds, Amos Pierpoint.

9B:5 Inventory of Ann Lambert.
9B:6 Amount: £104.13.0. Appraisers: John Edwards, Charles Tylly.

9B:7 Inventory of William Welch, Sr. (p, TA). Amount: £82.10.1. Date: 23 February 1703. Appraisers: John Alexander, Richard Holmes.

9B:8 Inventory of Daniel Beale (SM).
9B:9 Amount: £109.6.8. Appraisers: William Watts, Peter Watts.

9B:10 Inventory of Mr. Robert Rousby.
9B:11 ...
Amount: £26.16.4. Date: 2 December 1703. Appraisers: Geo. Muschamp, Adam Bell.

9B:12 Inventory of Christopher Horrell.
9B:13 ...
Amount: £116.7.7. Appraisers: Thomas Davis, William Hogden.

Inventory of John Lewis (TA). Date: 20 November 1703. Kin: Thomas Lewis.

Page 31

9B:14 List of debts: Thomas Lewis, Hugh Paxton, Mr. Robert Smith. Amount: £68.10.2.

9B:15 Appraisers: Richard Jones, Jr., Richard Hynson.

Inventory of William Balford (TA). Amount: £27.4.4.

9B:16 Date: 29 July 1703. Appraisers: John Lyon, John Abbot.

Inventory of David Steward (AA).

9B:17 Amount: £78.2.0. Date: 26 November 1703. Appraisers: Edward Carter, Stephen Warman.

9B:18 Accounts of William Neale (TA) by his widow & administratrix Elisabeth Neale. Amount of inventory: £12.7.0. Payments to: John Carr, Charles Whale, Thomas Sockwell for Capt. Blackiston, Mr. Vincent Hemsley. Amount of payments: £19.10.1.

9B:19 Accounts of Lawrence Tattersell (SM) by his executor James Tant. Amount of inventory: £38.0.0. Received from: Henry Taylor. Payments to: Mr. Gylick. Amount of payments: #1420. Date: 13 March 1703/4.

Accounts of (N) Harning (SM) by his executrix Ann Sykes. Amount of inventory: £18.9.0. Payments to: Ann Foster, Edward Hill, Geo. Rigg,

9B:20 William Watts, Rebecca White, James Keech, Mr. Brooke, Mr. Jos. Hall. Amount of payments: £23.19.6. Date: 10 December 1703.

Accounts of William Chamberlain (CE) by his administratrix Mary Chamberlain. Amount of inventory: #5650. Payments to: Thomas Robinson, Matthew Vheyden, John Carvil, James Frisby, John Jaward, Richard Mercury. Amount of accounts: #8174. Date: 17 November 1703.

9B:21 Accounts of John Atthey (CE) by his executrix Mary wife of Jonathon Beck. Amount of inventory: £112.0.10. Payments to: Benjamin Brams, Michael

Earle, Edward Smally, John Hynson, Samuel Manning. Amount of accounts: #10434. Date: 3 February 1703/4.

Inventory of Dennis Connor (AA). Date: 16 May 1704. Amount: £7.7.1. Appraisers: Amos Pierpoint, David Tooll.

9B:22   Inventory of John Benstead. Date: 22 April 1702. Amount: £20.4.0. Appraisers: William Carr, Silvester Abbatt.

Court Session: 1678

10:1   27 March. Edward Inglish (merchant, CE) administrator of Roger Thorpe (merchant, CE) exhibited LoA from Majoralty of London attested by Sir Francis Chaplin (Lord Mayor, alderman or senator) relating to an invoice of goods consigned by said Thorpe to John Blackfan (merchant, CH) by Thomas Wells & Co. (merchants, London) & PoA from said Wells attested by Josiah Jones (Tabellion Publick). Letter from said Chaplin:

10:2   Thomas Welles (age 25, merchant, London) appeared. Mentions: Golden Lyon Leonard Webber master, goods consigned by said Thorpe to said Blackfan.

10:3   Date: 16 November 1677. Invoice dated: 23 November 1675.

10:4-5   ...

10:6   Assignment to Mr. Ed. Inglish. PoA.

10:7   ...

10:8   Signed: Tho. Welles. Witnesses: John Liddiard, Porten Paul. Notary: Josi. Jones.

28 March. Capt. Jonathon Sibrey (high sheriff, CE) exhibited summons to Edward Inglish (merchant, CE) to show cause to George Parker attorney of Ralph Forth who administration of estate of Roger Thorpe should not be revoked & granted to said Parker (CV) for use of said Forth (leather seller, London) as principle creditor.

10:9   Edward Inglish (merchant, CE) administrator of Roger Thorpe (CE) is to show cause to George Parker (g, Cliffts, CV) attorney of Ralph Forth (leather seller, London) administrator of said Thorpe in ENG, why administration should not be revoked.

10:10   Said Inglish was granted continuance.

Susannah Ainsworth (SM) widow & executrix of George Ainsworth (SM) exhibited inventory.

10:11   George Parker procurator for Dr. Henry Lewis (AA) sole surviving executor of William Slade (AA) exhibited that the Commissioners of AA would not take the security of James Orrurcke who married Mary widow of John Ricks & executrix of her father William Slade for rest of orphans' (her siblings') portions. Commission ordered to take said security.

10:12   Alice Skydmore (AA) widow & administratrix of Edward Skydmore (AA) exhibited a letter of Capt. Richard Hill (dated 9 March last) that one of the appraisers John Ricks is dec'd & that the other appraiser Dr. Henry Lewis is very sick. New appraisers: Ralph Hawkins, William Hawkins. Capt. Richard Hill to administer oath.

Capt. Richard Hill (AA) exhibited that Lancellot Todd (AA) was sworn on 27 February last

10:13   as administrator of his brother John Todd (AA). Appraisers Thomas Bland & Andrew Norwood were sworn on 20 February last. Inventory of said John Todd was exhibited.

30 March. John Wynns (chyrurgeon, St. George's Hundred, SM) executor of John Ribton (Cumberland, ENG) was granted continuance.

10:14   Thomas Todd (Mop. Jacke Bay, VA) executor of his father Capt. Thomas Todd (BA, died in London ENG) exhibited inventory. Also exhibited was LoA from Rt. Rev. Gilbert Archbishop of Canterbury.

10:15   [Paragraph in Latin]
10:16   ...
10:17   Signed: Marcus Cottle.

10:18   3 April. Daniell Clarke (g, DO)
         executor of Edward Sauvage (DO)
         exhibited his will, proved by Jasper
         Howley & Robert Ellys. Appraisers:
         Thomas Newton, William Thomas. Stephen
         Gary (g) to administer oath.

10:19   8 April. John Heard (SM) executor of
         Jeffery Hudson (SM) exhibited his will &
         letter from Nicholas Geulick (clerk).
10:20   Said will was made before said Hudson
         went to Eastern Shore marche. Said
         Heard was granted administration.
         Appraisers: Matthew Cartwright, Thomas
         Basset. John Jourdain (g) to administer
         oath.

10:21   Elisabeth Ricard (KE) sole executrix of
         her son Christopher Hall exhibited his
         will & letter from Lt. Col. Thomas
         Taillor (AA) dated 30 March last. Said
         Taylor to prove said will.

10:22   9 April. James Smallwood (CH)
         administrator of his brother John Evans
         (CH) exhibited inventory.

         Richard Boughton (clerke, AA) exhibited
         letter dated 13 March last on behalf of
         Commissioners of AA, regarding letter
         directed to take security for remainder
         of estates of (N) Slade & (N)
         Stinchcombe.
10:23   Commissioners stated that it was
         improper for them to take security
         without special commission.

         Bartholomew Ennalls (g, DO)
         administrator of John Hallyfield (DO)
10:24   exhibited inventory.

         Thomas Notley, Esq. (Governor)
         administrator of Morgan Taylor (CH)
         exhibited that in 1675, he had proved
         his account. Mentions: creditors in
         ENG, bill of exchange of Sir Robert
         Yeoman (knight, baronet, Bristoll) in
         favor of Hon. Charles Calvert (then

10:25   Governor).
    ...

10:26   9 April. Michaell Tawney (g, CV)
    deposed that Jeremiah Williams (CV) made
    a will. Said Williams constituted his
    landlord Robert Taylor (CV) as executor.
10:27   Summons to said Taylor.

    10 April. Col. George Wells (BA)
    executor of James Ogdon (AA) exhibited
    accounts. Discharge was granted.

    Henry Henley (CH) administrator of
    Richard Harris (CH) exhibited accounts.

10:28   11 April. Col. George Wells (BA) on
    behalf of self & his mother Johanna
    Goldsmith joint executors of Maj.
    Samuell Goldsmith (her husband & his
    step-father) exhibited accounts.
    Discharge was granted.

    James Phillips (BA) administrator of
    James Cogill (BA) exhibited accounts.
    Discharge was granted.

10:29   12 April. James Denton (BA), in suit of
    William Westbury now administrator of
    Thomas O'Daniell unadministered by said
    James, exhibited inventory & accounts.
    Discharge to be granted to said Denton
    when said Westbury received the portion
    due his wife Margaret (eldest daughter &
    heiress of dec'd).

10:30   Michaell Miller (g) procurator for Anne
    Lowder (KE) exhibited that her husband
    Edward Lowder (KE) was "most
    barbariously murdered" & died intestate.
    Said Anne was granted administration on
    his estate. Appraisers: Philip Connor,
    John Winchester. William Lawrence (g)
    to administer oath.

10:31   Michaell Miller (g) procurator for
    Hannah Gibson (KE) exhibited will of
    John White (KE), constituting said
    Hannah as sole executrix. Witnesses are
    unable to travel as far as the Office.
    Samuell Tovy (g) to prove said will.

Thomas Marsh (high sheriff, KE) sole surviving executor of Ralph Williams (g, AA) exhibited an additional accounts.

10:32 13 April. Col. Baker Brooke (member of Council, CV) exhibited oath of Elisabeth Orson (CV) relict & executrix of Thomas Sherridine (CV), sworn on 23 March last.

John Saunders (CH) was granted administration on estate of his near kinsman Francis Keene (CH), who died a bachelor & brother- or sisterless & without other relation within the Province except said Saunders. Appraisers: Richard Chandler, William Chandler. John Stone (g) to administer oath.

10:33 James Phillips (BA) administrator of James Cogill (BA) was granted administration on estate of Shelton Berry (BA), who died a bachelor & no relations in the Province, as principle creditor. Said Berry left an inconsiderable estate.

10:34 William Rawlls (KE) who married executrix of estate of her father Edward Coppedge (KE) was granted continuance.

George Parker (g, Cliffts, CV) exhibited that William Done
10:35 (CV) died intestate & the widow refuses to administer the estate, fearing that the estate is insolvent. Said Parker was granted administration, as principle creditor, on behalf of the widow. Appraisers: William Parker, John Hance (Cliffts). Capt. Samuell Bourne to administer oath.

10:36 Robert Benjar (BA) executor of estate of his wife's mother Margaret Therrell (BA) exhibited inventory.

Joseph Hopkins (g, CE) exhibited will of William Huddle (CE), proved.

Joseph Hopkins (g, CE) exhibited oath of Edward Gunnell (BA) administrator of Joseph Seeres (CE), sworn on 19 October

last. Appraisers John James, & John
Gibbs
10:37   were sworn same day. Sureties: George
Oldfield, John Gibbs. Edward Gunnell
(merchant, BA) administrator of Joseph
Seeres (merchant, CE) exhibited
inventory.

Joseph Hopkins (g, CE) exhibited oath of
Mary Deale (CE) administratrix of her
husband Thomas Deale (CE), sworn on 2
December last. Appraisers William
Salsbury & Nicholas Shawe were sworn on
9 January.
10:38   Said Mary exhibited inventory.

Mary Warde (TA) relict & executrix of
Matthew Warde (g, TA) exhibited
inventory.

Love Daniell (Point Lookout, SM) widow &
executrix of Constantine Daniell (SM)
exhibited inventory.

Richard Whitton (CE) exhibited letter &
bill from Richard Leake
10:39   (CE, dec'd) to John Harris & William
Dunkerton. Said Whitton has had a long
sickness.

Maj. Thomas Long (high sheriff, BA)
exhibited the commission of 26 April
1677 to swear John Willmot executor of
estate of John Melem.
10:40   Said John Wilmott refused to take said
oath. Date: 11 August 1677. William
Dennit (witness), William Gaine
(witness), & Rowland Thornborough
(clerk) proved the will. Date: 2
January 1677.

Maj. Thomas Long (high sheriff, BA)
exhibited
10:41   oath of John Boring (BA) administrator
of Roger Sidwell (BA) unadministered by
relict of said Roger & late wife of said
John, sworn on 23 October last.
Sureties: John Arden, John Leakings.
Appraisers John Arden & John Leakings
were sworn on 9 October. John Boaring
(BA) exhibited inventory.

15 April. Richard & Sarah Collins (TA)
joint administrators of her husband
William Hambleton

10:42 (TA) exhibited inventory.

Philip Lynes (g) for Jane Lee (CH) widow
& administratrix of James Lee (CH)
exhibited accounts. Said administratrix
is inform. Discharge was granted.

Phillip Lynes (g, CH) exhibited LoA in
ENG granted to Anne Greene sister &
administratrix of Luke Greene (trader,
CH), who died "in parts beyond the seas"

10:43 & PoA to William Nicholas (mariner,
Bristol), proved before Thomas Notley,
Esq. (now Governor) & PoA from said
Nicholas to said Lynes. [Paragraph in
Latin]

10:44 Signed: Marcus Cottle. Date: October
1676, per William Meredith, William
Jenning, Tho. Dawe.

10:45 PoA of said Anne Greene (spinster) &
sister to Luke Greene (p, Nanjemy,
Potomack River, CH, dec'd) to William
Nicholas (mariner, Bristol).

10:46 Date: 13 October 1676. Witnesses:
William Andrewes, William Meredith, Tho.
Dawe, Jos. Hiscox.

10:47 William Andrewes & Joseph Hiscox brought
PoA to William Nicholas. Date: 9 April
1677. Signed: Thomas Notley. PoA from
William Nicklus to Philip Lynes.

10:48 ...
10:49 Date: 9 April 1677. Witnesses: John
Kewellyn, Jon. Hamillton, John Manley,
Richard Gardner. John Cable (CH) had
exhibited inventory.

10:50 Said Phillip Lynes was granted
administration on estate of Luke Greene
unadministered by John Cable. Col.
John Douglas to take bond.

16 April. Commissioners of CE exhibited
accounts of Capt. Edmund Cantwell (DE)
administrator of Daniell Mackary (CE).

10:51 Date: 14 March 1677.

Cornelius Comagies (g, KE) exhibited
bond of Joane Davies (KE) administratrix
of her husband John Davies (KE), with
sureties: self, William Harris.

10:52   Said Comagies exhibited inventory on behalf of widow.

Henry Harris (DO) administrator of Denis O'Bryan (DO) exhibited inventory. He also exhibited that Anne O'Bryan widow conveyed away sundry goods, which are un-inventoried.

10:53   Sheriff (DO) to summon said Anne to render accounts of said goods.

17 April. Samuell Tovy (g, KE) exhibited bond of William Bateman (KE) administrator of William Stanley (KE), with sureties: John Trewe, Thomas Boone. Said Tovy exhibited inventory on behalf of administrator.

10:54   Samuell Tovy (g, KE) exhibited will of Christopher Andrews (KE), proved. Said Tovy exhibited bond of William Bateman (KE) administrator of said Andrews, with sureties: John Trewe, Thomas Boone. Said Tovy exhibited inventory.

10:55   Henry Hosier (g, KE) exhibited bond of Hannah Johnson (KE) administratrix of her husband Jacob Johnson (KE), with sureties: William Harris, Richard Lowder. Said Hosier exhibited inventory on behalf of administratrix.

Henry Hosier (g, KE) exhibited bond of Cornelius Comagies & Edward Frye for Mary Kenniday administratrix of her husband James Kenniday (KE).

10:56   Said Hosier exhibited inventory on behalf of administratrix.

19 April. Margery Good (CV) was granted administration on estate of her husband Edward Good (CV). Appraisers: George Blinkhorne, Robert Ceely. Richard Ladd (g) to administer oath.

10:57   Robert Solomon for Capt. Gerrard Slye (high sheriff, SM) sole executor of William Watts (SM) exhibited his will, proved by Abraham Price. (Other witness is absent.)

10:58   Said Slye was granted administration. Appraisers: Nehemiah Blackistone, Thomas

Lomax. Capt. John Coode to administer oath.

10:59   23 April. Executors of Isaac Abrahams (TA) exhibited supplemental inventory.

Edward English (merchant, CE), by letter from Mr. Henry Stocket (AA), exhibited that Edward Chicken (KE) died intestate, a bachelor & without relations visible in the Province. Said Inglish was granted administration, as principle creditor. Joseph Hopkins (g, CE) to administer oath.

10:60   24 April. Charles Hutchins procurator for Anne Cuffyn (DO) exhibited that her husband David Cuffyn (DO) made a will. Bartholomew Ennalls or Henry Bradle (gentlemen) to prove will, by witnesses: said Hutchins, Thomas Daniell.

10:61   27 April. Col. William Burgess (AA) exhibited accounts of Rachaell Stimson (DO) relict & executrix of Neale Clarke (DO). Discharge was granted.

         29 April. Will of John Gill (taillor, SM) was exhibited,
10:62   on behalf of his brother George Gill executor (dwelling in ENG). Witnesses: William Stone, William Cornwalleys.

Abraham Bishop & Francis Morlin (TA) exhibited that they were sureties to Nicholas Shawe (CE) administrator of his brother

10:63   William Shawe (TA) unadministered by his widow Joyce (since dec'd), & exhibited accounts for sake of orphans. Discharge was granted.

10:64   ...

10:65   2 May. Elisabeth Grammar (CV) exhibited verbal will of her husband John Grammar (CV). Said Elisabeth was granted administration. Appraisers: Charles Boteler, John Henning. Richard Ladd (g) to administer oath.

Court Session: 1678

10:66   3 May. Alice Skydmore (AA) widow &
        administratrix of Edward Skydmore (AA)
        petitioned for new appraisers in CE:
        Ebenezar Blackiston, Isaac Harness.
        Edward Inglish (g) to administer oath.

        Henry Bradle (DO)
10:67   executor of Thomas Sewall (DO) exhibited
        inventory.

        4 May. William Coursey (g, TA)
        administrator of Sophia Beedle (AA)
        widow petitioned for a copy of her will
        for debtors in ENG, on behalf of her
        daughter Sophia.

10:68   7 May. LoA were sent to George Gill
        (dweller in ENG) brother & executor of
        John Gill (taylor, SM) via Capt. Robert
        Goland (merchant, commander of
        Rapahanack).

        Richard Ladd (g, CV) who married
        Rozamond relict & executrix of Joseph
        Horsely (CV) exhibited accounts.
        Discharge was granted.

        Richard Ladd (g) for Mary MackDowell
        (Cliffts, CV) widow of William
        MackDowell (Cliffts, CV) was granted
        administration.
10:69   Appraisers: John Clarke, George Ceely.
        Said Ladd to administer oath.

        George Parker (g, CV) exhibited a
        certificate from majoralty of City of
        London of:
10:70   ...
        •   bond of Roger Thorpe to Anne Yeend.
        •   Thorpe's counterbond to his sureties
            Ralph Forth, etc.
        •   procuration from said Forth sent to
            said Parker.
        •   copy of renunciation of Thorpe's
            kindred in ENG of right of
            administration.
        Before Sir Thomas Davies knight, Lord
        Mayor & alderman or senator of City of
        London.
        •   Henry Nye (scrivener, London),
10:71   ...
            age 30, deposed that he saw Roger

Page 42

Thorpe, Ralph Forth, John Forth, &
William Wiggun enter a bond dated 11
April 1674 to Anne Yeend & a
counterbond.

10:72 ...

He also cited an action by executors
of said Yeend dated 2 July 1675
against said Ralph Forth Also,
Anthony Wright cited as a notary.
Date: 9 October 1677.

10:73 Signed: Wagstaffe. [Paragraph in
Latin.]

10:74 Witnesses: Henry Nye, Lawrence Hatsell.
[Paragraph in Latin.]

10:75 Condition that Roger Thorpe, Ralph
Forth, & John Forth together with
William Wigan (sope boyler, London)
bound to Anne Yeend. Signed: Roger
Thorpe. Witnesses: Henry Nye, Lawrence
Hatsell. [Paragraph in Latin.] Signed:
Ant. Wright.

10:76 Came before Anthony Wright (notary,
London) on 9 October 1677: Mr. Ralph
Forth (citizen, leather seller, London)
creditor & administrator of Roger Thorpe
(merchant, dec'd) & made PoA to Mr.
George Parker (g, MD)

10:77 to recover from Edward Inglish, et. al.

10:78 Signed: Ralph Forth. Witnesses:
Benjamin Hodges, John Randall, Leon.
Webber. Ant. Wright (notary).

10.79 Joseph Thorpe, Mary Thorpe (alias Mary
Jackson), Martha Thorpe (alias Martha
Hammet), Sarah Thorpe (alias Sarah
Ogden), Hester Thorpe (alias Hester
Phillips), & Hannah Thorpe (spinster)
natural brother & sisters of Roger
Thorpe (London, dec'd) renounce
administration on his estate. Mentions:
ship Baltemore. Administration was
granted to Ralph Forth as principle
creditor. Property that was given to
Mr. Francklin is revoked. Mr. Godfrey
Lee, Mr. Robert Chapman, & Mr. Francis
Nixon (public notaries, procurators of
Arches Court of Canterbury) to appear
for them, before Sir Leoline Jenkins
knight, Doctor of Laws, Master, Keeper
of Prerogative Court of Canterbury, or
his surrogate.

10:80 Date: 20 October 1676. Signed: Joseph
Thorpe, Mary Jackson, Martha Hammet,

Sarah Ogdine, Esther Phillips, Hannah Thorpe. Witnesses: James Clough, Joseph Bacon, J. Keryon. Marcus Cottle (reg.).

10:81
Robert Taillor (CV) & Michaell Tawney (CV) appeared in response to summons regarding verbal will of Jeremiah Williams (CV) whereof he was constituted executor. Said Robert Taylor (p) renounced administration, & assigned it to Michaell Tawney (merchant), as principle creditor. Witnesses: William Stone, Mich. Taney.

10:82
Said Michaell Tawney was granted administration on estate of said Jeremiah Williams. Appraisers: Christopher Bayne, Peter Oulson. Roger Brooke (g) to administer oath.

Edward Inglish (merchant, CE) administrator of Edward Chicken (KE) exhibited additional goods. New appraisers (KE): Benjamin Ricks, (N) Sparkes. Maj. James Ringgold to administer oath.

10:83
George Parker vs. Edward Inglish (merchant, CE). Said Inglish had filed accounts.

Edward Inglish for John White (CE) executor of William Tyson (KE) exhibited accounts.

8 May. Capt. Richard Hill (AA) exhibited oath of Mary relict & executrix of John Rix (AA), sworn on 27 March last. Appraisers William Jones & John Peasly were sworn same day. Capt. Richard Hill (AA) exhibited will of John Ricks

10:84
proved.

Martha O'Kaine (SM) widow & administratrix of Rickart O'Kaine (SM) exhibited inventory.

Richard Ladd (g, CV) exhibited oath of Susanna Flood & Alice Graves executrices of Demetrius Cartwright (CV), sworn on 24 January last. Also, oath of appraisers John Hollins & John Turner, sworn same day.

10:85 Edward Inglish (g, CE) administrator of
Roger Thorpe (merchant, CE), who died at
sea on board ship Baltimore, exhibited
accounts. George Parker attorney for
Ralph Forth (London) was granted liberty
to except. George Parker (g, Cliffts,
CV) was given a copy of said accounts.
George Parker (g, CV) attorney for Ralph
Forth (leather seller, London) exhibited
exceptions to inventory & accounts.

10:86-87 ...
10:88 Mentions: debt of Anne Yeend,
10:89 John Allen.

10:90 9 May. Thomas Carlile & John Watson
(merchants, SM) executors of John
Cunningham (SM) exhibited accounts.

10:91 Edward Inglish (merchant, CE) was
granted a copy of exception by George
Parker (CV) against estate of Roger
Thorpe.

Edward Inglish (merchant, CE)
administrator of John Allen (merchant,
CE) unadministered by John Vanhecke,
exhibited accounts, for use of executors
in ENG. Discharge was granted.

10 May. Arthur Ludford exhibited that
John Martin (p) died at his house in CV,
10:92 & before his death, gave his estate to
said Ludford. Estate is very
inconsiderable. Said Ludford is
empowered to collect said goods &
chattels & to keep for his use, unless
other demands are made.

Edward Inglish (merchant, CE)
administrator of Roger Thorpe (merchant,
CE) exhibited additional accounts
10:93 & filed answer to exceptions of George
Parker (CV) attorney of Ralph Forth.

10:94 ...
10:95 Mentions debts: (N) Edmonds (gone away,
insolvent), (N) Allen (gone away,
insolvent), (N) Stennart (gone away,
insolvent), (N) Radford, (N) Adams.
Mentions judgements vs.: Tho. Bennet,
Elisabeth Greene.

10:96   Signed: Ro. Carvile procurator for E.
          English. George Parker (g, Cliffts, CV)
          was granted a copy of the answer.

10:97   11 May. Edward Inglish administrator of
          Roger Thorpe exhibited accounts, for use
          of Timothy Harmer & William Pococke
          (executors of John Allen (dec'd)),
          Thomas Bibby, Richard Ryly, & Thomas
          Welles (merchants, London) creditors to
          said Thorpe, & George Parker attorney to
          Ralph Forth (alderman of London) &
          admitted administration as chief
          creditor, by renunciation of kindred of
          said Roger, & copy of said Parker's
          exceptions. Judge took accounts,
          exceptions, & answer.

10:98   ...

10:99   Mentions: debts of Tho. Edmonds, Tho.
          Allen, & Cornelius Stennart. All 3 men
          are run out of the Province. Mentions:
          bills of Brewer Radford & Richard Adams,
          judgement vs. Tho. Bennet & Elisabeth
          Greene.

10:100   Mentions: Anne Yeend, Newton Thorpe.
          Said Inglish allowed certain amounts.

10:101   Mentions: Gregory Marloe, Capt. Strong,
          Capt. Knott, Timothy Harmer, William
          Pococke, (N) Bibby, Richard Ryly, Tho.
          Welles, Edward Pynne, (N) Chezeldyne,
          (N) Parker, (N) Ridgely, (N) Thorpe,
          Jane Crouch, (N) Hopkins, sheriff for
          Roger Thorpe, Sarah Philips, (N) Bennet,
          (N) Greene, (N) Crouch,

10:102   storekeeper of Newton Thorpe, George
          Parker attorney of Ralph Forth. Capt.
          Samuell Bourne to swear said Parker as
          administrator of (N).

          Edward Inglish administrator of Roger
          Thorpe exhibited a debt due from John
          Cleaver. Said debt was overlooked by
          administrator

10:103   & his attorney (N) Ridgely. Discharge
          was granted to said Inglish on estate of
          said Thorpe.

          Peter Watts (St. George's Hundred, SM)
          executor of Robert Cager (St. George's
          Hundred, SM) exhibited additional
          accounts.

10:104 13 May. Randolph Hinson & William Hatton (gentlemen, both of Poplar Hill, SM) exhibited that Zachary Wade (g, CH) made will, constituting said Hinson & Hatton as executors. Said Hatton tendered renunciation. Date: 12 May 1678. Witnesses: William Cornwalleys.

10:105 Maj. Benjamin Rozer to prove said will.

Randolph Hinson (SM) administrator of Thomas Hatton (SM) was granted administration on estate of Robert Hatton (SM). William Hatton (g) to administer oath.

10:106 14 May. Nathan Smith (g, AA) administrator of Thomas Howard (AA) exhibited accounts. Discharge was granted.

15 May. Elisabeth Beck (CH) widow & administratrix of Richard Beck (CH) exhibited appraisers (N) Hayes & (N) Castleton are by sickness & death unable to appraise said estate. New appraisers: John Wood, John Godson.

10:107 Maj. Benjamin Rozer to administer oath.

Robert Castleton eldest son of Mary Castleton (CH) widow & executrix of Robert Castleton (CH) exhibited the will of the dec'd, for his mother. Maj. Benjamin Rozer to prove said will. Said Mary was granted administration. Appraisers: Garret Sinnot, John Wood.

10:108 Said Rozer to administer oath.

Stephen Gary (g, DO) exhibited oaths of Thomas Newton & William Thomas appraisers of Edward Sauvage (g, DO).

16 May. Thomas Spincke (merchant, SM) administrator of Jane Paine (widow,
10:109 SM, dec'd) exhibited accounts. Discharge was granted.

17 May. Capt. George Cowley (TA) exhibited will of Robert Turner (TA), proved. Sarah Illingsworth executrix was sworn on 10th instant.

Court Session: 1678

10:110   18 May. Joseph Fowler (SM)
administrator of William George (SM)
exhibited accounts.

21 May. Robert Carvile & Christopher
Rousby procurators for Randolph Revell
(SO) & his wife Katherine vs. Andrew
Jones nephew & administrator of James
Jones & his wife Sarah (SO, both dec'd).
Libel exhibited. Mentions: Randall
Revell (g, plaintiff, SO) & his wife
Katherine executrix of Sarah Jones
executrix of James Jones (p, SO).

10:111   Said James made his will, bequeathing
land to said Sarah Jones & his cousin
Andrew Jones. Said James made said
Sarah his sole executrix & George
Johnson & Charles Hutchins overseers.
About October 1677, said James died.
Said Sarah died not long after, having
made a nuncupative will,

10:112   bequeathing to said Katharine Revell,
chattel to wife of Leonard Jones.

10:113   Mr. William Steevens was directed to
prove will of said James on 8 November
last.

10:114   Sheriff (SO) to summon plaintiffs,
defendant, and Thomas Daniell, Dorothy
Philips, John Evans, & John Watts
(witnesses to

10:115   nuncupative will).

Thomas Vaughan (g, TA) exhibited
commission of last day of April 1677 for
Matthew Warde (g) to prove will of John
Beard. Said Warde is since dec'd,
before will was proved.

10:116   Said Vaughan is executor with Elisabeth
Beard then widow, for the son of said
Vaughan, who is sole heir of said Beard.
Said relict is newly remarried to a
wasteful spendthrift. Anthony Mayl (g)
to prove said Beard's will. Appraisers:
Simon Irons, James Murphey. Said Mayl
to administer oath.

10:117   22 May. Sarah Barnes (Cliffts, CV)
relict & executrix of Nicholas Carr
(Cliffts, CV) exhibited inventory.

25 May. Randolph Hinson (St. George's
Hundred, SM) administrator of Thomas

Hatton (g, SM) & Robert Hatton (SM)
exhibited 2 additional accounts.

10:118   Benjamin Rozer, Esq. (CH) exhibited will
of Zachary Wade (g, CH), proved.
Randolph Hanson, one of executors, was
granted administration.

10:119   Appraisers (SM): Richard Lloyd (g),
Capt. John Cambell. Appraisers (CH):
Richard Hudson, William Smith. Maj.
Benjamin Rozer to administer oath.

William Hatton (g, SM) exhibited oath of
Henry Phippes & Robert Graham appraisers
of John Jones (attorney of Provincial
Court,
10:120   were sworn 15 November.

27 May. Kenelme Cheseldyne (Attorney
General, SM) executor of John Jones (g,
SMC) exhibited inventory.

John Waterton (g, BA) exhibited
10:121   oath of Jane Ebden widow &
administratrix of William Ebden (BA),
sworn on 2 April 1678. On 8 May, she
gave bond. Appraisers
10:122   Richard Simms & Thomas Richardson were
sworn on 6 April. Date: 8 May 1678.
Inventory of William Ebden (BA)
exhibited.

30 May. Jane Gray (alias Jane Jones)
wife of Thomas Jones (St. Innago's
Hundred, SM) administratrix of Alexander
Winsore (g, St. Innago's Hundred, SM)
exhibited accounts.
10:123   Discharge was granted.

ultimate May. Joane Waughop (Piney
Point, SM) widow & executrix of John
Waughop (Piney Point, SM) petitioned for
appraisers. Appraisers: William Hatton
(g), Peter Watts. Richard Lloyd (g) to
administer oath.

1 June. Robert Asiter son & heir of
William Asiter (St. Clemens Bay, SM) vs.
his stepmother Anne Asiter widow &
administratrix of said William.
Exceptions to inventory & accounts
exhibited.

10:124   Said Robert is only heir, age 22.

10:125   If said Anne does not appear & exhibit
accounts, then administration is to be
granted to said son & Capt. John
Jourdaine to take bond.

6 June. Bridget Powell (TA) widow &
executrix of William Powell (TA)
exhibited accounts. Mentions: infirmity
of said widow.

10:126   7 June. Thomas Bland procurator for
Hester Goffe (CV) widow of William
Goffe, who unfortunately drowned, was
granted administration. Appraisers
(AA): said Bland, George Holland. Col.
Thomas Taylor (AA) to administer oath.

10:127   8 June. Anne Asiter (St. Clemens Bay,
SM) widow & administratrix of William
Asiter (St. Clemens Bay, SM) exhibited
accounts.

John Howell (CE) executor of John
Vanhacke (CE) exhibited that his sister
Sarah Vanhacke (widow of said dec'd, now
dec'd) has a female orphan (infant).
Said Howell was granted administration
on estate of said Sarah, on behalf of
said orphan Sarah.

10:128   Said John Howell is over age 17, but
under age 21; his guardian is Capt.
Jonathon Sibrey. Joseph Hopkins to
summon said Howell & administer oath.

10:129   Capt. Jonathon Sybrey & John Howell
(CE) appeared. Said Sybrey is
father-in-law to said John & his brother
Nathaniell Howell (under age), joint
executors of their father Capt. Thomas
Howell (CE) & executors of their
brother-in-law John Vanhacke (CE).
Accounts were exhibited.

10:130   Joane Workman wife of Anthony Workman
(KE) exhibited a letter from Maj.
Joseph Wickes (KE). 2 months ago, a
commission was directed to take bond of
Sarah Brown (widow, KE) on
administration of her husband's estate.
Said Brown refused to give security, &
estate lies in jeopardy. Said widow
remarried "a strange man" who has

runaway & taken her with him & some of the chattel. The widow left behind the child.

10:131 Date: 5 May 1678. Anthony Workman (KI) was granted administration on estate of Edward Browne (KE), as greatest creditor, for use of Morgan Browne (orphan left to his grandfather's care, who is ancient). The other 2 orphans are with the fugitives. Appraisers: Thomas Osbourne, Valentine Southerne. Said Wickes to administer oath.

10:132 10 June. John Pollard (DO) administrator of Thomas Newman (DO) exhibited accounts.

11 June. John Waterton (g, BA) exhibited oath of John Owen (BA) administrator of Richard Winley (BA), sworn on 6 April 1678. Date: 25 April 1678.

10:133 Sureties: William Westbury, Tho. Richardson. Said Owen exhibited inventory.

Maj. Benjamin Rozer (CH) exhibited will of Robert Castleton, Sr. (CH), proved.

10:134 Maj. Benjamin Rozer (CH) exhibited oath of Garret Synnot & John Wood appraisers of estate of Robert Castleton, sworn on 21 May 1678.

Elisabeth Beck widow was sworn on 30 March 1678, with securities: Kenelme Mackloghlin, Richard Clowter.

10:135 John Wood & John Godson appraisers of estate of Richard Beck were sworn on 15 May 1678.

John Cammell, Richard Lloyd, Richard Hodgson, & William Smith appraisers of estate of Zachary Wade were sworn on 27 May 1678.

12 June. Thomas Walker (high sheriff, SO) exhibited that John Markham

10:136 (SO) was slain by Indians at the house of David Williams, leaving no relation in the Province but a brother in Accomack VA who refuses administration

because the estate is so small. Said
Thomas Walker was granted
administration, as principle creditor,
on behalf of the brother. Appraisers:
Andrew Jones, Daniell Haste. William
Brewerton (g) to administer oath.

10:137 Sheriff (AA) to summon James Rigby (AA)
sole executor of William Dreury (AA) to
exhibit accounts.

Joseph Hopkins (CE) exhibited oath of
Martha Huddle (CE) widow & executrix of
William Huddle, sworn on 4 May 1678.
10:138 Thomas Hawker & Richard Adams appraisers
of estate of William Huddle (CE) were
sworn same day. Said Martha exhibited
inventory.

Michaell Tawney (g, CV) administrator of
Jeremiah Williams (CV) exhibited
inventory.

13 June. Mary Warde (CH) relict &
executrix of George Grodtwell (CH) &
sister & administratrix of Richard
Foulkes (CV) unadministered
10:139 by said George exhibited inventory, by
her now husband William Warde &
accounts.

10:140 James Wheeler (CH) who married Elisabeth
widow & executrix of Thomas Corker (CH)
exhibited accounts.

10:141 Richard Ladd (CV) exhibited oath of Mary
Mackdowell administratrix of William
Mackdowell (Clifftes, CV).
10:142 Sureties: George Ceely, John Clarke.
John Clarke & George Ceely appraisers
were sworn. Inventory was exhibited.

10:143 Richard Ladd (g, CV) exhibited oaths of
Charles Botler & John Henning appraisers
of estate of John Grammer (CV), sworn on
10 May 1678.

Richard Ladd (g, CV) exhibited oaths of
Robert Blinckhorne & George Ceely
appraisers of estate of Edward Good (CV)
& Margery Good administratrix.
Sureties: Robert Blinkhorne, George

Ceely.

10:144   Samuel Bourne (g, CV) exhibited oath of
George Parker (Cliffts, attorney of
Provincial Court, CV) administrator of
William Done (Clifts, CV). Surety:
William Parker. Appraisers William
Parker & John Hance

10:145   were sworn on 13 April last. Said
Parker exhibited inventory. Said Parker
exhibited renunciation of Katherine Done
widow of said William.

10:146   Date: 18 May 1678. Signed: Cathe. Done.
Witnesses: William Parker, Thomas Bland,
Richard Boughton.

10:147   John Welsh (sheriff, AA) exhibited
accounts of estate of orphans of Roger
Gross (AA).

Thomas Blandford who married Tabitha
relict & executrix of William Mills (CV)
exhibited accounts.

10:148   Mentions: creditors, legatees, children.

Elisabeth Beckwith relict &
administratrix of Thomas Skinner (DO)
exhibited accounts.

Humphry Warren & John Fanning (CH)
exhibited inventory of George Credwell
(CH). Date: 23 October 1677.

10:149   George Godfrey & Robert Midleton
exhibited inventory of Thomas Corkes
(CH). They were sworn on 19 May 1677.

Humphry Warren & John Fanning exhibited
inventory of Richard Fowke (CH). Date:
23 October 1677.

14 June. Alice Gugat (CV) wife of John
Gugat was granted administration on
estate of her late husband Samuel
Graves. Appraisers: Robert Taylor, John
Turner. Mr. Richard Ladd to administer
oath.

10:150   Capt. John Quigley (SM) exhibited that
his kinsman John Deery (inn holder, SMC)
made will constituting said Quigley sole
executor & that Garet Vansweringen (inn

holder, SMC) had administration on his estate, as principle creditor.

10:151 Richard Dalton to summon said Vansweringen, to show cause why said Quigley should not be granted administration.

John Wedge (TA) who married relict of John Chadborne (CE, died 3 years ago) exhibited that the widow feared trouble & charge to administer the small estate. Said Wedge was granted administration, for the widow & orphan.

10:152 Appraisers: Richard Pullen, Richard Adams. Edward English to administer oath.

Philip Steevenson (TA) exhibited will of William Price (TA), proved by John Tillison & Hugh Paxston.

10:153 Thomas Walker (high sheriff, SO) exhibited oath of Cornelius Johnson & Henry Hayman appraisers of estate of David Williams sworn on 19 April last. John Coventon administrator was sworn same day. Sureties: Nehemia Coventon, Sr., Nehemia Coventon, Jr., John Ingram.

John Coode (g, SM) exhibited oath of Capt. Gerrard Sly executor of William Watts (SM) & oaths of Nehemiah Blackiston & Thomas Lomax appraisers of said estate. Inventory was exhibited.

10:154 Bartholomew Ennalls & Henry Bradley (gentlemen, DO) exhibited will of David Coffyn (DO), proved by Charles Hutchings & Thomas Daniell. Anne Coffyn executrix was sworn. Appraisers: Charles Hutchings, Thomas Daniel.

15 June. William Stephens for Samuel Jones (SO) exhibited will of his father Sanders Jones (SO). Said William Steevens to prove will by witnesses Ellis Colman, Henry Hall, & Anne Patricks.

10:155 Appraisers: Robert Richardson, Thomas Poynter. Said Steevens to administer oath.

James Mills (BA) sole remaining executor of Capt. Samuel Boston (BA) petitioned for new appraisers: James Philips, James Ives. Henry Haslewood (g) to administer oath. Former appraiser was John Ireland.

Thomas Gilbert for Elisabeth Tall (DO) widow of Anthony Tall (DO) exhibited his will.

10:156 Stephen Gary to prove, by witnesses John Mackells & John Alford. Appraisers: John Alford, John Edwards.

Capt. Richard Hill administrator of Edward Gardner (AA) exhibited accounts.

Capt. Richard Hill administrator of Philip Dawson (AA) exhibited accounts.

Capt. John Cobreth (Clifts, CV) one of administrators of Thomas Pagett (Clifts, CV) for self & John Hunt exhibited accounts.

10:157 Discharge was granted.

Charles Boteler & John Henning exhibited inventory of John Gramer (CV).

10:158 Robert Neves & William Deane exhibited inventory of William Davis (KE). Bond by Cornelius Comegys & Henry Hosier was exhibited.

William Steevens (g, SO) exhibited will of Nicholas Rice, proved by Thomas Daniell & Thomas Wilson. Richard Crockett & John Evans executors were sworn. Appraisers David Browne & James Dashiell were sworn.

William Steevens (g) exhibited bond of Elisabeth Hudson administratrix of Nicholas Hudson (SO). Sureties: Edward Steevens, Edward Wale.

10:159 Inventory was exhibited, by appraisers Edward Wale & John Vigerous.

William Steevens exhibited bond of Robert Richardson (SO) administrator of John Teye, sworn on ultimate November 1675.

10:160 James Mills (BA) administrator of Robert Maddox exhibited inventory & accounts. Continuance was granted to include in inventory goods in SO.

17 June. Michaell Miller for Hannah Gibson (KE) sole executrix of John White petitioned for appraisers: William Harris, Richard Lowder. Henry Hosier (g) to administer oath.

18 June. Will of Sarah Jones was exhibited, proved.

James Mills administrator of Samuel Boston exhibited accounts.

10:161 19 June. William Crosse procurator for Edward Man (g, TA) administrator of Philip Harwood (DO) & administrator of Thomas Reade (DO) exhibited that said Man fell from his horse & is lame. Continuance was granted.

20 June. Capt. Philemon Loyd (TA) was granted administration on estate of Edward Sacker (Wye River, DO), a bachelor sine relations, as principle creditor. Appraisers: William Younge, Peter Sydes. Philip Steevenson to administer oath.

10:162 Robert Carvile procurator for Rand. Revell & his wife Katherine (SO) was granted a copy of the answer of Andrew Jones (late of SO) regarding nuncupative will of Sarah Jones.

Anne Assiter was granted discharge on estate of William Assiter.

Philip Lynes (g, CH) petitioned that Thomas Warner (CH, dec'd) & his wife Elisabeth Warner (dec'd) were indebted to petitioner.

10:163 They have been dec'd for 2 years. Said Warner died a widower without relations except 2 orphans bound out by County Court. Said Philip Lines was granted administration. Appraisers: Thomas Baker, Richard Dodd. Col. John Douglas to administer oath.

Sheriff (AA) to summon Cornelius Howard (AA) administrator of John Grange (BA) to exhibit accounts.

10:164 24 June. Katherine relict of John Lewis (SM) exhibited accounts.

25 June. Henry Lewis exhibited receipt of Paule Dorrell & William Jones orphans of George Dorrell (AA) from Dr. Henry Lewis & Thomas Turner (AA), due from estate of their father. Date: 24 February 1677. Signed: Paul Dorrell, William Jones. Witness: Geo. Howell, Theophilus Hacket. Discharge was granted.

10:165 28 June. Robert Ridgeley procurator for Andrew Jones exhibited "interrogatorys" of witnesses of will of Sarah Jones.

29 June. Thomas Todd (VA) executor of his father Thomas Todd (BA) exhibited letter dated 1 May 1678, citing lost LoA from Bishop of Canterbury. Copy of LoA and will was requested.

10:166 1 July. John Cood (g, SM) granted administration on estate of Henry Sprye (merchant), who drowned in Wicakomaco River on 29 June last & died childless,
10:167 as greatest creditor. Appraisers: Kenelme Chesledyne, David Hoult. William Hatton (g) to administer oath.

George Yate (AA) was granted administration on estate of Richard Willson (also Richard Wilson, BA), who died with no wife nor child nor other relation in Province, as greatest creditor.
10:168 Said George is unable to travel to Office. Appraisers: Francis Watkins, Rowland Nance. Anthony de Mondidier (also Anthony DeMondidier, BA) to administer oath.

George Yate (g, AA) was granted administration estate of Robert Willson (g, BA),
10:169 as greatest creditor. Appraisers: Francis Watkins, Rowland Nance.

Anthoney Demontegore (g, BA) to administer oath.

5 July. James Mills executor of Samuel Boston (BA) cited that he exhibited accounts on 18 June last.

10:170 Marmaduke Semme (SM) administrator of Samuel Dickeson exhibited accounts.

Thomas Jeffe (AA) administrator of his father Thomas Jeffe exhibited bond.

Henry Hosier (g, KE) exhibited the bond of William Harris (KE) administrator of Richard Mason (KE). Michaell Miller & Henry Hosier, Jr. exhibited inventory of
10:171 Richard Mason (KE). Date: 16 March 1677.

Jonas Davis & Edward Steevenson administrators of William Rice (TA) exhibited inventory, made in presence of Richard Wolman & Philemon Loyd (gentlemen).

James Ringold (g, KE) exhibited will of Francis Tench (KE), proved by Thomas Warren & John True. Mary widow & executrix was sworn on 8 June,
10:172 & appraisers Henry Hosier & William Deane were sworn on 25 February 1677. Mary Tench exhibited inventory.

James Ringold (g, KE) exhibited oath of Samuel Tovye administrator of John Wright (KE), with sureties: William Bateman, Thomas Boone. Inventory was exhibited.

10:173 James Ringold (g, KE) exhibited bond of Samuel Tovye (g, KE) administrator of William Norman, with sureties: William Bateman, Thomas Boone. Inventory was exhibited.

10:174 James Ringold (g, KE) exhibited will of Richard Fittingham (KE), proved by John Wright. Samuel Tovye executor was sworn on 8 November 1677. Inventory was exhibited, appraised by: William Bateman, Richard Louder.

George Cowley (g, TA) exhibited oath of Ann Earle executrix of Thomas Earle (TA).

10:175 Katherine relict & administratrix of John Luvys (West of SM, SM) exhibited accounts. Mentions: residue due orphans. Said Katherine is now wife of Thomas Shore.

8 July. Richard Loyd (g, SM) exhibited oath of William Hatton (g) & Peter Watts appraisers of John Wacop (SM), sworn on 19 June last.

10:176 10 July. Philip Connor & John Winchester exhibited inventory of estate of Edward Lowder (KI). Anne Lowder administratrix of Edward Lowder (KE) exhibited bond, with sureties: William Rawles, John Winchester.

11 July. William Lawrence (g, KE) for Mary Blangey, wife of Luvis Blangey, relict & administratrix of Tobias Wells exhibited her accounts.

10:177 Mary Pope administratrix of Thomas Pope (CH) exhibited accounts & requested that Philip Lynes (CH) render accounts.
10:178 Said Lynes is tending to defraud creditors by pretense of fees paid to officers in VA & of a debt to Murty Fanning Hill the Minister Clipsham. Mentions payments to: Thomas Notley,
10:179 orphans of (N) Smith, Maior Benjamin Rozer. Discharge was granted.

10:180 12 July. Randolph Hanson exhibited inventory of estate of Zachary Wade (CH).

Randolph Hinson administrator of Robert Hatton deposed that Robert Hatton made a verbal will, bequeathing to his brother Thomas Hatton, who intermixed his estate with his own & said Thomas died before probate of said will.

10:181 William Hatton (g, SM) exhibited oath of Randolph Hanson administrator of Robert Hatton (SM). Said Robert's estate is

contained in inventory of estate of
Thomas Hatton.

William Hatton (g, SM) executor of his
brother Richard Hatton exhibited
accounts.

10:182   16 July. Elisabeth Beck widow of
Richard Beck (CH) exhibited inventory,
by appraisers Thomas Wood & John
Godhall. Said Elisabeth (an illiterate
woman) exhibited that her husband died
much in debt,
10:183   & exhibited accounts.

May Castleston (CH) executrix of Robert
Castleston (CH) exhibited inventory, by
appraisers Garrett Sinnett & John Wood.
10:184   She also exhibited accounts. Mentions:
children.

10:185   Temperance Clouder relict of John
Ashberry (CH) was summoned to exhibit
his will, at request of son & heir.

Mathew Cartwright & Thomas Barsett
administrators of Jeffery Hudson (SM)
exhibited his inventory, dated 27 April
last.

18 July. Ebenezar Blackiston exhibited
will of Anne Toulson (CE). Said
Ebenezar & his wife are executors,
10:186   & are unable to travel as far as Office.
Joseph Hopkins (g) and/or Edward English
(g) to prove will.

Hugh Marnacke (an infant, under age,
Nansemond, VA) with his mother Katherine
Roberts exhibited
10:187   that said Hugh is son of Hugh Marnacke
(Nansemond, dec'd). Said Hugh (dec'd)
was of the blood of Macom Thomas
(Pocomoke, SO, formerly of Nansemond)
per deposition of Allexander King taken
before Col. William Coleburne (SO) &
William Brereton (SO) & oath of Daniel
Gery, Robert Bunckley, & John Murfey,
Sr. taken in court of Nansemond on 19
April 1676 & certified by Joseph Peasley
(Deputy Clerk, Nansemond Co.). Said
Macom Thomas was killed by his servant,

who was since executed. Said Hugh, Jr. is heir at law.

10:188 Notice to Court of Chancery of a writ of mandamus. Mentions: William Steevens (g) administrator of said Thomas.

10:189 Robert Ridgely procurator for Capt. John Quigley vs. Geritt Vansweringen. Exhibit of libel for revoking LoA of John Deery to said Vansweringen. Nicholas Painter, Richard Dalton, & Edmund Deeremott summoned to testify. Said Vansweringen to exhibit inventory.

10:190 19 July. Anthony Mayl (TA) exhibited oaths of James Murphey & Symon Irons appraisers of estate of John Beard (TA). Said Irons was disabled by sickness; Edmund Fuller sworn in his place. Thomas Vaughan executor also sworn. Also exhibited was renunciation of Elisabeth Beard as executrix.

20 July. William Hatton & Peter Watts exhibited inventory of
10:191 John Waushop.

25 July. Gerit Vansweringen to swear Katherine relict of John Levys (SM) regarding her account of his estate.

27 July. Alice Bond relict of William Drury (AA) petitioned that said William bequeathed the greatest portion of his estate to his daughter Christian Drury (since dec'd) & made James Rigby executor.
10:192 Said Alice petitioned for LoA on estate of said Christian, there being no other relation. Mentions: Dr. Henry Lewis (commissioner), Richard Wharfield (appraiser), & Addam Shipley (appraiser). Said Rigby summoned to account for estate of said William Drury, at suit of Hugh Merriken (brother of the half blood to Christian Drury (daughter of said William)).

10:193 29 July. John Quigley vs. Geritt Vansweringen. Answer by said Vansweringen. Summons to: Henry Carewe (N) Pennington (g), (N) Manning wife of

Hugh Manning (St. Michael's Hundred, SM), Nicholas Painter, Edmund Deeremott, Richard Dalton. Said Vansweringen exhibited inventory,
10:194 appraised by John Blomfeild & Thomas Junis.

ultimate July. Jane Ebden (BA) widow of William Ebden (died October last) petitioned that her husband left her with 3 small children.
10:195 Said Jane exhibited accounts, which are overpaid. Mr. John Waterton (g, BA) to take her oath, as her 2 young children are sick.

10:196 1 August. Hugh Merriken (AA) son & heir of John Merriken (AA) exhibited that his father died intestate & that his mother Christian never administered his estate.
10:197 She remained a widow for 3/4 years before marrying William Drury (AA). Said Hugh Merriken was granted administration on estates of John Merriken & Christian Drury.
10:198 Appraisers: William Hawkins, Ralph Hawkins. Henry Lewis to administer oath.
10:199 Said Hugh Merriken vs. James Rigby executor of William Drury (AA). Said Drury married Christian mother of said Merriken. Said Rigby summoned.

Elisabeth Manning, Henry Carewe, & Francis Pennington examined as per Gerit Vansweringen.

2 August. Nicholas Painter examined
10:200 per Gerit Vansweringen.

Joanna Farrar executrix of Robert Farrar (SM) exhibited accounts. Discharge was granted.

6 August. John Quigley (merchant, VA) vs. Geritt Vansweringen administrator of John Deery.
10:201 Examinations to be published.

7 August. John Foster who married Mary executrix of William Chandler (AA) was summoned to show why Mary Chandler

(daughter of dec'd) should not have her legacy.

13 August. Col. Vincent Lowe exhibited oath of Alexander Larimore (TA) administrator of Nicholas Lurkye & his wife Mary. Securities: Ralph Dawson, William Gascoine.

10:202 Alixander Larrimore exhibited inventory of Nicholas Lurkye, appraised by Richard Gould & Ralph Nicholson.

Jane Williams (Piney Point, SM) widow of William Williams (attorney of Provincial Court)

10:203 was granted administration on his estate. Appraisers: Capt. John Coode, John Wasson.

16 August. Joanna Trawer executrix of Robert Farrer exhibited her accounts. Continuance was granted, in order for her to put the accounts in order.

10:204 John Quigley (merchant, VA) vs. Garret Vansweringen. Said John, one of executors of John Derry (inn holder, SMC), deposed that on 2 December 1677, said Deery

10:205 made his will; said Deery having no kindred here. Nicholas Painter (g, clerk to Hon. William Calvert, Esq. (Principle Secretary)) wrote will. Bequests: sister Ellinor Deery (IRE), brother Owen Quigley (IRE), cousin said John Quigley.

10:206 Executors: same said three. Proved before Thomas Notley, Esq. (Governor) by oaths of Nicholas Painter & Edmond Dormott.

10:207 Garrett Vansweringen is cited as administrator of said estate.

10:208 Witnesses (to will): Nicholas Painter,
10:209 Edmond Dermot, Richard Dolton.
10:210 Will of John Derry (inn holder, SMC).
10:211 Bequests: sister Ellinor Derry (IRE), brother Owen Quigley, cousin John Quigley (merchant).

10:212 Executors: said three. Date: 2 December 1677. Proved by Nicholas Painter on 13 June 1678.

10:213 Proved by Edmond Dermott.

10:214 ...
10:215 Mentions: Edmond Dermott kingsman [sic] to said John Quigley.
10:216 Signed: Chr. Rousby. Interrogation of Nicholas Painter, Edmund Dermott, & Richard Dolton.
10:217-8 ...
10:219 ...
- Nicholas Painter, age 23, deposed on 19 July 1678
10:220 ...
   that he was called by Richard Dolton who was at house of Richard Chilman.
10:221 ...
10:222 ...
- Edmond Dermott, age 25/6, deposed on 19 July 1678.
10:223 ...
10:224 ...
- Richard Dolton, age 24/5, deposed on 19 July 1678.
10:225 ...
10:226 Cross-examination of Nicholas Painter,
10:227-8 ...
10:229 who deposed on 2 August 1678.
10:230-2 ...
10:233 Cross-examination of Edmond Dermott & Richard Dalton.
10:234 ...
10:235 ...
- Edmond Dermott deposed on 3 August 1678:
10:236 ...
   Mentions: Elisabeth Manning, Mr. Carewe, Mr. Blomfeild.
10:237-8 ...
10:239 Interrogation on behalf of Garrat Vansweringen (g) administrator of John Derry.
10:240 ...
10:241 ...
- Elisabeth Manning (St. Michael's Hundred), age 35/6, deposed on 1 August 1678.
10:242 ...
10:243 ...
- Henry Carewe, age 40, deposed on 1 August 1678.
10:244 ...
10:245 ...
- Francis Pennington, age 36, deposed on 1 August 1678.

• Henry Carewe further deposed.

10:246 Robert Ridgely procurator for John Quigley (merchant, VA) vs. Gerrat Vansweringen (g, SMC). Both appeared on 16 August 1678.

10:247-254 ...

10:255 Will declared null and void.

10:256 Ellinor Derry (as next of kin of whole blood) to be notified that she may be administratrix de bonis non of estate of said John Derry. Mr. Peter Wadding for Michaell Rochford to convey notice to said Ellinor.

21 August. Vincent Lowe exhibited oath of Alexander Larimore administrator of Nicholas Larkie (TA) & his wife Mary (TA), sworn on 13 May 1678.

10:257 Richard Gold & Ralph Nickson appraisers of Nicholas Larky sworn same day.

Stephen Gary (DO) exhibited that the will of Anthony Tall (DO) was to be proved by John Alford & John Miccell, and that there is no written will. Elisabeth widow of said Tall, age above 60, desires proof of nuncupative will. Said Gary to prove. Appraisers: John Alford, John Edward.

10:258 Mary Hall (AA) widow of Patrick Hall was granted administration on his estate. Appraisers: Robert Franckling, Edward Thorley. Thomas Taillor, Esq. to administer oath.

10:259 Capt. Richard Hill (AA) exhibited will of William Harness (AA), proved by Nathaniel Heathcoate & John Welsh. Susanna executrix refused to take oath. Said will to be recorded for security of Jacob & Elisabeth Harness. Mentions: children of dec'd.

10:260 Temperance Clouder relict of John Ashberry (CH) exhibited that last June, she entrusted will of said John to Philip Lynes (CH), requesting him to procure LoA. Said Lynes to deliver will to John Stone (g, CH), who is to prove said will. Appraisers: Rob. Robins, Kenelme Macloughlin.

William Shirtecliffe (SM) administrator of Joseph Shirtecliffe administrator of his brother John Shirtecliffe exhibited accounts.

10:261

William Shertcliffe (SM) administrator of his mother Anne Shertcliffe exhibited accounts.

10:262   22 August. Randell Revell vs. Andrewe Jones. William Steevens (g), Morgan Jones & his wife Elisabeth, & John Evans & his wife Mary were summoned.

William Steevens (g) to prove will of Stephen Bond (SO). Appraisers: Capt. Lt. Daniell Curtice, Ensign Henry Miles. Said Steevens to administer oath.

10:263   23 August. Richard Crockett (SO) & John Evans (SO) executors of Nicholas Rice (SO) were granted administration on his estate.

William Jones & William Pearly exhibited inventory of John Ricks (AA).

Richard Hill (AA) exhibited bond of Alice Skidmore, with sureties: Henry Lewys, Ralph Hawkins. Date: 18 July 1678.

10:264   Said Alice is widow & administratrix of Edward Skidmore. Inventory (AA) appraised by Ralph Hawkins & William Hawkins. Inventory (CE) appraised by Ebenezar Blackiston & Isaac Harnes.

10:265   30 August. George Parker (Clifts, CV) administrator of William Done (Clifts, CV) exhibited that goods & chattel are in hands of Richard Hill & Thomas Dryfeild, who will not prove any accounts. Said Hill & Dryfeild summoned.

10:266   John Owen (BA) administrator of Richard Winley exhibited accounts.

Inventory of Samuel Graves (CV) was exhibited by appraisers Robert Taylor & John Turner.

10:267 Mary DesJardins widow of Jean Des
Jourdins (chirurgeon, KE) renounced
administration.

10:268 Witness: William Cornwaleys. James
Balderston & Josias Lanham were granted
administration on estate of said Jean
Jardins, as principle creditors. Col.
Henry Coursey to take security.

10:269 ultimate August. Richard Ladde (CV)
exhibited oath of Robert Taylor & John
Turner as appraisers of Samuel Graves
(CV), sworn on 1 July. Said Ladde also
took bond of John Guyatt with sureties:
John Turner, Henry Hollis.

10:270 Thomas Taillor, Esq. exhibited oath of
Hester Gough widow & administratrix of
William Gough (CV). Sureties: William
Jones (doctor in physick), John Larkin
(inn holder). Appraisers: Thomas Bland,
George Holland. Said Hester exhibited
inventory.

10:271 4 September. Act for Prevention of
       Fraud & Perjury regarding
10:272 Nuncupative Wills.
10:273 ...

10:274 5 September. Richard Cornish (Boston,
NE) brother of John Cornish (Boston, NE)
exhibited that Thomas Snell took LoA on
14 February last. Said Snell to deliver
inventory.

10:275 Margarett widow of Michael Rotchford
(merchant, SM) exhibited his will,
proved by Abraham Roades (SM). Frances
wife of said Roades is other witness, &
is sick & unable to walk. Henry Carewe
(3rd witness) is absent, visiting the
sick.

10:276 Said Margarett was granted
administration. Appraisers: Robert
Carvile (recorder, SMC), Geritt
Vansweringen (alderman, SMC). Mentions:
mother of dec'd, brother of dec'd,
sister of dec'd, Sam. Heron (merchant),
Richard Covill, Barnaby Dunch.

10:277 7 September. Charles Bayley (AA) who
married Mary (now dec'd) executrix of

John Hawkins (AA) was granted
administration on his estate.
10:278 Appraisers: Robert Franklin, William
Carre. Nathaniel Heathcoate to
administer oath.

16 September. James Rigby (AA)
exhibited accounts of estate of William
Drury.

James Mills (BA) executor of Samuel
Boston (BA) exhibited accounts & was
granted continuance.

10:279 Thomas Walker (SO) administrator of John
Markeham (SO) exhibited bond, with
sureties: Nehemiah Coventon, Andrewe
Jones. Also exhibited inventory,
appraised by Andrewe Jones & Daniell
Hast, sworn by William Brewton on 2 July
1678.

10:280 On 23 July, Justices of CV examined
accounts of Mary Spencer wife of Francis
Spencer executrix of Joseph Anderson
(CV): Said Mary certified to accounts of
said John Anderson. Signed: John
Darnall, Capt. Samuel Bourne, Maj.
Henry Jowles, Mr. Richard Ladd, Mr.
Thomas Sterling, Mr. Robert High, Mr.
William Parker.

10:281 23 September. Lancellott Todd (AA)
administrator of George Langley (AA)
exhibited accounts. Discharge was
granted. Mentions: orphans.

Lancellott Todd (AA) administrator of
John Todd (AA) exhibited accounts.
Discharge was granted.

10:282 24 September. Lancellott Todde (AA)
petitioned that he was surety to widow
of his brother Thomas Todd (AA), & said
widow has since married William
Stafford, who wastes the estate of the
orphans. Said Sarah Stafford summoned
to prove accounts.

10:283 25 September. Charles Hollingworth (TA)
petitioned for search for will of John
Singleton (TA) & LoA to executors, with

oaths of John Elliott, John Broadrib, &
Cornelius Comegys. Administration was
granted in 1676 to Charles Hollinsworth
& Henry Wilcox (overseers) on behalf of
Mary & Judith Hawden.

10:284 27 September. William Chandler (high
sheriff, CH) exhibited summons to Edward
Maddox administrator of Henry Frankcham
(CH). Said Edward exhibited inventory
of said Henry Frankham.

10:285 John Hanson (CH) executor of Richard
Midgley (CH) exhibited accounts.

10:286 28 September. Edward Inglish (CE)
exhibited bond of John Wedge (KE)
administrator of William Chadbourne
(CE), with sureties: Isaac Harney,
Richard Pulling. Said Inglish sworn
Richard Pullen & Richard Adams as
appraisers on 12 August. John Wedge
(KE) exhibited inventory, appraised by
Richard Pullin & Richard Adams.

10:287 William Chandler (CH) exhibited summons
to Temperance Clouder to prove will of
John Ashberry.

1 October. Joseph Hopkins (g, CE)
exhibited bond of John Howell (CE)
administrator of Sara Vanhacke, with
sureties: Thomas Hawker, George Warner.
Appraisers: James Hetborne, Benjamin
Gunnery.
10:288 Joseph Hopkins (g) to administer oath.

Josias Lanham & James Balderston
administrators of Jean DesJardins (KE)
petitioned for appraisers: Charles
Howell (chirurgeon), William Bateman.
Col. Henry Coursey to administer oath.

10:289 2 October. Andrewe Jones produced
Morgan Jones (clarke) & John Evans as
witnesses to be interrogated. Mary
Evans & Elisabeth Jones, 2 other
witnesses, are sick & not able to travel
to Office. William Brereton (SO) to
interrogate said Mary & Elisabeth.

Court Session: 1678

5 October. Joanna Frarrar (SM) widow &
executrix of Robert Frarrar (SM)
exhibited accounts.
10:290 Continuance was granted.

Richard Marsham & George Lingan (CV)
executors of Charles Gosfright
(merchant, CV) exhibited his will,
proved by Thomas Gant & William Bolter.
10:291 Said Marsham & Linghand were granted
administration. Appraisers: Francis
Hutchins, William Bolter. Maj. Samuel
Lane to administer oath.

9 October. Andrew Jones petitioned that
it was uncertain whether William
Brereton (g) had returned from VA to SO,
& that James Dashiele
10:292 (g) to interrogate Mary Evans &
Elisabeth Jones.

John Gibbs who married Anne relict &
administratrix of Edward Best (CE)
exhibited accounts. Mentions: caveat by
James Stavely.

10 October. Elisabeth relict &
executrix of Col. Thomas Brooke (CV)
exhibited additional
10:293 inventory.

12 October. John Fanning (CV) was
granted administration on estate of
William Thompson, who died at house of
said Fanning. Said Fanning is next of
blood in the Province. Appraisers:
Francis Wyne, Robert Midleton. Humphrey
Warren (g, CH) to administer oath.

10:294 John Waterton (CE) exhibited accounts of
Jane Edbden administratrix of William
Ebden (CE). Discharge was granted.

Michaell Taney (CV) administrator of
Jeremiah Williams (CV) exhibited
accounts. Discharge was granted.

10:295 John Browning (CE) administrator of John
Gilbert exhibited additional accounts.

14 October. Mary Dynes relict of
Richard Dod (CH) exhibited that said

Page 70

Richard made will, bequeathing all to said Mary during her lifetime, then to his 2 sons John & Richard equally. Maj. Benjamin Rozer

10:296 to prove said will. Said Mary was granted administration. Appraisers: Joseph Cornel, Thomas Baker. Said Rozer to administer oath.

Michaell Miller (KE) vs. estate of Patrick Gordon (KE). Caveat.

10:297 James Stavely administrator of (N) Salmon vs. (N) Browning administrator of John Gilbert (CE). Caveat.

James Stavely administrator of (N) Stiles vs. John Gibbs who married relict of (N) Best (CE). Caveat.

Capt. Richard Hill (AA) petitioned regarding summon by George Parker administrator of William Done, that he said Hill had a grievous fit of sickness.

10:298 Mentions: Col. Thomas Taylor, Thomas Dryfeild, Mr. Parker. Date: 5 October 1678.

10:299 John Ireland administrator of Margarett Penry (CE) exhibited accounts.

Inventory of John Cage (CH), by appraisers Robert Henly & Robert Roelands.

10:300 Thomas Clipsham who married relict of John Cage (CH) petitioned for copy of LoA & will of said Cage.

Stephen Murty administrator of John Balley (SM) exhibited that he has a judgement vs. John Russell (Cliffts). Continuance was granted.

10:301 Maj. Benjamin Rozer exhibited will of Thomas King (CH), proved by John Douglas & Richard Edlen. Appraisers Robert Robins & John Wheeler were sworn.

County Court of CH exhibited accounts of Mary Ward administratrix of Richard Foukes (CH).

10:302   Said Mary Ward administratrix of Richard Foulkes was granted discharge. Francis Teyne is bound to William Ward who married Mary for residue due to orphans.

10:303   Stephen Burle (AA) administrator of his father Robert Burle exhibited accounts.

James Stavely administrator of Thomas Salmon (CE) exhibited accounts.

10:304   James Stavely administrator of Nath. Stiles (CE) exhibited accounts.

16 October. James Rumsey (CV) executor of Henry Inclock (CV) exhibited accounts.

10:305   James Rumsey (CV) who married Anne relict & executrix of John Bigger (CV) exhibited additional accounts. Mentions: bill of Andrew Tennahill.

Philip Lynes (CH) petitioned for LoA of Robert Downes
10:306   (CH). Said Downes left 2 children, in care of Maj. Benjamin Rozer & other justices of CH, who ordered them to the petitioner.
10:307   Mentions: goods in hands of petitioner of Elisabeth White (dec'd). Mentions items in hands of: Richard Way, Christopher Breames, Anne Pinner, Cuthbeard Musgrove, Edward Ming, Richard Vaughan,
10:308   Richard Pinner. Robert Downes (CH) died intestate & left Margarett relict who administered estate & is now dec'd, & left Robert Downes (son) & Elisabeth Downes (daughter) in care of her husband Christopher Warner. Said widow is now dec'd, & said Warner has remarried, and is now runaway from the Province.
10:309   Said Lynes is empowered to collect all goods owned by said Robert Downes.

Inventory of David Coffin (DO), by appraisers Charles Hutchins & Thomas Daniell, dated 29 July 1678.

Ralph Shawe & William Henfre exhibited inventory of Samuel Clarke.

Court Session: 1678

10:310 John Stone (g, CH) exhibited bond of
John Sanders administrator of Francis
Keene (CH), with sureties: Margery
Stone, William Wells. Date: 21 July
1678.

10 October. Edward Man administrator of
Thomas Read (TA) petitioned that George
Reid (TA), under pretense of a legacy,
detains goods of said estate & refuses
to render any account.
10:311 Said Reid summoned.

29 October. Rachell Sturme (TA) widow
appointed William Bishop (TA) to
administer estate of her husband Richard
Sturme, as chief creditor. Date: 11
October 1678. Witnesses: John Jackson,
John Simmons.
10:312 Appraisers: Stephen Tully, Richard
Jones. Thomas Hinson to administer
oath.

John Keely petitioned to Thomas Notley,
Esq. (Governor) that "my father" died
5/6 years ago, leaving his mother as
administratrix. My mother died about 1
year later, leaving 3 children (2 sons &
1 daughter, youngest age 10) &
maidservant. The two brothers were
bound to James Rigbie & sister with a
neighbor.
10:313 No one has administered the estate. Any
one of the petitioners (the 3 children)
could be granted administration, if they
are over age 17. AA to care for the
heirs.

1 November. Lancellot Todd (brother of
dec'd, AA) procurator for Sarah Stafford
wife of William Stafford & relict &
administratrix of Thomas Todd (AA)
10:314 exhibited accounts. Mentions: orphans.

10:315 William Michell (AA) petitioned that he
& Dr. William Jones (now dec'd) were
overseers of estate of Thomas Roper
(AA). The widow Mary has since married
John Hammon (AA), who is likely to
embezzle the estate. Said Mary is
summoned to render accounts, & secure
the child's portion.

10:316 Elisabeth Wintcles widow petitioned that she has been continually sick & indisposed of body & unable to travel to Office, & requests LoA via Mr. Richard Wollman. Capt. Philemon Loyde to prove the will. Appraisers: William Tanney, Robert Noble.

10:317 2 November. Elisabeth Standle executrix of William Standle petitioned for Mr. Richard Ladd to take oath of Charles Carty, to swear said Elisabeth as executrix, & to swear John Manning & Robert Dixon as appraisers.

10:318 4 November. Col. William Burges (AA) was granted administration on estate of William Jones (practitioner of Physick, AA), who died leaving a widow (who is a lunatic) & children (under age 17), as greatest creditor. Mentions: bond of Joseph Taylor (merchant, London).

10:319 Appraisers: Maj. Samuel Lane, Francis Stockett. Lt. Col. Thomas Taillor to administer oath. Said Taillor to examine the widow.

10:320 8 November. Mary Trwe relict & executrix of Francis Finch (KE) petitioned

10:321 that the petitioner & her husband are both very sick & unable to travel to Office. Henry Hosier (g) to take accounts of said estate, for sake of orphans' shares.

11 November. William Sharp executor of John Webb petitioned for

10:322 Capt. Samuel Bourne to prove said will.

14 November. Thomas Griffin (SM) one of overseers of Richard Chillman renounced administration on his estate. Witnesses: Anthony Evans, Nic. Painter.

10:323 16 November. John Holding (SM) who married Rebecca Neale one of daughters & coheirs of Samuel Neale (SM) exhibited that said Samuel constituted Thomas Pinke & John Barnes as executors. They have #2400 of tobacco for each orphan. Said Barnes is willing to pay child's

portion of said Sarah as well as
daughter to her father as heir to her
brother. Said Sarah is of age 18 &
married to said Barnes.

10:324   19 November. Henry Exon was granted
administration on estate of Richard
Hutchins (SM), as chief creditor.
Security: John Barnes. Appraisers: John
Barnes, John Garnish.

Thomas Highway was granted
administration on estate of Nathaniel
Parsons (SO). Appraisers: George
Haffort, Samuel Coopper. William
Steevens to administer oath.

Mary Dod (CH) was granted administration
on estate of Richard Dod (CH).
10:325   Appraisers: Thomas Baker, Joseph
Cornell. Maj. Benjamin Rozer to
administer oath.

Jane Busse (CV) widow of Henry Busse
(CV) was granted administration on his
estate, who died leaving 2 small
children. Appraisers: George Busse,
George Younge. Maj. Henry Joayles to
administer oath.

10:326   26 November. John Sunderland (CV)
exhibited that James Maxwell (AA), died
leaving a widow & 1 son. Said widow
married Patrick Hall (AA), who was
granted administration on said estate,
with securities: Thomas Knighton, James
Humes. Said Humes is since dec'd, &
petitioner married his widow. Said Hall
is since dec'd, & widow wastes the
property of said orphan, who is now 17.
Petition for Col. Taillor to secure the
estate of said orphan & to put it in
hands of a guardian of choosing of the
orphan.
10:327   Samuel Bourne & Thomas Sterling to prove
lost will of Robert Rider (CV).

Alice Gouldson widow & executrix of
Daniel Gouldson (CV) was granted
administration on his estate. Capt.
Samuel Bourne to prove said will.
Appraisers: Francis Hutching, Samuel

Goosey.   Said Bourne to administer oath.

2 December.   Edward English (g) to prove
will of Isaac Harnes (CE).

John Farr (AA) was granted
administration on estate of Jacob
Walker, as chief creditor.
10:328   Appraisers: Thomas Ford, William Horne.
Col.   Thomas Taillor to administer oath.

5 December.   Anne Herbert (CV) widow of
William Herbert was granted
administration on his estate, who died
leaving 1 son & 1 daughter.   Appraisers:
John Stone, John Chaney.   Mr.   Roger
Brooke to administer oath.

10:329   17 December.   Johanna Gourden (KE) widow
of Patricke Gourden petitioned for
administration on his estate, she being
disabled of her limbs through sickness &
incapable to travel to Office.
Appraisers: MM Isaac Winchester, Francis
Ashberry.   Mr.   William Lawrence to
administer oath.   Maj.   Joseph Wicks
10:330   to represent said Johanna.   Date: 28
November 1678 at KI.   Said Johanna was
granted administration.

18 December.   Bernard Johnson (CV) was
granted administration on estate of
Gervas Shawe (CV),
10:331   who died leaving a widow who refused
administration, as greatest creditor.
Maj.   Henry Joayles to take widow's
renunciation.   Appraisers: John Gelasse,
Gabriell Trusty.   Said Joales to
administer oath.

10:332   26 December.   Joanna Farrar (SM) widow &
executrix of Robert Farrar (SM) was
granted discharge.

1 January.   Henry Stockett petitioned
that Mr. Stavely supplied accounts on
estates of (N) Stiles & (N) Salmon
10:333   & that those accounts may not be
advantageous to said Stockett.   Said
Stockett has distemper.   Petitioner
requests Col.   Thomas Taillor to make
his accounts concerning said estates, so

that he may notify the executors in ENG.
Date: 18 December 1678.

10:334   13 January. Henry Bonnde petitioned on
behalf of his sister (N) Douglas for
Maj. Benjamin Rozer to prove will of
her husband Col. John Douglas. Date: 8
January 1678/9 at Newtowne. Commission
to be sent via Mr. Vansweringen.

10:335   Sheriff (CV) to summon Roger Brooke (CV)
executor of Edward Keene (CV) to render
accounts.

John Pollard (DO) administrator of
Thomas Newman (DO) was granted
discharge.

21 January. John Welshe petitioned
10:336   for access to papers of Mr. Samuel
Dabanck (undersheriff, SM).

10:337   John Welsh (sheriff, AA) or Lt. Col.
Thomas Taillor commissioned to examine
papers of said Dabanck. Said Mr.
Samuel Debanke died at house of Henry
Exon at St. John's, in Assembly time, &
papers examined in presence of Mr.
Edward Golding & Mr. Thomas Frances on
7 December:

10:338   Mentions: Thomas Taylor (merchant, AA),
Edward Parrish, Henry Howard, James
Thomson not to Mr. Rigeley against
Francis Wyne, summons by Mr. Boughton to
James Orruck, (N) Homewood & (N) Arnoll
& (N) Watkins & (N) Hillin, Symon
Cubnall servant to John Homewood, Mr.
Welsh vs. Mr. Homewood, Mr. Thomas
Bland, Mr. Beamont,

10:338½   John Homewood & Hen. Homewood, Robert
Carvile (merchant) to pay John Watkins,
Fr. Stockett, William Stafford to pay
Mr. William Cornewallis, estate of
James Browne, George Parker, John Howard
vs. Cornelius Howard, William Russell
bond to Robert Carvile, Hugh Merrikin
bond to James Rigby, letter of Mrs. de
la Roche to Henry Handslipp. Signed:
Ro. Carvile.

10:339   Susanna Ainsworth (SM) widow & executrix
of George Ainsworth (SM) was granted
discharge.

Margery Good (CV) widow & executrix of Thomas Good (CV) was granted discharge.

10:340 William Steevens (Pocomoke, SO) exhibited will of Steeven Bond (SO), proved by Sam. Beauchamp & Robert Hall. Jane Bond executrix was granted administration.

Margarett Smith widow of Francis Smith (AA) assigned administration to John Beamon.

10:341 Date: 18 November 1676. Signed: Margrett Smith. Witnesses: Thomas Lightfoot. Said Beamon was granted administration. Appraisers: Edward Lunn, James O'Rurrke. Capt. Richard Hill to administer oath.

Exhibited inventory of Stephen Bond (SO), by appraisers Daniel Curtis & Henry Miles, sworn by William Steevens (Pocomoke).

10:342 John Butcher (CH) was granted administration on estate of John Woodward (CH), who made nuncupative will, bequeathing all to Mr. Michell Forsted who refused to accept it & his wife is runaway with another man before he died, & has not returned. Said Butcher is a creditor. Appraisers: Thomas Hussey, Thomas Crackeson. Maj. Benjamin Rozer to administer oath.

Col. Thomas Taillor (AA) on behalf of Elisabeth Coale widow & executrix of William Coale, to prove said William's will.

10:343 Maj. Samuel Lane (AA) on behalf of Mary Thorley widow & executrix of Edward Thorley to prove said Edward's will.

23 January. Edward English (CE) to prove will of Jacob Singleton (CE). Appraisers: William Elms, Richard Pullen. Ebenezar Blackiston sole surviving executor was granted administration, on behalf of John Singleton (father of dec'd, ENG). Said English to administer oath.

10:344   29 January. John Beamon (AA) was granted administration on estate of Francis Smith (AA). Appraisers: Edward Lunn, James Orronck. Capt. Richard Hill to administer oath.

Barnard Johnson (CV) exhibited will of Isaac Vantricht (CV), on behalf of Jochem Kirested. Roger Brooke (g) to prove.

10:345   Col. Thomas Taillor to examine accounts of John Foster.

Gilles Tomkins (CH) exhibited will of William Brookes (CH). Capt. Humphrey Warren to prove.

15 February. Robert Roberson (TA) was granted administration on estate of Thomas Hynson on behalf of widow.

10:346   17 February. Thomas Bankes exhibited additional goods of estate of George Beckwith (CV). Appraisers: Capt. Henry Darnall, John Darnall (g). Said goods to be distributed to children of said Beckwith: John Miles who married eldest daughter Elisabeth (of age). Said Bankes to give bond for portions to other children: Charles, Barbara, Margarett.

10:347   19 February. Mary Allen (CV) widow of Patrick Allin (CV) was granted administration on his estate. Appraisers: Jame Michell, Francis Malden. Richard Ladd (g) to administer oath.

Margarett Stagge relict of John Gittings (CV) exhibited additional payments to be added to accounts of said Gittings:
10:348   (N) Atkey, (N) Rovotom. Mentions: children.

Margarett widow of Thomas Stagge (CV) & relict of John Gittings was granted administration on estate of said Stagge.
10:349   Appraisers: John Mills, William Davis. Capt. Henry Darnall to administer oath.

Margaret Hall widow & executrix of Walter Hall (g) was granted administration on his estate & appraisers were Robert Carvile & Garrat Vansweringen. Since then Mr. Carvile "is gone up the bay and not as yet returned".

10:350 New appraisers: Thomas Courtney, Gilbert Turberfeild (gentlemen).

James Thompson (CV) was granted administration on estate of Edward Player (CV). Appraisers: Patrick Due, Richard Boughen. George Lingan to administer oath.

10:351 Richard Masham one of executors of Charles Gosfright exhibited inventory.

Bernard Johnson exhibited inventory of Gervase Shawe, appraised by James Nuthall & John Galosh.

Mr. Richard Gardiner exhibited PoA to collect debts due estate of Major Weire.
10:352 Signed: Geo. Jones, Honoria Jones (alias Honoria Veire). Richard Gardner procurator for Honoria Jones relict & executrix of John Ware (Rappahannock Co. VA) exhibited his will. Said Gardner is unable to travel to Office. Said Gardner was granted administration on said estate. Clement Hill (g) to administer oath.

10:353 22 February. John Walston (BA) was granted administration on estate of John Leonard (BA), who died with no wife nor child nor any relation in this Province. Appraisers: Robert Jones, James Philips. Col. George Wells to administer oath.
10:354 Exhibited inventory of Walter Hall (SM), appraised by Thomas Courtney & Gilbert Turbervile.

25 February. John Addison administrator of Nicholas Proddy (CH) who was sole executor of Jeremiah Dickenson (CH) exhibited accounts of said Dickenson.
10:355 Thomas Dickenson (son of said Jeremiah) to receive a copy.

28 February. Mary widow of Morgan Jones
(St. Jerome's, SM) was granted
administration on his estate.
Appraisers: Robert Large, Christopher
Sprye.

10:356   Edward Gunnell (BA) administrator of
Joseph Seares (CE) exhibited accounts.
Discharge was granted.

Exhibited bond of John Fanning (CH)
administrator of William Thompson, with
sureties: Thomas Clipsham, Henry
Reynolds. Date: 11 November 1678.

10:357   1 March. Exhibited inventory of Sarah
Vanheck (CE) widow, appraised by
Benjamin Gundry & Ja. Hebron.

Exhibited bond of George Yate (AA)
administrator of Robert Wilson, with
sureties: John Larkin, Rowland Nance.
Date: 12 November 1678.

Exhibited bond of John Butcher (CH)
administrator of John Woodward, with
surety: Henry Hawkins. Date: 21
November 1678.

10:358   Exhibited inventory of William Jones
(physitian, AA), appraised by Samuel
Laine & Francis Stockett.

3 March. Exhibited inventory of John
Beard (TA), appraised by James Murphy &
Edward Foollen

Exhibited inventory of Samuel Clarke
(CH), appraised by William Hensey &
Ralph Shawe.

Capt. Gerrard Sly (SM) administrator of
Richard Chilman (SMC) exhibited his
bond,
10:359   with surety: Thomas Garrard. Date: 7
March 1678.

Exhibited inventory of James Cox (AA).
Col. Thomas Taillor to order Dr. Henry
Lewis (AA) to take a true account.

Elisabeth Foster (TA) administratrix of Seth Foster (TA) exhibited accounts.

10:360   7 March. Exhibited inventory of William Standley (CV), appraised by John Manning & Robert Dixon, sworn by Richard Ladd (g).

Capt. Jonathon Sibrey (CE) on behalf of Mary Brockhurst widow of William Brockhurst (CE) was granted administration on his estate. Appraisers: Richard Nash, John Hiland. Augustine Herman to administer oath.

10:361   Maj. Henry Joales (CV) exhibited bond of Barnard Johnson administrator of Jarvis Shawe, with sureties: James Nuttwell, John Galash. Date: 24 January 1678.

Mary Ward widow & executrix of Mathew Ward (TA) exhibited that appraiser Thomas Hynson is now dec'd. New appraisers: Richard Jones, Robert Smith. Henry Coursey to administer oath.

Michell Miller (KE) was granted administration on estate of William Lee (KE), as greatest creditor. Appraisers: William True, Patrick Sulevant. Henry Hosier (g) to administer oath.

10:362   8 March. Michael Miller (g, KE) administrator of William Lee exhibited his bond, with surety: Capt. Jonathon Sibrey.

Col. William Burges to prove will of Susanna Harnise (AA).

Margery Roelants relict of Robert Roelants (CH) was granted administration on his estate. Appraisers: John Fanning,
10:363   Thomas Clipsham. Col. Benjamin Rozer to administer oath.

Sheriff (TA) to summon John Mitchell & his wife to produce will of George Aldrige (TA). Fees to be charged to William Gary (TA).

Michaell Miller (KE) vs. John Lewis (KE). Said Lewis to show cause why he detains will of John Rye (KE).

10:364 10 March. Thomas Hacker & Edward Beck executors of Johm Dixson (CE) were granted administration on his estate. Edward English (g) to take bond.

Elisabeth Lewis widow & executrix of Dr. Henry Lewis (AA) exhibited his will. Capt. Richard Hill to prove. Appraisers: William Hawkins, Richard Guyn. Said Hill to administer oath.

10:365 12 March. Thomas Trewman (g, CV) was granted administration on estate of John Oxman (CV).

George Parker (CV) vs. William Cromwell (BA) & Nicholas Ruston (BA). Defendants to render accounts of Robert Willson (BA).

Nicholas Hackett (TA) was granted administration on estate of Francis Bridges (died in VA), as principle creditor.

10:366 Nicholas Hackett (TA) vs. Thomas Price (SO). Defendant to exhibit accounts of estate of said Bridges.

Nicholas Hackett (TA) administrator of Francis Bridges gave bond, with sureties: Symon Iron, Robert Brian. Date: 14 March 1678.

15 March. Thomas Bland (AA) vs. Cornelius Howard (AA). Defendant to render accounts of estate of John Grange (BA).

10:367 18 March. John Larkin (the Ridge, AA) was granted administration on estate of Enoch Boulton (AA), as greatest creditor. Elisabeth Boulton widow renounced administration. Date: 15 March 1678. Witnesses: Ri. Boughton, Geo. Holland. Appraisers: Robert Wade, Richard Tyding. Nath. Heathcoate (g) to administer oath.

Court Session: 1678

10:368 21 March. Robert Carvile procurator for Randall Revell & his wife Katherine vs. Andrew Jones administrator of James Jones. Arbitrators: David Browne, William Breereton, Charles Hutchings, Morgan Jones. Sheriff (SO) to **10:369** summon said Andrew.

24 March. Sarah Newton widow of Thomas Newton (DO) appointed her son Edward Newton to administer said estate.
10:370 Date: 23 March 1678. Witnesses: William Trego, Jr., Edward Gould. Said Edward Newton was granted administration. Appraisers: William Trego, William Dorsey. Stephen Gary to administer oath.

10:371 5 March. Elisabeth Tassall (DO) widow of Francis Tassall (DO) was granted administration on his estate. Appraisers: Thomas Flower, John Kirke. John Brooke (chirurgeon) to administer oath.

10:372 7 March. Gerrard Sly (SM) exhibited that Richard Chillman (SM) made a will, constituting Thomas Loquer (an infant) executor & John Garnish & Thomas Griffin overseers. Said Griffin renounced administration. Said Garnish can't find security. Said Sly was granted administration, as greatest creditor, during minority of infant.
10:373 Security: Thomas Gerrard.

8 March. Charles Bayley administrator of Mary Hawkins (AA) exhibited warrants for appraisers Robert Francklin & Walter Carr. Said Francklin could not attend. New appraisers: Walter Carr, Samuel Garland. Nathaniel Heathcoate (g) to administer oath.

10:374 10 March. Charles Hollingsworth (KE) one of overseers of John Singleton was granted administration.

Michaell Miller (KE) on behalf of William Key was granted administration on estate of Edward Reynolds (KE). Appraisers: Josias Lanham, James

Page 84

Balderstone. Maj. James Ringold to administer oath.

Michaell Miller (KE) on behalf of William Key exhibited will of Roger Shacock (KE).
10:375 Maj. James Ringold to prove.

Stephen Gary exhibited will of Anthony Tall (DO), proved on 15 June 1678. Elisabeth Tall widow was granted administration. Appraisers: John Alford, John Edwards.
- John Hudson, age 26, deposed on 16 October 1678 that
10:376 ...
  Anthony Tall (DO) made a nuncupative will in April 1678, devising his lands to his son Philip Tall.
- John Miceell, age 46, deposed on 16 October 1678 the same.

10:377 13 March. William Steevens (g, SO) on behalf of Jane Bond executrix of her husband Stephen Bond was granted administration on his estate.

John Foster administrator of William Chandler (AA) exhibited accounts, sworn before Col. Thomas Taillor. Distribution: orphans of said Chandler. Discharge was granted.

10:378 14 March. Edward Man (TA) administrator of Thomas Read exhibited that he has not found any additional goods.

Edward Man (TA) exhibited accounts of Robert Harwood.

Roger Brooke (CV) exhibited additional accounts of Edward Keene.

Court Session: 1679

11:1 19 March 1678/9. Will of Baker Brooke (de la Brooke Mannor, CV, Surveyor General & Judge of Provincial Court) was exhibited, proved by. Henry Carew & Gerritt Vansweringen. Anne Brooke (widow) was granted administration.

Court Session: 1679

Henry Darnall to take oath.

27 March 1679. Col. William Burges
(AA) exhibited will of Susanna Harnesse
(AA), proved. Said Burges
11:2 was granted administration on behalf of
Jacob Harniss & Elisabeth Harniss
executors. Appraisers: Capt. Richard
Hill, Thomas Francis (g).

Col. William Burges (AA) exhibited will
of John Robynson (AA) on behalf of Mary
Robynson executrix. Said Mary was
granted administration. Appraisers:
John Grey, John Belt.

Col. William Burges (AA) exhibited will
of Capt. Thomas Besson, Sr. (AA) on
behalf of Hester Besson executrix. Said
Hester was granted administration.
Appraisers: Capt. Nicholas Gassaway,
Thomas Francis (g).

11:3 28 March. Margarett Hall (Crosse
Mannor, SM) widow & executrix of Walter
Hall (g, Crosse Mannor, SM) exhibited
that said Walter was bound to Thomas
Bankes (Pointe Patience, CV) on said
Bankes' administration of George &
Francis Beckwith (Pointe Patience, CV).
Said Margarett petitioned for said
Bankes to render accounts & that she be
released of her husband's bond.

11:4 29 March. Margarett Hall (Crosse
Mannor, SM) exhibited that she is
guardian in locage (?) to Philip
Gittings (under age 21) son & heir of
John Gittings (CV, dec'd) by his wife
Margery sister to said Margarett Hall.
Executrix of said Gittings is Margarett
Stagge.
11:5 Said Stagge is summoned to render
accounts on estate of said Gittings & to
pay said Hall the child's portion due
said Philip.

31 March. James Phillips (BA) was
granted administration
11:6 on estate of John Stanford (BA), as
principle creditor. Said Phillips is
unable to travel to Office. Appraisers:

Page 86

John Walston, William Osborne. Col.
George Wells to administer oath.

James Phillips (BA) was granted
administration on estate of James
Browinck (BA),
11:7   as principle creditor. Said Phillips is
unable to travel to Office. Appraisers:
John Walston, William Osborne. Col.
George Wells to administer oath.

Ben. Randall vs. estate of John
Erackson. Caveat entered.

Phylemon Loyd vs. estate of John
Bradbourne (his mother's late overseer).
Caveat entered.

11:8   5 April. William Rawles & his wife
Elisabeth administratrix of Edward
Coppidge (KE) exhibited accounts. Said
Rawles are unable to travel to Office.
Thomas Marsh (g, KE) to examine accounts
and take oath.

Isaac Winchester administrator of
Richard Moore (KE) exhibited accounts.
Said Winchester is unable to travel to
Office. Thomas Marsh (g, KE) to examine
accounts and take oath.

11:9   Elisabeth Christison (TA) widow &
executrix of Wenlock Christison (TA)
exhibited his will. Capt. Phylemon
Loyd to prove said will.

2 April. Robert Ridgely procurator for
Andrew Jones (SO) petitioned that
William Brereton (SO) examine Mr.
William Steevens (g) & Mary Evans
regarding will of Sarah Jones (SO).

3 April. Hester Beard (AA) widow of
John Beard (AA)
11:10   was granted administration on his
estate. Appraisers: William Ramsey,
James Saunders. Col. William Burges to
administer oath.

(N) Covington administrator of David
Williams (SO) exhibited inventory, by
appraisers Cornelius Johnson & Henry

Hayman.

11:11   Col. George Wells (BA) exhibited oath of John Walstone (BA) administrator of John Leonard, sworn 1 March 1678/9. Sureties: James Phillips, William Osborne. Appraisers Robert Jones & James Phillips sworn same day. Inventory was exhibited.

11:12   Col. George Wells exhibited oath of William Osbourne administrator of John Gun (BA), sworn on 1 March 1678/9. Sureties: James Phillips, John Walstone. James Phillips & Nicholas Hampsted, appraisers of said John Gunne, were sworn same day.

John Raddish (merchant, CH) vs. estate of William Loveday (p, CH). Mentions: Joane wife of dec'd. Said Raddish is greatest creditor.

11:13   4 April. John Porter (chyrurgeon, Bristol, ENG) exhibited that Peter Wadding, James Pope, & James Cox (merchants, said city) sent merchandise to the Province, to be managed by said Cox, who is since dec'd in MD. Said Wadding & Pope gave PoA to said Porter. Said Porter was granted administration on estate of said Cox, on behalf of said Wadding & Pope & the kindred of said James Coxe in ENG. Bondsman: Philip Batch (master of the Richard). LoA.

11:14   ...

11:15   Date: 14 September 1678. Witnesses: Philip Batch, John Roger, Thomas Ope. Said Ope deposed on 24 March 1678/9. Signed: William Burges.

11:16   6 April. Capt. William Digges & Nic. Sewall, Esq. exhibited will of Thomas Notley, Esq. (late Governor), constituting Charles Lord Baltimore as executor. Said peer was granted administration, and assigned it to Nic. Sewall, Esq. & Col. Benjamin Rozer. Appraisers: John Darnall, Gerrard Slye (gentlemen). Capt. William Digges to administer oath.

Court Session: 1679

11:17   ...

11:18   9 April. Margarett Stagg relict &
executrix of John Gittings (CV)
exhibited final accounts.

11:19   Richard Ladd (CV) exhibited oath of Mary
Allen widow & executrix of Patrick Allen
(CV), sworn on 4 April 1679. Sureties:
Samuell Holdsworth, James Maycall.
Appraisers James Maycall & Francis
Malden sworn same day.

Sarah Steevens (BA) widow of Giles
Steevens was granted administration on
his estate. Appraisers: Oliver Haile,
Ambrose Gellet. Maj. Thomas Long to
administer oath.

11:20   11 April. An Aldridge (TA) widow of
George Aldridge (TA) petitioned for
Capt. Phylemon Loyd (TA) to prove his
will.

Nathaniell Heathcote (g, AA) exhibited
bond of John Larkin (AA) administrator
of Enoch Boulton. Sureties: George
Yate, John Tate.

11:21   Appraisers Richard Tydeing & Robert Wade
sworn 26 March 1679.

Anne Brooke widow & executrix of Baker
Brooke, Esq. (Dele Brooke Mannor, CV)
petitioned for appraisers: Lt. Col.
Henry Darnall, Charles Boteler
(gentlemen). John Hallee (g) to
administer oath.

Mary Thorley (AA) exhibited will of
Edward Thorley (AA). Said Mary was
granted administration.

Stephen Burley (AA) administrator of
Robert Burley (AA) exhibited accounts.

11:22   Discharge was granted.

Edward Parish (AA) was granted
administration on estate of Samuell
Debanck (AA). Appraisers: Thomas
Francis (g), John Watkins. Col.
William Burges to administer oath.

12 April. Sara widow of William Ford
(DO) exhibited
11:23   his will, proved, constituting Thomas
Taylor (DO), Benjamin Hunt, John
Edmundson, & William Sharpe executors,
on behalf of her younger son Josias
Ford. Said executors refuse
administration. She is very infirm &
cannot travel or stir abroad. Edward
Pinder was granted administration on
behalf of said Sara. Stephen Gary (g)
to take executors' renunciation.
11:24   Appraisers: John Rawlins, John Brooke
(chyrurgeon).

Anne Mason (DO) exhibited will of Miles
Mason (DO). Stephen Gary (g, DO) to
prove. Appraisers: John Edwards, John
Button.

Peter Stookes (DO) administrator of
George Boulton (DO) was granted
discharge.

Anne Evans (SM) exhibited
11:25   the will of Thomas Evans (SM), with LoA.

19 April. Hugh Merrekin (AA) was
granted administration on estate of
Christian Drury (AA). Appraisers:
William Hawkins, Richard Gwin. Capt.
Richard Hill (AA) to administer oath.

John Butcher (CH) exhibited inventory of
estate of John Woodward (CH), by
appraisers Thomas Craxon & Thomas
Hussey.

22 April. Sheriff (AA) to summon Capt.
Richard Hill (AA) administrator
11:26   Samuell Whethers & his wife, to render
accounts.

Capt. Richard Hill (AA) exhibited oath
of John Beamon administrator of Francis
Smith (AA), sworn on 14 April 1679.
Sureties: Rob. Smith, John Richlouse.
Inventory was exhibited, by appraisers
Edward Lunn & James Orrouck.

11:27   23 April. Lydia Watkins (AA) widow of
Thomas Watkins (AA) was granted

administration on his estate. Mr.
Nathaniell Heathcoate to prove his will.

Magdalen widow of James Penn (SM) was
granted administration on his estate.
Appraisers: John Steevenson, John
Danbridge. Richard Gardner (g) to
administer oath.

Maj. Samuell Lane (AA) exhibited will
of George Simmons (AA). Mr. John Welsh
to prove said will. Appraisers: Charles
Abevan, Richard Deavors.

11:28   Inventory of Mr. Thomas Stagg (CV) was
exhibited, by appraisers John Miles &
William Davis.

25 April. Thomas Jackson (CV) who
married Mary Harbud daughter of William
Harbud (CV) exhibited that his
father-in-law William Harbud & his
mother Sarah Harbud are dec'd.
Appraisers: Thomas Tasker, Thomas
Cosden. Roger Brooke (g) to administer
oath.

11:29   26 April. William Laurence exhibited
inventory of Patrick Gordon (KE), by
appraisers Isaac Winchester & Francis
Ashbury. Also exhibited was bond of
Johanna Gordon with sureties: Isaac
Winchester, Francis Ashbury.

28 April. Semelia Garretson widow of
Ruthen Garretson (BA) was granted
administration on his estate.
11:30   Appraisers: Edwarde Bedle, Robert Jones.
Henry Haslewood to administer oath.

James Miles (BA) exhibited that James
Ives & Dr. John Ireland were appointed
to appraise the estate of Samuell Boston
& said Ireland has departed the county.
James Philips was appointed in his
stead. James Ives has since died.
George Smith was appointed in his stead.

11:31   Thomas Bankes (CV) exhibited additional
inventory of George Beckwith (CV), by
appraisers Henry Darnall & John Darnall.
Also exhibited was a final account.

Court Session: 1679

29 April. John Michener (CV) exhibited
inventory of Michaell Crawley (CV), by
appraisers James Nuttall & Barnard
Johnson, sworn by Maj. Henry Joales
(CV).

1 May. Clement Hill (g, SM) exhibited
bond of Richard Geardner (SM)
administrator of Maj. John Weire
11:32   (Rappahannock Co., VA).

Inventory of Kezia White (SM) was
exhibited, by appraisers Joseph Pile &
Joshua Guibert. Administrator is John
Bearecroft.

Col. George Wells (BA) exhibited
inventory of John Stanford (BA), by
appraisers William Osborne & John
Walstone.

11:33   Inventory of Jacob Brownings (BA) was
exhibited, by appraisers William Osborne
& John Wallstone, sworn by George Wells
(g). Also exhibited was bond of James
Philips administrator, with sureties:
William Osbourne, John Wallstone.

Col. George Wells (g, BA) exhibited
bond of James Philips administrator of
John Stanford, with sureties William
Osborne & John Walstone, sworn 7 April
1679.

Col. George Wells (BA) exhibited
inventory of John Gunn (BA), by
appraisers James Phillips & Nicholas
Hempstead.

11:34   Sheriff (SM) to summon Pope Alvey to
exhibit will of Joseph Alvey (SM).

George Parker (attorney of Provincial
Court) on behalf of Leonard Coates & his
wife Martha relict of William Russell
(inn holder, AA) was granted
administration on his estate.
Appraisers: George Parker, John Sollers.
Maj. Samuell Lane to administer oath.

11:35   2 May. James Coursey (TA) exhibited
will of Thomas Harlings (TA). William

Page 92

Coursey (g, TA) to prove said will.

James Coursey (TA) for Elenor Bradborne relict of John Bradborne (TA) exhibited her renunciation. Said Elener gave PoA to Robert Carvile & James Coursey.

11:36   Said Elener also desired William Bishop (TA) as administrator, who is a creditor. Date: 18 March 1678. Signed: Eleanor Bradborne. Witnesses: Roger Weddill, Thomas Crosse, Ja. Coursey.

11:37   Said James Coursey on behalf of Symon Wilmer (merchant) vs. said estate. Caveat entered. Judge ruled that, since Capt. Phylemon Loyd had formerly entered a caveat, that he, as greatest creditor, had a right to administration, by custom.

11:38   Richard Woolman (g, TA) to take bond of said Loyd.

James Coursey (g, TA) administrator of John Scott (TA) exhibited accounts.

11:39   Capt. Henry Darnall exhibited bond of Margarett Stagg administratrix of Thomas Stagg, with sureties: John Evans, John Miles. Date: 19 April 1679.

3 May. James Thompson (CV) exhibited inventory of Edward Player, by appraisers Richard Bongheir & Patrick Dew, sworn by George Lingam.

5 May. Inventory of John Greaer (CV) was exhibited, by appraisers Samuell Goosey & Nicholas Buttrum.

11:40   Robert Carvile procurator for Thomas Marsh (g, KE) exhibited that Mary de Rumple relict & administratrix of John Clemens (TA) had exhibited accounts. Said Marsh married one of the daughters of said Clemens. Said Mary is summoned to make oath on said accounts, so said Marsh may receive his wife's child's portion & security for remainder due other orphans. James de Rumple is now her husband.

7 May. John Baker (SMC) for Ann Spence widow & executrix of David Spence (SO)

11:41   exhibited his will. Capt. Thomas
Walker (SO) to prove said will.

9 May. Thomas Walker (high sheriff, SO)
exhibited summons to Andrew Jones (SO)
administrator of James Jones.

11:42   10 May. Mary Brockhurst (CE) widow
exhibited that a poor man died in her
house, leaving a small estate,
bequeathing legacies & constituting the
petitioner as executrix. Augustine
Herman to prove will of Thomas Lewin.

11:43   Rowland Williams (CE) for Mary
Brockhurst widow & executrix of William
Brockhurst (CE) petitioned for
appraisers: William Price, John Hiland.
Augustine Herman (CE) to administer
oath.

John Peerce son & heir of John Peerce
(chyrurgeon, CV) exhibited his will,
proved by Robert Lee. Said son was
granted administration. Appraisers:
Thomas Sprigge, Andrew Abbington.

11:44   Lt. Col. Henry Darnall to administer
oath.

12 May. Inventory of Michaell Rochford
(SM) was exhibited, by appraisers Robert
Carvile & Gerrit Vansweringen.

Robert Carvile (recorder, SMC) for
Randell Revell (SO) & his wife Katherine
vs. Andrew Jones (SO) executor of his
uncle James Jones & administrator of his
aunt Sarah Jones. Petition for copies
of depositions.

11:45   Answer of Andrew Jones. Said James
devised a moyety of said land to said
Sarah & other to said Andrew. At death
of said Sarah, estate was undivided.

11:46   Said Andrew indicated that by law said
Sarah was not capable of disposing of
that estate, in joint tenancy. By law,
said estate in joint tenancy is to go to
the survivor. Said Andrew said that
said Randall should have administration
of said Sarah. Questions:

11:47   Mentions: said Thomas Daniell to write
will, Katherine Revell,

11:48   bequest to wife of Leonard Jones.

11:49 ...
11:50 Randall Revell & his wife Katherine
       exhibited interrogations. Thomas
       Daniell deposed that Sara Jones
       (Wicokomaco) died October last, & she
       was not well satisfied with her kinsman
       Andrew Jones.
11:51 ...
11:52 ...
    • Dorothy Philips deposed.
11:53 ...
11:54 ...
    • Jane Watts deposed.
11:55 ...
11:56 Cross-examination questions by Andrew
       Jones.
11:57-58 ...
11:59 ...
    • Mr. Steevens deposed.
11:60 ...
11:61 ...
    • John Evans, age 40, deposed.
11:62 ...
       Mentions: that Katherine Revell went
       to house of Nicholas Rice.
11:63 ...
    • Morgan Jones (minister of the
       Gospel), age 42, deposed.
11:64 ...
       Mentions: Mary Fishpoole at house of
       Andrew Jones last November, Joane
       Watts, Rice Thomas,
11:65 ...
       Dorothy Philips, Elisabeth Jones
       (wife of deponent), Thomas Daniell.
11:66 ...
    • Mary Evans, age 36, deposed
11:67 ...
       on 22 April 1679.
    • Thomas Shanke, age 29, deposed on 1
       October 1678 that he was a servant
       to James Jones husband to said Sara.
       Mentions: Joane Watts is maid to
       Mrs. Katherine Revell.
11:68 ...

11:69 12 May. Randall Revell & his wife
       Katherine vs. Andrew Jones. Robert
       Ridgeley procurator for Andrew Jones
       petitioned for copies.

14 May. Stephen Gary (g, DO) exhibited
will of Samuell Prethett (DO).
11:70   Inventory was exhibited by appraisers
William Trego, Jr. & William Dossey.

Stephen Gary (g, DO) exhibited bond of
Edward Newton administrator of Thomas
Newton, with sureties: John Dossey,
William Dossey.   Date: 17 April 1679.
11:71   Inventory was exhibited, by appraisers
William Trego, Jr. & William Dossey.

Stephen Gary (g, DO) exhibited will of
Miles Mason (DO), proved.

16 May. Henry Hollis (CV) was granted
administration on estate of John Moretun
(CV), who unfortunately drowned,
11:72   as principle creditor. Appraisers:
Simon Edwards, James Morris. Capt.
Richard Ladd to administer oath.

Robert Francklin (high sheriff, AA)
exhibited summons to Capt. Richard Hill
administrator of Samuell Whethers & his
wife Elisabeth
11:73   to render accounts.

James Ellis (AA) on behalf of Elisabeth
Gross administratrix of Roger Grosse
(TA) was granted administration on his
estate. Appraisers: John Davies,
William Lawes. Capt. Phylemon Loyd to
administer oath.

Robert Francklin (high sheriff, AA)
exhibited
11:74   summons to Cornelius Howard
administrator of John Grange (BA) to
render accounts.

20 May. Inventory of Patrick Allen (CV)
was exhibited, by appraisers James
Macall & Francis Maldin, sworn by
Richard Ladd (g, CV).

John Dalton (TA) on behalf of Richard
Girling was granted administration
11:75   on estate of George Bayley (TA).
Appraisers: Thomas Alexander, John
Whittington. Capt. George Cowley to
administer oath.

Margaret Stagg (CV) relict & executrix
of John Gittings exhibited accounts.
Mentions: children.

11:76 21 May. Elisabeth Alvey (SM) exhibited
will of Joseph Alvey (SM), proved by
Henry Ferneley & Edward Cole. Said
Elisabeth executrix was granted
administration. Appraisers: William
Langworth, John Bayley, Sr. Clement
Hill (SM) to administer oath.

22 May. Sheriff (CE) exhibited summons
to Edward English (g) regarding his
administration of estate of Edward
Chicken (KE).

11:77 Sheriff (CV) to cause Richard Smith, Sr.
to prove will of John Grammer (CV).

Sheriff (CV) to summon Elisabeth Hollis
relict of John Grammer regarding her
husband's will, exhibited by Robert
Carvile procurator for William
Dorrington.

24 May. Sheriff (BA) to summon Jane
Gunnell (BA) to render accounts on
estate of her husband Thomas Overton
(BA).

James Stavely one of administrators of
Nathaniell Stiles (CE) exhibited that
appraiser John Dixon
11:78 is dec'd & appraiser William Salbury is
sick. New appraisers: Edward Jones,
Gideon Gundery. Capt. Jonathon Sibrey
to administer oath.

James Stavely (CE) exhibited that Edward
Inglish (g, CE) is administrator of
Edward Chicken (KE), but no inventory
has been exhibited.
11:79 Said Stavely was granted administration
on said Chicken's estate, unadministered
by said Inglish. Security: Michaell
Miller (KE). Appraisers: Edward Jones,
Gideon Gundary. Capt. Jonathon Sibrey
to administer oath.

Michaell Miller (g, KE) on behalf of
Maj. James Ringgold (g, KE) & Samuel

11:80 Tovy (g, KE)
exhibited will of William Key (KE) &
renunciation of said Ringgold & Tovy.
Mentions: Michaell Miller (high sheriff,
KE) & his subsheriff William Raules &
Josias Lanham (carpenter) bound to said
Key for building a courthouse & prison
in KE.

11:81 Date: 15 May 1679. Said Miller was
granted administration. Security: James
Stavely (CE). Appraisers: William
Bateman, Thomas Boone. Said Ringgold to
administer oath.

11:82 26 May. Randall Revell & his wife
Katherine (SO) vs. Andrew Jones (SO).
Regarding: estates of James Jones & his
wife Sarah. Continuance. Notice

11:83 to procurators Robert Carvile & Robert
Ridgely.

20 May. Capt. Phylemon Loyd (TA)
exhibited will of Edward Winkles (TA),
proved.

Capt. Phylemon Loyd (TA) exhibited will
of Richard Webb (TA), proved.

Capt. Phylemon Loyd (TA) exhibited will
of Philip Steevenson (TA), on behalf of
Anne Steevenson executrix.

11:84 Said Loyd to prove said will. Said Anne
was granted administration. Appraisers:
James Phyne, Symon Stevens. Said Loyd
to administer oath.

Capt. Phylemon Loyd (TA) exhibited will
of William Jones (TA) on behalf of
Rebecca Jones widow & executrix. Said
Loyd to prove said will. Said Rebecca
was granted administration. Appraisers:
James Scott, Thomas Collins. Said Loyd
to administer oath.

11:85 2 June. Inventory of James Pennington
(CV) was exhibited, by appraisers
Richard Smith, Jr. & Willam Hill.

Nathaniell Heathcoate (g, AA) exhibited
will of Thomas Watkins (AA), proved.

Nathaniell Heathcoate (g, AA) exhibited his renunciation as executor of Samuell Debuncke (AA).

11:86   3 June. Stephen Gary (high sheriff, DO) exhibited will of Henry Bradley on behalf of Mary Bradley sole executrix. Said Mary was granted administration. Appraisers: Bartholomew Ennall, Michaell Basse. William Stevens (g) to administer oath.

Anne James (KE) relict & administratrix of Edward Lowder (KE) exhibited accounts. Discharge was granted.

11:87   Maj. Samuell Lane exhibited oath of Leonard Loates & his wife Martha administrators of William Russell (AA), sworn 12 May 1679. Sureties: Thomas Ford, John Gale. Robert Conant (AA) accepted these sureties. Appraisers George Parker & John Sollers were sworn same day.

Maj. Samuell Lane (AA) exhibited inventory of Edward Thorley (AA).

11:88   Thomas Vaughan (TA) exhibited summons of Mary de Rumple relict & administratrix of John Clements (TA) to render accounts.

Inventory of George Utie (BA) was exhibited, by appraisers Miles Gibson & Edward Gunnell.

11:89   James Coursey (g, TA) on behalf of William Bishop (TA) administrator of Richard Sturme (TA) was granted continuance.

John Stanesby (high sheriff, BA) exhibited summons to William Cromewell & Nicholas Ruxton to render accounts on estate of Robert Wilson.

11:90   Inventory of Mathew Warde (TA) was exhibited, by appraisers Richard Jones & Robert Smith.

4 June. Inventory of William Russell (AA) was exhibited, by appraisers George Parker & John Sollers, sworn by Maj. Samuell Lane.

George Parker (g, CV) administrator of William Done (CV) exhibited accounts.

11:91 Maj. Samuell Lane who married Margaret administratrix of John Burridge (AA) exhibited accounts, but cannot travel to Office. Nathaniell Heathcoate (g, AA) to examine accounts & administer oath.

Lydia Watkins widow & executrix of Thomas Watkins (AA) petitioned for appraisers Henry Ridgely

11:92 & Jacob Harniss. Capt. Richard Hill (g) to administer oath.

Henry Darnall (g, CV) exhibited summons to Richard Smith, Sr. (CV) regarding will of John Grammer. He also exhibited summons to Elisabeth Hollis relict of John Grammer.

11:93 Thomas Bright (KE) on behalf of Mathew Eareckson was granted administration on estate of his brother John Eareckson (KE). Appraisers: Thomas Osbourne, Valentine Southerne. Joseph Weekes (g) to administer oath.

5 June. Capt. Richard Hill (g, AA) administrator of Elisabeth Whethers (AA) exhibited

11:94 accounts.

Robert Smith (TA) on behalf of Thomas Norris was granted administration on estate of Henry Pearle (TA), as principle creditor. Appraisers: John Broadribb, William Austine. William Bishopp (G) to administer oath.

11:95 John Welsh (g, AA) exhibited will of George Simmons (AA), proved. Maj. Samuell Lane & Nathan Smith executors were sworn. Appraisers Charles Abevan & Richard Deavors were sworn.

Court Session: 1679

Col. Vincent Lowe (Surveyor General, TA) exhibited will of William Godwin. Said Lowe to prove.

6 July [sic]. Peter Archer (CV) was granted administration on estate of Ann Keverne (spinster, CV).

11:96 Thomas Marsh (g, KE) exhibited commission to examine accounts of Isaac Winchester administrator of Richard Moore.

Thomas Marsh (g, KE) exhibited commission to examine accounts of Elisabeth Rawles executrix of Edward Coppidge (KE).

11:97 6 June. Mary de Rumple petitioned as relict & administratrix of John Clements, (TA). Said petitioner is feeble & ancient & by extremely hot weather is granted continuance.

11:98 Richard Gardner (g, SM) exhibited oath of John Steventon & John Dawbridge appraisers of James Pean (SM), sworn on 11 May 1679.

Clement Hill (g, SM) exhibited oath of William Lanworth & John Bayley, Sr. appraisers of Joseph Alvey, sworn on 29 May 1679.

Henry Darnall (g, CV) exhibited oath of Thomas Sprigg & Andrew Abbington appraisers of John Peerce (chyrurgeon, CV), sworn on 5 June 1679.

11:99 Capt. Richard Hill (AA0 exhibited oath of Alice Skidmore administratrix of Edward Skidmore (AA), sworn on 11 May 1679.

Capt. Richard Hill (AA) exhibited commission to take bond of Hugh Merrikin administrator of Christian Drury. Said Hugh cannot find security.

George Yates (AA) petitioned for new appraisers for estate of Robert Willson (BA): John Thomas, Rowland Nance.

Court Session: 1679

Anthony deMontidier to administer oath.

11:100 John Mould (CH) petitioned that he
married a daughter of Francis Posey (CH,
dec'd), whose widow married John
Villaine (CH, now dec'd), who died
possessed of 300 a. plus chattel. Said
Villaine made a will bequeathing ½ of
his estate to his wife & her 2 children
she had by him; the other ½ to his 2
children he had by his wife after the
death of said Villaine. Allexander
Smith married his widow & has the will
of said Villaine.
11:101 <does not exist>
11:102 Said Smith is summoned.

Col. William Burges (AA) exhibited will
of John Roberson, proved.
11:103 Also exhibited oath of Mary Roberson
executrix, sworn on 1 May 1679.
Appraisers John Grey & John Belt were
sworn same day. Inventory was
exhibited.

Col. William Burges (AA) exhibited oath
of Hester Beard administratrix of John
Beard (AA), sworn on 2 May 1679.
Sureties: Anne Gassaway, John Green.
11:104 Appraisers William Rumzey & James
Saunders sworn same day. Inventory was
exhibited.

Col. William Burges (AA) exhibited will
of Thomas Besson, Sr., proved. Hester
Besson executrix
11:105 sworn on 29 April 1679. Appraisers
Richard Tydings & James Saunders sworn
same day. Inventory was exhibited.

Col. William Burges (AA) exhibited oath
of Capt. Richard Hill & Thomas Francis
appraisers of Susanna Harnies (AA),
sworn on 10 May 1679. Inventory was
exhibited.

11:106 11 June. Warrant for resurvey of land
of Mr. Francis Ancktell in Choptank.
First survey was 22 August 1659. Ralph
Elston has built a dwelling on part of
land. Per John Hunt & Allexander
Laremore, there is another parcel of 100

a. belonging to Mr. Anckell adjoining
this land on the west. Land contains
440 a. Date: 23 May 1679, Wye River.
Signed: William Coursey.
11:107 Survey: <metes & bounds>
11:108 for 500 a.

Charles County Court. Date: 9 November
1663. Elisabeth relict of John Belaine
exhibited his will, proved before Mr.
Henry Adams & Mr. Thomas Matthewes, by
John Courte, Meverell Hulle, &
Allexander Smith.

John Addison (g, SM) exhibited
renunciation of Joan Loveday relict of
estate of William Loveday
11:109 (p, CH). Date: 4 April 1679.
Witnesses: James Finlay, Michaell
Parvinge. Before: John Stone. John
Munn (CH) procurator for John Raddish
was granted administration.
11:110 Appraisers: Henry Aspinall, Roger
Dickinson. John Stone to administer
oath.

Capt. Richard Hill (AA) exhibited oath
of Elisabeth Lewis widow & executrix of
Henry Lewis, sworn 26 April 1679. Also
exhibited was will, proved.
11:111 Appraisers William Hawkins & Richard
Gwin were sworn same day.

Sheriff (AA) to summon Cornelius Howard
to render accounts on estate of John
Grange (AA).

12 June. John Mechener (CV) one of
executors of Michaell Crauley exhibited
accounts.

11:112 14 June. Inventory of George Simmons
(AA) was exhibited, by appraisers
Charles Abevan & Richard Deavor.

Elisabeth Darnall (SM) relict of John
Darnall (SM) was granted administration
on his estate. Appraisers: John
Goldsmith, John Suttle. John Lewellin
(g, SM) to administer oath.

18 June. Edward English (g, CE) exhibited inventory of Edward Chicken, by appraisers Benjamin Ricard & Robert Park.

11:113 Also exhibited was accounts of said Edward Chicken (KE).

Will of Jacob Singleton (CE) was exhibited, proved. Inventory was exhibited, by appraisers Richard Pullin & William Elmer.

11:114 Will of John Dixon (CE) was exhibited, proved. Inventory was exhibited, by appraisers Benjamin Gundry & Gideon Gundry, sworn by Edward English (g, CE).

Edward English (g, CE) exhibited bond of Thomas Hawker & Edward Beck, with sureties: John Willis, Benjamin Gundry.

11:115 Will of An Tolson (CE) was exhibited, proved.

Will of Isaac Harnise (CE), was exhibited, proved.

Jonathon Sibrey (high sheriff, CE) exhibited summons of Edward English (g, CE) to render accounts of Edward Chicken (KE).

11:116 Edward English (g, CE) on behalf of Edmond Cantwell (New Castle on Delaware River) exhibited nuncupative will of John English, constituting said Cantwell as executor. Said Edward to prove. Said Cantwell was granted administration. Appraisers: George Oldfeild, Richard Edmonds. Inventory of goods & chattels under hands of John Francklin, William Porter, & Thomas Spry was exhibited.

23 June. Inventory of Miles Mason (DO) was exhibited, by appraisers John Ebden & John Butten,

11:117 sworn by Stephen Gary (g, DO).

25 June. Inventory of William Ford (DO) was exhibited, by appraisers John Brooke & John Rawlling. Also exhibited was

renunciation of executorship by 2 of
executors Thomas Taylor & Benjamin Hunt
on 17 April 1679.

11:118   Edward Pinder to administer estate on
behalf of Sarah Ford widow. Witnesses:
Batt. Taylor, Grace Jones.

William Sharpe & John Edmondson
11:119   2 of executors of William Ford renounce
executorship on 14 May 1679. Witnesses:
James Charlcraft, John Graye.

Sheriff (DO) to summon John Keirke &
Thomas Flower appraisers of Francis
Tassall (DO) to show why they will not
certify their appraisal.

27 June. John Homewood (AA)
11:120   was granted administration on estate of
Thomas Homewood (AA), on behalf of
orphans. Appraisers: Robert Davidge,
William Hawkins. Capt. Richard Hill to
administer oath.

Nathaniell Heathcoate (g, AA) exhibited
accounts of Samuell Lane & his wife
Margaret on estate of John Burridge
(AA).

11:121   Sheriff (CV) to summon Richard Johnes
(CV) administrator of John Meares (CV)
to render accounts.

28 June. Inventory of William Harbut &
his wife Sarah (CV) was exhibited, by
appraisers Thomas Tasker & Thomas
Cosden.

30 June. Samuell Tovy (g, KE) exhibited
accounts on his administration of
Vincent Atchinson (KE).

11:122   Samuell Tovy (g, KE) exhibited accounts
on his administration of John Wright
(KE).

Samuell Tovy (g, KE) exhibited accounts
on his administration of William Norman
(KE).

Samuell Tovy (g, KE) exhibited accounts
on his administration of Richard

Fillingham (KE).

11:123 3 July. Inventory of William Brockhurt (CE) was exhibited, by appraisers John Hiland & William Price.

Augustine Herman (g, CE) exhibited bond of Mary Brockhurst, with sureties: William Dore, John Hyland.

Will of Thomas Lewin (CE) was exhibited, proved.

11:124 Inventory of James Pean (SM) was exhibited, by appraisers John Steeventon & John Dabridgcourt.

4 July. Will of John Grammer (CV) was exhibited, proved.

8 July. Inventory of Henry Lewis (AA) was exhibited, by appraisers William Hawkins & Richard Guin, sworn by Capt. Richard Hill (g).

11:125 Cornelius Howard (AA) administrator of John Grange (BA) exhibited accounts.

9 July. Col. Vincent Lowe (Surveyor General, TA) on behalf of Arthur Norwood who married widow of John Eason (TA)
11:126 was granted administration on his estate. Appraisers: Robert Napp, Richard Golde. Said Lowe to administer oath.

14 July. George Cowley (g, TA) exhibited inventory of estate of George Bayley (TA), by appraisers Thomas Allexander & John Wittington.
11:127 Also exhibited was bond, dated 23 June 1679, of Richard Girling administrator, with sureties: John Wittington, John Staneley.

17 July. Capt. Gerard Slye (SM) administrator of William Watts (SM) exhibited accounts.

19 July. Stephen Gary, exhibited oath of Edward Pindar administrator of William Ford (DO)

11:128   for use of Sarah Ford widow of said
William, sworn 23 April 1679. Sureties
(said Pindar): John Brooke, Edward
Steevens. Also oath of appraisers John
Rawlins & John Brookes (chyrurgeon),
sworn same day.

Stephen Gary (DO) exhibited summons to
John Kirke & Thomas Flowers appraisers
of estate of Francis Tassall.

11:129   Said inventory was exhibited. Elisabeth
Tassall widow of Francis Tassall
petitioned

11:130   that she is envied by her neighbors & so
threatened, that she be allowed her
1/3rd & a portion for her young child

11:131   (under age 21). John Kirke appraiser
was granted administration, & to give
bond to widow. Bartholomew Ennalls to
take said bond.

11:132   Inventory of Thomas Evans (SM) was
exhibited, by appraisers Jacob Looten &
Robert Cran.

Inventory of Thomas Overton (BA) was
exhibited, by appraisers John Stanesby &
William Hollis. Also exhibited was bond
of George Gunnell administrator of said
Overton, with sureties: John Stansby,
William Hollis.

11:133   Abigall Wright administratrix of Arthur
Wright (DO) exhibited accounts.

21 July. Richard Johns (Clifts, CV) one
of executors of John Meares exhibited
accounts.

23 July. Elisabeth Holt (St. John's
Hundred, SM) widow & administratrix of
David Holt (SM) was granted
administration on his estate.
Appraisers: William Hatton, Henry
Phipps. Kenelme Cheseldine to
administer oath.

11:134   Bond was taken, with surety: Thomas
Speake.

Kenelme Cheseldine (Attorney General,
SM) executor of John Jones was granted
continuance.

24 July. John Coode (SM) administrator of Henry Spry exhibited accounts.

26 July. William Rawles & his wife Elisabeth administratrix of Edward Coppidge (KE) exhibited accounts, but are not
11:135 able to travel to Office. James Ringgold (g, KE) to examine & administer oath.

Isaac Winchester administrator of Richard Moore (KE) exhibited accounts, but is not able to travel to Office. Thomas Marsh (g, KE) to
11:136 examine & to administer oath.

Anthony Workeman administrator of Edward Browne (KE) exhibited accounts, but is not able to travel to Office. Joseph Weecks (g, KE) to examine & administer oath.

11:137 Sara Deane relict & administratrix of Thomas Warren (KE) exhibited accounts, but is not able to travel to Office. Henry Hosier (g, KE) to examine & administer oath.

Joane Woorkeman relict of Robert Dunne (KE) exhibited accounts.

Michaell Miller (KE) exhibited will of William Key. James Ringgold (g, KE) to prove.

11:138 28 July. George Gunnell (BA) administrator of Thomas Overton exhibited accounts.

Henry Elliot who married Jane administratrix of John Halfehead exhibited accounts. Discharge was granted.

John Dabridgcourt who married Ann (SM) executrix of Edward Clarke exhibited accounts.

11:139 Inventory of Joseph Alvey (SM), by appraisers William Langworth & John Bayly.

Elias Nutthall who married a daughter of George Beckwith vs. Thomas Bankes administrator of said Beckwith. Plaintiff desires child's distribution.

11:140 Request for price of tobacco. Request for security for portions due Charles, Margaret, & Barbara Beckwith.

Robert Carvile procurator for Henry Ward vs. James Rumsey executor of Henry Trulock. Said Ward is a creditor, & obtained 2 judgements on 9 April 1676. Exceptions to accounts are cited.

11:141 Mentions: Thomas Starling, Christopher Rousby.

11:142 Said James Rumzey to have a copy of exceptions.

Robert Carvile (SM) attorney for Daniell Jenifer (g) vs. James Thompson (CV) administrator of William Greene. Plaintiff exhibited exceptions to accounts.

11:143 Mentions: orphans.

11:144 29 July. John Herd (SM) executor of Jeffery Hudson (SM) exhibited accounts. Discharge was granted.

Richard Keene (CV) was granted administration on estate of Thomas Booty (CV). Appraisers: William King, John Evans. John Griggs to administer oath.

11:145 Stephen Murty (SM) administrator of John Bayley exhibited accounts.

30 July. Dorothy Homan (SM) administratrix of Herbert Homan (SM) exhibited accounts. Discharge was granted.

31 July. Mary Blangey relict & administratrix of Disburrough Bennet (KE) exhibited accounts, but is unable to travel to Office. William Lawrence (g, KE)

11:146 to examine & administer oath.

Additional inventory of Nicholas Proddy (CH) was exhibited, by appraisers John Wheeler & Thomas Shuttleworth. John

Court Session: 1679

Addison (SM) exhibited accounts. Discharge was granted.

11:147 Inventory of Rutten Garettson (BA), by appraisers Edward Bedell & Robert Jones. Bond of Semelia Garretson was exhibited, with sureties: Edward Bedell, Robert Jones.

John Stanesby (high sheriff, BA) exhibited citation ot Jane Gunnell administratrix of Thomas Overton. Date: 17 June 1679.

Maj. Thomas Trueman (CV) administrator of his brother Nathaniell Trueman exhibited that he is ready to satisfy debts of said estate.

11:148 Garret Vansweringen (SMC) administrator of William Baker exhibited accounts. Discharge was granted.

1 August. Inventory of Daniell Goldson (CV) was exhibited, by appraisers Samuell Goosey & Francis Hutchings.

John Sunderland (Cliffts, CV) administrator of James Humes exhibited accounts.

Love Jones administratrix of Constant Daniell (SM) exhibited accounts. Discharge was granted.

11:149 William Bishop (TA) exhibited will of Thomas Hynson, proved. Appraisers Richard Jones & John Cheir were sworn 19 June 1679. Ann Hynson executrix was sworn same day. Inventory was exhibited.

11:150 Mary Tilghman (TA) widow of Richard Tilghman (TA) was granted continuance.

4 August. Inventory of William Lee (KE) was exhibited, by appraisers Patrick Sulivant & William True.

Inventory of John Moorton (CV) was exhibited, by appraisers Symon Edwards & James Morris.

John Guyat & his wife Alice (CV) exhibited accounts of Samuell Graves (CV).

11:151 Will of Daniell Gouldson (CV) was exhibited, proved. Capt. Samuel Bourne (CV) exhibited oath of Alice Gouldson executrix of Daniel Gouldson, sworn on 17 June 1679. Appraisers Francis Hutchings & Samuell Goosey sworn same day.

11:152 Capt. Richard Ladd (CV) exhibited oath of Henry Hollis administrator of John Mooretun (CV), sworn on 17 May 1679. Surety: Symon Edwards. Appraisers Simon Edwards & James Morris sworn same day.

Will of John Webb (TA) was exhibited, proved.
11:153 Elisabeth Macdowell relict of Robert & administratrix of William Standly (Pattexant River, CV) exhibited accounts.

Elisabeth Strong (Clifts, CV) relict of William Macdowell exhibited accounts.

George Parker (CV) sued for LoA on estate of Roger Thorpe (merchant, CE) & desired Capt. Samuell Bourne to administer oath. Said Bourne said
11:154 that said Parker would not take oath, but merely disclaimed his right to said estate.

5 August. sheriff (BA) to summon Peter Ellis & his wife administratrix of William Palmer (BA) to render accounts.

Henry Hosier (g, KE) to swear Mary True on accounts of her husband Francis Finch.

Robert Ellis administrator of John Underwood (TA) exhibited accounts, but cannot travel to Office. William Bishop (g, TA) to examine said accounts & administer oath.

11:155 Francis Malden (CV) & Henry Barnes (CV) exhibited accounts of estate of Owen

Griffith. Discharge was granted.

6 August. Robert Carvile procurator for
Henry Ward vs. estate of Henry Trulock.
James Rumsey (CV) exhibited answer.

7 August. Edward Pack (CV) & John Feild
(CV) executors of Martha Hill exhibited
accounts.

11:156 11 August. Henry Howard (AA) exhibited
will of John Pawson (city of York, ENG),
constituting his brother Henry Pawson
executor. Said Howard exhibited PoA
from said Henry. [Paragraph in Latin.]
11:157-159 ...
11:160 Signed: Richard Dennis (notary).
Witnesses: Charles Woolf, Thomas Sugden.

Inventory of Thomas Homewood (AA) was
exhibited, by appraisers William Hawkins
& Robert Davidge.
11:161 Richard Hill exhibited oath of William
Hawkins & Robert Davidg appraisers of
Thomas Homewood. Date: 8 July 1679.

Elias Beach & his wife Sara exhibited
accounts of estate of Richard Cole (SM).

Robert Ridgely (SM) on behalf of Ann
Hardye exhibited her petition:
11:162 as widow of Robert Hardye (p,
Wiccocomico River, SO), said dec'd left
petitioner with 7 small children: 1 by a
former husband, 5 by dec'd born in his
lifetime, & 1 born since his death. He
left no servant & inconsiderable stock.
His will was exhibited,
11:163 witnessed by John Windey & William
Brereton. Date: 4 August 1679. Said
Ann was granted administration.
Appraisers: William Keene, Thomas
Humphryes. William Brereton to
administer oath.

11:164 Robert Ridgely for Capt. Thomas Walker
(SO) administrator of John Markham was
granted continuance.

Robert Ridgely administrator of John
Evans (SO) executor of Nicholas Rice was
granted continuance.

13 August. John Hammond administrator of Richard Russell (AA) exhibited accounts.

11:165 Mary Hammond relict & administratrix of Thomas Roper (AA) exhibited accounts, but is unable to travel to Office. Richard Hill to examine said accounts & administer oath.

Anne Hawkins relict & executrix of Stephen White (AA) exhibited accounts, but is unable to travel to Office.
11:166 Richard Hill (g) to examine said accounts & administer oath.

Margarett Worrall relict & administratrix of Richard Ambrose (CH) exhibited accounts. Robert Henley (g) to examine said accounts & administer oath.

15 August. Richard Clarke (CV) for his wife Susanna Clarke relict & executrix of Francis Streete exhibited accounts.

11:167 Samuell Abbot (TA) exhibited accounts on estate of Nickolas Holmes.

John Pattison (TA) administrator of John Blower exhibited accounts.

16 August. Inventory of Isaack Vantrick (CV) was exhibited, by appraisers Samuell Goosey & Symon Wooton.

Henry Henley administrator of Richard Harris (CH)
11:168 was granted discharge & exhibited security for distribution to orphans.

Inventory of Thomas Booty (CV) was exhibited, by appraisers William King & John Evans.

Inventory of Henry Bradley (DO) was exhibited, by appraisers Bartholomew Ennalls & Michaell Busse.

18 August. Thomas Flowers (DO) executor of Anthony Handaker exhibited his will.
11:169 Bartholomew Ennalls to prove said will.

Said Flowers was granted administration.
Appraisers: John Walker, Alexander
Fisher. Said Ennalls to administer
oath.

11:170   Petition of John Kirke (DO)
administrator of Francis Tassall (DO)
for Bartholomew Ennalls (g, DO) to take
security.
11:171   Mentions: Francis Tassall (youngest
child of dec'd), Elisabeth Tassall
(widow) who
11:172   renounced administration on said estate.

20 August. John Peerce executor of his
father John Peerce (CV) was granted
continuance.

Allen Smith (CH) who married relict of
John Bolaine was summoned to exhibit
will of said Bolaine. Said will was
exhibited & commission issued to Thomas
Mathews &
11:173   Henry Adams (g), dated 29 October 1663,
to prove said will. John Mould to have
a copy of said will.

21 August. William Ward (CH) who
married Mary relict & administratrix of
George Credwell exhibited accounts.

William Ward (CH) who married Mary
relict & administratrix of George
Credwell administrator of Richard Fowkes
exhibited accounts.

11:174   Richard Marsham (CV) one of executors of
Charles Gosfreight was granted
continuance.

11:175   Richard Marsham for Jone Jenkins
administratrix of William Jenkins (CV)
was granted continuance.

23 August. Robert Carvile procurator
for Henry Ward vs. estate of Henry
Trulock. James Rumsey executor
appeared. Ruling: exceptions allowed.

Robert Carvile procurator for
11:176   Daniel Jenifer vs. estate of William
Greene. James Thompson administrator

Court Session: 1679

appeared. Ruling: exceptions allowed.

Richard Collins who married Sara executrix of William Hambleton (TA) exhibited accounts.

25 August. John Howell (CE) for Edward English administrator of Edward Chicken (KE) was granted discharge.

John Howell (CE) administrator of Sara Vanhecke exhibited accounts.

11:177 Alexander Larimore (TA) administrator of Nicholas Larkey exhibited that he is ready to pay debts & to pay distribution to orphans.

Martha Derry petitioned that Martha Huddell was summoned to render accounts on estate of petitioner's former husband. Petitioner has been very ill disposed of body.
11:178 Continuance was granted.

Maj. Thomas Long (BA) petitioned that Ralph Gearth made a nuncupative will at petitioner's home, bequeathing all to petitioner's wife. Said Long was granted administration. Appraisers: Jacob Jinifer, Thomas Peirt.
11:179 Lt. John Boring to administer oath.

John Boring (BA) administrator of Roger Cidwell petitioned that he has been very sick & unable to travel. Maj. Thomas Long to examine accounts & administer oath.

11:180 Jonas Bowing administrator of Lewis Bryan (BA) exhibited accounts, but is unable to travel to Office. Lt. John Boring to examine accounts & administer oath.

11:181 26 August. William Wintersell administrator of Alex. Pollard (TA) exhibited accounts.

Inventory of William Jones (TA) was exhibited, by appraisers Thomas Collins & James Scott.

Thomas Vaughan executor of John Beard
exhibited that he is ready to pay debts.

27 August. Elisabeth Munkiastor widow
of James Munkister (CH)

11:182 was granted administration on his
estate. Appraisers: Edward Ming,
Christopher Breames. John Stone (g, CH)
to administer oath.

20 August. Robert Carvile one of
executors of Elisabeth Moy exhibited
accounts.

1 September. Capt. Richard Hill (AA)
was granted continuance on estate of
David Griffith,

11:183 he being much impaired by sickness.

Anne Dawson (AA) widow of Abraham Dawson
(AA) was granted continuance.

Will of Robert Hardye was exhibited,
proved. William Brereton (SO) exhibited
oath of Ann Hardy (SO) administratrix of
Robert Hardye, sworn on 25 August 1679.
Also exhibited oath of William Keene &
Thomas Humphris, appraisers of said
estate, sworn on same day.

11:184 Inventory was exhibited.

Will of David Spence was exhibited,
proved. Thomas Walker exhibited oath of
Ann Spence executrix, sworn on 9 August
1679.

Will of Henry Bradly (DO) was exhibited,
proved.

11:185 William Stephens (DO) exhibited oath of
Mary Bradley executrix, sworn on 1 July
1679. Also exhibited oath of
Bartholomew Ennalls & Michaell Bussy,
appraisers sworn same day.

2 September. Bartholomew Ennalls
exhibited bond of John Kirke, with
sureties John Edwards & James Peterkin,
on estate of Francis Tassall (DO).

John Hudson (DO) exhibited accounts on
estate of his father John Hudson (DO).

Court Session: 1679

11:186   John Evans & Richard Crockett joint executors of Nicholas Rice (SO) exhibited accounts.

John Wedge (KE) administrator of William Chadbourne (CE) exhibited accounts.

4 September. George Parker (g, CV) on behalf of Sibell Joales now wife of Henry Joales & administratrix of William Groome exhibited accounts. Capt. Samuell Bourne to examine & administer oath.

11:187   George Parker (CV) on behalf of Leonard Coates (AA) exhibited additional accounts of Thomas Chandler. Residue to: orphans.

Thomas Bland (AA) vs. Cornelius Howard administrator of John Grange (BA). Exceptions exhibited. Said Bland is one of creditors of said estate.

11:188   Mentions: Richard Uggins, (N) Warfeild. Signed: John Thompson (clerk).

11:189   Robert Ridgely attorney for John Baker (inn holder, SMC) vs. Samuell Tovy (g, KE) administrator of Vincent Atchinson (KE). Exceptions exhibited.

11:190   Robert Carvile procurator for said Tovy exhibited answer.

11:191   ...

11:192   5 September. Inventory of Capt. John Jourdain (SM) was exhibited, by appraisers Clement Hill & Richard Gardner, sworn by Capt. Coode (SM).

6 September. Cuthbert Scott (SM) administrator of John Jourdein exhibited accounts.

8 September. John Mitchill was granted administration on estate of Henry Jones (SM), who died without relation in the Province. Appraisers: John Wyn, John Evans.

11:193   Sheriff (SM) to summon Jane Williams (SM) widow of William Williams to render accounts on his estate.

10 September. Inventory of William Loveday (CH) was exhibited, by appraisers Henry Aspinal & Roger Dickenson.

15 September. Inventory of John Eareckson (KE) was exhibited, by appraisers Thomas Osbourne & Valentine Sotherne.

Isaack Winchester (KE) administrator of Richard Moore (KE) exhibited accounts.

11:194 Isaack Winchester on behalf of Johannah Gourdon widow & executrix of Patrick Gourdon exhibited accounts. Said Johannah is bedridden.

18 September. Marmaduke Semme (SM) administrator of Abell James (SM) exhibited accounts.

20 September. Elisabeth Holt administratrix of David Holt exhibited inventory, by appraisers William Hatton & Henry Phipps, sworn by Kenelme Cheseldine (g).

Edward Lunn (AA) who married Elisabeth relict & administratrix of William Cooke (AA) was granted administration on his estate.
11:195 Appraisers: Nicholas Greenberry, William Cockey. Edward Dorsey (AA) to administer oath.

Summons to John Halls (CV) to render accounts on estate of George Beckwith.

Petition of Elias Nutthall who married Elisabeth Beckwith (one of daughters of George & Frances Beckwith).
11:196 Regarding: distribution of estate. Mentions: administrators John Halls & Thomas Bankes.

11:197 23 September. Vincent Mancell (SM) administrator of Richard Foster was granted discharge.

Bartholomew Ennalls (g, DO) administrator of John Hallyfeild (DO)

Court Session: 1679

exhibited inventory.

John Lewellin (g, SM) exhibited bond of
Elisabeth Darwell widow of John Darwell
on his estate. Inventory was exhibited,
by appraisers George Goldsmith & John
Suttle, sworn by John Lewellin (g).

John Kirke (DO) exhibited a list of
goods delivered to relict of Francis
Tassall.

11:198 25 September. Gilbert Turbervile (SM)
was granted administration on estate of
John Davis (SM), as greatest creditor.

26 September. William Crommell (BA) was
granted administration on estate of
Richard Mascall (BA). Appraisers:
William Davis, William Ball. Maj.
Thomas Long (g, BA) to administer oath.

11:199 29 September. John Halls (CV) exhibited
a list of goods of estate of George
Beckwith for distribution to orphans.

Jane Williams (SM) widow of William
Williams exhibited accounts on his
estate.

Inventory of Dr. John Peerce was
exhibited, by appraisers Thomas Sprigg &
Andrew Abbington.

3 October. Col. Phylemon Loyd (TA) for
Sara Lawes widow of William Lawes (TA)
was granted administration on his
estate. Appraisers: John Browne, Peter
Ellis. Said Loyd to administer oath.

11:200 Richard Lightwood, Esq. (TA) was granted
administration on estate of Thomas Allen
(TA). Sureties: Henry Fox, William
Gascall. Appraisers: John Hunt,
Alexander Laremore. James Murphy (g,
TA) to administer oath.

4 October. Thomas Jeffe (AA)
administrator of his father Thomas Jeffe
(AA) exhibited accounts.

6 October. James Balderston (KE) exhibited accounts on estate of Dr. Desjourdaine.

11:201 Col. William Burges (AA) procurator for Robert Langley was granted administration on estate of James Ives (BA). Mentions: Martha (now dec'd) widow of said James, said Langley (creditor to said James, merchant, London), said James sold 300 a. per Col. George Wells. Appraisers: William Hollis, Peter Ellis. Said Burges to administer oath.

11:202 Robert Langley (g, London) gave a PoA to Col. William Burges, before William Scorey (notary). Date: 27 March 1679.

11:203 Witnesses: Thomas Brookehouse, Porten Paul. Sealed before: Rich. Burke, Thomas Elves.

11:204 Indenture between James Ives (p, BA) & his wife Martha & Robert Langley (g, London). Mentions: land <metes & bounds>

11:205 called "Everton".

11:206-207 ...

11:208 Witnesses: George Wells, Henry Haslewood. Date: 14 March 1674. Signed: John Turpin (clerk).

11:209 Said Martha was privately examined. Signed: George Wells.

Capt. Richard Hill (AA) exhibited oath of Henry Ridgely & Jacob Harnisse, appraisers of Thomas Watkins, sworn 18 July 1679. Inventory was exhibited.

11:210 Capt. Richard Hill exhibited accounts of Mary Hammond relict & administratrix of Thomas Roper (AA). Date: 2 August 1679.

Maj. Thomas Long exhibited accounts of John Boring administrator of Roger Cidwell (BA).

Maj. Thomas Long exhibited oath of Sarah Steevens administratrix of Giles Steevens, sworn 20 April 1679. Sureties: John Arden, Jacob Jenipher.

11:211 Also exhibited is oath of Oliver Haile & Ambrose Gellet, appraisers of Guiles

Steevens, sworn same day. Inventory was exhibited.

John Boreing (g, BA) exhibited oath of Maj. Thomas Long administrator of Ralph Gearth, sworn 7 September 1679. Sureties: said John Boring, Thomas Pearle. Also exhibited was oath of Jacob Jynifer & Thomas Peirt, appraisers, sworn same day. Inventory was exhibited.

11:212 Maj. Thomas Long exhibited oath of William Cromwell administrator of Richard Mascall (BA). Sureties: Thomas Long, William Ball. Also exhibited oath of William Ball & William Davis, appraisers.

7 October. Will of Anthony Handaker (DO) was exhibited, proved. Inventory was exhibited, by appraisers John Walker & Alexander Fisher, sworn by Bartholomew Ennalls (DO).

11:213 Capt. Richard Hill (AA) exhibited accounts of William Hawkins who married Anne administratrix of Stephen White & their oath.

Capt. Richard Hill (AA) exhibited his accounts on estate of David Griffith.

John Boring (g, BA) exhibited oath of Jonas Bowing administrator of Lewis Bryan.

Henry Hosier (g, KE) exhibited accounts of Sara Deane administratrix of Thomas Warren & oath.

11:214 Henry Hosier (g, KE) exhibited accounts of Mary True executrix of Francis Finch & oath.

John Hanson (CH) executor of Richard Midgely exhibited accounts. Discharge was granted.

Henry Bonner (CH) on behalf of Elenor Bayne was granted administration on estate of Matthew Hill (CH), on behalf of orphans. Appraisers: John Fanning, Thomas Clipsam. Robert Henley (g, CH) to administer oath.

11:215 8 October. Capt. Richard Hill (g, AA) on behalf of Flora Hawkins widow of Ralph Hawkins was granted administration on his estate. Appraisers: John Bird, Humphry Boone. Said Hill to administer oath.

Will of Jeremiah Eaton (KE) was exhibited, proved.

11:216 Inventory of Roger Shacock (KE) was exhibited, by appraisers Josias Langham & James Balderston.

Inventory of Edward Renells (KE) was exhibited, by appraisers Josias Langham & James Balderston.

Inventory of William Key (KE) was exhibited, by appraisers William Bateman & Thomas Boone.

Will of Robert Hoode (KE) was exhibited, proved.

11:217 9 October. Inventory of William Palmer (BA) was exhibited, by appraisers William Hollis & Miles Gibson.

7 October. Col. William Burges (AA) exhibited his accounts on estate of Dr. William Jones.

10 October. Peter Ellis (BA) exhibited his accounts on estate of William Palmer.

George Gunnell (BA) was granted discharge on estate of Thomas Overton.

11:218 John Gray (AA) exhibited his accounts on estate of Thomas Jones (AA).

Cornelius Comagys administrator of William Davis (KE) exhibited accounts.

Cornelius Comagys on behalf of his wife Mary relict & administratrix of James

Kenneday (KE) exhibited accounts.

William Berry executor of Thomas Marsh (KE) exhibited his will. Maj. James Ringgold (g, KE) to prove.

11:219 Jone David administratrix of John David (KE) exhibited accounts, but is unable to travel to Office. Cornelius Comagys (KE) to examine & administer oath.

Hannah Gibson executrix of John White (KE) exhibited accounts, but is unable to travel to Office. Henry Hosier (g, KE) to examine & administer oath.

11:220 Hannah Johnson administratrix of Jacob Johnson (KE) exhibited accounts, but is unable to travel to Office. Henry Hosier (g, KE) to examine & administer oath.

William Bateman administrator of Christopher Andrews (KE) exhibited accounts, but is unable to travel to Office. Maj. James Ringgold to examine & administer oath.

11:221 Maj. Thomas Taillor (DO) on behalf of Abigall Turner widow of Henry Turner was granted administration on his estate. Appraisers: John Sulberry, (N) Peterkin. Said Taillor to administer oath.

11 October. Katherine Cooke administratrix of Robert Winsmore (DO) exhibited accounts, but is unable to travel to Office.
11:222 William Steevens (g, DO) to examine & administer oath.

Katherine Cooke administratrix of Henry Mountague (DO) exhibited accounts.

Inventory of Baker Brooke, Esq. (CV) was exhibited, by appraisers Col. Henry Darnall & Maj. Charles Boteler.

11:223 13 October. Ebenezar Blackiston executor of William Toulson (CE) exhibited accounts.

Ebenezar Blackiston administrator of
William Pike (CE) exhibited accounts.

Mary Ward (TA) executrix of Matthew Ward
exhibited accounts. Discharge was
granted.

11:224 15 October. Inventory of Thomas Barnes
(KE) was exhibited, by appraisers John
Winchester & Morgan William.

John Grigs (CV) exhibited oath of
William King & John Evans, appraisers of
Thomas Booty (CV).

Anne Haslewood administratrix of John
Avery (DO) exhibited accounts, but is
unable to travel to Office. Thomas
Taillor (DO) to examine & administer
oath.

11:225 16 October. James Mills (BA) on behalf
of Lawrence Taillor was granted
administration on estate of Owen
Williams (BA). Appraisers: Peter Ellis,
Robert Jones, Jr. Henry Haslewood (g,
BA) to administer oath.

James Mills (BA) on behalf of Elinor
Jackson widow of Edward Jackson was
granted administration on his estate.
11:226 Appraisers: Robert Jones, Jr., Edward
Bedle. Henry Haslewood (g, BA) to
administer oath.

17 October. Will of William Jones (TA)
was exhibited, proved. Col. Phylemon
Loyd (TA) exhibited oath of Rebecca
Jones executrix of William Jones, sworn
on 6 June 1679. Appraisers James Scott
& Thomas Collin were sworn same day.

11:227 Will of George Alldridge (TA) was
exhibited, proved.

Col. Phylemon Loyd (TA) exhibited will
of Philip Steevenson (TA), proved. Anne
Steevenson executrix was sworn on 17
June 1679.

William Coursey (g, TA) exhibited will
of Thomas Haylings, proved. John Chafe

executor was sworn on 30 May 1679.

11:228 Thomas Hynson (g, TA) exhibited oath of
William Bishop (g, TA) administrator of
Richard Sturme, sworn on 30 November
1678. Appraisers Stephen Tully and
Richard Jones sworn same day. Inventory
was exhibited.

Richard Woollman (g, TA) exhibited bond
of William Bishopp (g, TA) on estate of
John Bradbourne to Col. Philemon Loyd.

11:229 William Bishop (TA) exhibited oath of
Thomas Norris (TA) administrator of
Henry Pearle, sworn on 26 June 1679.
Appraisers John Broadribb & William
Austine were sworn same day.

Col. Phylemon Loyd (TA) exhibited oath
of Elisabeth Winkcles executrix of
Edward Winkcles (TA), sworn on 19
November 1678.

8 October. Thomas Bland (AA) vs.
Cornelius Howard (AA) administrator of
John Granger (BA). Said Howard
exhibited answers to exceptions of said
Bland.

11:230 Mentions: Richard Huggins & accountant
were executors of John Sisfon who left 2
orphans (under age) in custody of said
Huggins & the accountant.

11:231 Said Huggins died leaving considerable
estate to his wife who married said John
Granger, who wasted estate of said
orphans & said Huggins. Signed: Kenelme
Chesledyne.

11:232 Robert Carvile & Kenelme Cheseldyne
procurators for Randall Revell & his
wife Katherine vs. Robert Ridgely &
Christopher Rouseby procurators for
Andrew Jones. Date: 2 September.
Mentions: James Jones (p, SO) made will
in 1673, constituting his wife Sara
executrix, devising to said Sara & his
cousin Andrew Jones. Said James died in
October 1677. Said Sara died before
James' will could be proved, leaving
nuncupative will bequeathing to said
Katherine,

11:233   wife (N) of Leonard Jones, Andrew Jones
as heir-at-law of said James, Joane
Watts, Dorothy Philips.

11:234   Morgan Jones (Minister of the Gospel),
Elisabeth wife of said Morgan. Ruling:
words of said Sara were not said before
3 witnesses, as per Act for Preventing
of Perjuryes nor anyone required to take
notice nor put in writing. Therefore,
said Sara died intestate & therefore
said James died intestate.
Administration was confirmed to said
Andrew his heir-at-law & next-of-blood
within this Province.

11:235   Said Andrew to make full satisfaction to
said Katherine. [Ed. note: There was no
ruling regarding the point of joint
tenancy.]

17 October. John Stone exhibited oath
of Henry Aspinall and Roger Dickinson,
appraisers of William Loveday (CH),
sworn on 22 June 1679. Said Stone also
exhibited oath of John Muns
administrator of said Loveday, sworn on
21 June 1679. Sureties: George Newman,
Thomas Hemfray.

11:236   John Stone (g, CH) exhibited will of
John Ashbrooke, proved. Temperance
Clouder (CH) executrix was sworn on 24
January 1678. Robert Robins and Kenelme
Mackloughlin appraisers were sworn, but
they never did an appraisal.

John Stone (g, CH) exhibited oath of
John Saunders administrator of Francis
Keene. Richard & William Chandler were
cited as appraisers; they are runaway
and cannot be sworn.

11:237   18 October. Inventory of John Paramore
was exhibited, by appraisers William
Jones (SO) and Henry Bishop (SO).

Katherine widow of John Garnish (inn
holder, SMC) exhibited his will,
constituting said Katherine as
executrix. Said Katherine renounced
administration

11:238   and recommended Henry Exon (inn holder,
SMC) to be administrator. Witnesses:

Gerritt Vansweringen, James Boulley.
Said Exon was granted administration.
Kenelme Cheseldine procurator for Thomas
Matthews (Cherry Poynt, VA) exhibited
debt against said estate. Richard
Smith, Jr. (CV) exhibited debt against
said estate. John Barnes had formerly
entered a caveat against said estate.
Sureties: Gerrit Vansweringen, Daniell
Clocker. Appraisers: said Vansweringen
John Baker.

11:239 18 October. Jane Elliott (SM) widow of
Henry Elliott (SM) exhibited his will,
proved by Henry Exon & Phylip Land.
Said Jane was granted administration.
Appraisers: Thomas Courtney, John Evans.
Geritt Vansweringen to administer oath.

22 October. Kenelme Cheseldine for
Alice Surton (SM) widow of Francis
Surton (SM) was granted administration
on his estate. Appraisers: Robert
Graham, John Wattson. Said Cheseldine
to administer oath.
11:240 Surety: John Baker.

Kenelme Cheseldine (Attorney General)
exhibited oath of Geritt Vansweringen &
John Baker, appraisers of John Garnish
(SMC). Date: 18 October 1679.

23 October. James Dossey (CV) who
married Martha executrix of Thomas
Morris exhibited accounts.

24 October. Inventory of Nathaniell
Parsons (SO) was exhibited, by
appraisers George Hasfurt & Samuell
Cooper.

11:241 Mary Davis (CH) widow of Walter Davis
was granted administration on his
estate. Appraisers (CH): Thomas
Clipsham, Humphrey Waring. Robert
Henley (CH) to administer oath.

Mary Davis (CH) administratrix of
Richard Smoote (CH) exhibited accounts.

11:242 28 October. Elisabeth Darwall
administratrix of John Darwall (CH)

exhibited accounts, but is unable to travel to Office. John Lewellin (g, CH) to examine & administer oath.

Richard Meekings administrator of George Bacon (DO) exhibited accounts.

CV Co. Court at Calverton on 21 October 1679. Commissioners: Capt. Samuell Bourne, Mr. Roger Brooke, Col. Henry Jowles, Mr. Thomas Starling.

11:243   Examined accounts of Thomas Bankes administrator of George Beckwith (CV). [See f. 254.]

29 October. Elias Nutthall (CV) to summon Thomas Bankes administrator of George and Frances Beckwith.

30 October. Gerett Vansweringen administrator of John Derry (SM) exhibited accounts.

31 October. Gustavius White on behalf of his wife Philis administratrix of Thomas Howes (CV) exhibited accounts.

11:244   3 November. Col. Benjamin Rozer for Thomas Wharton (CH) exhibited will of Sylvanus Gilpin, constituting said Wharton executor. Said Rozer to prove.

4 November. Thomas Bankes exhibited that he sees no reason to pay tobacco at 8 shillings 4 pence per hundred when he pays 10 shillings per hundred.

Robert Ridgely (SM) attorney for Elias Nutthall who married Elisabeth (one of daughters of George Beckwith (dec'd)) vs. Thomas Bankes (CV) administrator of said George and Frances Beckwith (CV). Exceptions exhibited by Ridgely.

11:245   ...
11:246   Petition by said Nutthall.
11:247   Ruling: said Bankes to pay said Nutthall his wife's portion.

6 November. Richard Royston (Great Choptank, TA) exhibited that William Crosse (TA) is indebted to Richard Draper

11:248 (girdler, London).
- Exhibit of letter to: Sir James
Edwards Knight Lord Mayor & alderman
or senator of London.   Richard
Draper, Sr. (girdler, London), age
64, and Richard Draper, Jr.
(girdler, London), age 27, exhibited
that they demanded payment from
William Crosse (scrivener,
Blandford).

11:249 ...
Said Crosse became bankrupt.

11:250 ...
William Crosse (Blandford) received
from Mr. Richard Draper (London),
mentioning Mr. George Bradford.
Date: 1 April 1671. Verified by:
Richard Draper, Jr.

11:251 ...
Said Royston exhibited PoA from said
Richard Draper. Mentions: John
Tregonwell, Esq. and other
creditors.

11:252 ...
11:253 ...
Date: 12 December 1673. Witnesses:
Joseph Motts, Guil. Scorey (notary).
Said Royston was granted administration
on estate of William Crosse.
Appraisers: John Rouseby, Richard
Peacocke.

11:254 Col. Vincent Lowe to administer oath.

10 November. Robert Ridgely procurator
for (N) Nutthall vs. Christopher Rousby
procurator for Thomas Banckes (CV)
administrator of George and Frances
Beckwith. Continuance was granted said
Banckes.

11:255 11 November. Robert Ridgely procurator
for (N) Nutthall vs. Christopher Rousby
procurator for Thomas Banckes (CV)
administrator of George and Frances
Beckwith. Continuance was granted said
Banckes.

14 November. Bernard Johnson
administrator of Gervis Shaw (CV)
exhibited accounts. Discharge was
granted.

11:256 17 November. Inventory of Richard
Hutchins (SMC) was exhibited, by
appraisers John Barnes and John Garnish.

18 November. Henry Exon (SMC)
administrator of Richard Hutchings (SM)
exhibited accounts.

Thomas Evans exhibited will of Gregory
Roule (SMC), proved by Thomas Nottingham
and John Angell. Said Evans was granted
administration. Appraisers: James
Pattison, Robert Drury. Clement Hill
(g) to administer oath.

11:257 21 November. Elias Nutthall vs. Thomas
Banckes (CV) administrator of George and
Frances Beckwith. Letter to: Philip
Calvert, (Chancellor). Said Bankes to
answer exceptions. Mentions: additional
estate, estate in AA & CV.
11:258 Signed: C. Baltemore (your nephew).
Continuance was granted said Banckes.
Signed: John Thompson (clerk).

11:259 22 November. Edward Dorsey (g, AA)
exhibited oath of Edward Lunn who
married Elisabeth relict of William
Cooke, sworn 27 October 1679. Sureties:
Richard Gwin, William Cockey.
Appraisers Nicholas Greenbury and
William Cockey were sworn same day.
Inventory was exhibited.

26 November. Peter Watts executor of
Robert Cager (SM) exhibited accounts.

11:260 27 November. Thomas Sterling (CV)
exhibited will of Thomas Jackson (CV),
constituting said Sterling executor.
Said Sterling renounced administration.
Witnesses: George Parker, James
Cranford, John Brashire.
11:261 George Parker (CV) procurator for John
Cobreath was granted administration on
said estate, as greatest creditor.
Appraisers: Richard Stallings, John
Sunderland. Capt. Samuell Bourne to
administer oath.

Sheriff (CV) to summon Robert Brassure
(CV) and his wife Alice, Richard Poole

(CV), and Henry Jenkins (CV).

11:262 29 November. Anne Willson (CV) widow of William Willson was granted administration on his estate. Appraisers: William King, John Peerce. John Griggs (g) to administer oath.

11:263 Richard Marsham and George Lingham (CV) executors of Charles Gosfright were granted continuance.

5 December. Clement Hill exhibited oath of James Pattison and Robert Drury, appraisers of Gregory Rouse (SM), sworn on 26 November 1679.

Gerritt Vansweringen exhibited oath of Thomas Courtney and John Evans, appraisers of Henry Elliott, sworn on 22 October 1679.

11:264 2 December. Mary Browne (CV) widow & executrix of Thomas Browne (CV) exhibited his will. Col. Henry Jowles to prove said will.

3 December. Joane Hilton (TA) widow of Robert Hilton (TA) exhibited her renunciation of his estate.

11:265 Witnesses: John Thompson, James Boullay. Richard Wollman for Richard Carter was granted administration, as greatest creditor.

11:266 Appraisers: Daniell Walker, Peter Dennis. Col. Phylemon Loyd to administer oath.

6 December. Thomas Flowers (DO) executor of Anthony Hardacre exhibited accounts.

John Lewellin (SM) exhibited accounts of Elisabeth Darwell administratrix of her husband John Darwell (SM). Discharge was granted.

11:267 8 December. Inventory of Morgan Jones (SM) was exhibited, by appraisers Robert Large and Christopher Sprye.

9 December. Mary Dines (CH) widow of Thomas Dines (CH) was granted administration on his estate.

11:268 Appraisers: Thomas Baker, Joseph Conwell. Henry Adams (g) to administer oath.

12 December. John Lemaire (CH) administrator of Samuell Hutchinson (CH) exhibited accounts. Henry Adams (CH) exhibited oath of Thomas Baker and Thomas Atkins, appraisers of said Hutchinson, sworn 12 February 1678/9. Inventory was exhibited.

11:269 15 December. Walter Kirby (KE) was granted administration on estate of Charles Banckes (KE), on behalf of his one son Charles Banckes.

11:270 Appraisers: Richard Pedder, Lewis Merredeth. Joseph Weekes (g) to administer oath.

John Chafe (TA) executor of Thomas Haylings was granted administration on his estate. Appraisers: Daniell Glover, Matthew Smith. Col. Henry Coursey to administer oath.

11:271 William Bishopp (TA) was granted administration on estate of John Bradborne (TA). Appraisers: Daniel Glover, Mathew Smith. Col. Henry Coursey to administer oath.

Thomas Banckes was ordered to pay Jacob Seth (TA) who married Barbara her child's portion of estate of George and Frances Beckwith (CV).

11:272 16 December. Margarett Stagg (CV) administratrix of Thomas Stagg (CV) exhibited accounts.

19 December. J. Loveday (sheriff, CV) exhibited summons to Robert Brassure and his wife Alice (CV), Richard Poole (CV), and Henry Jenkins (CV) to render accounts of items of estate of Thomas Jackson (CV).

Court Session: 1679

20 December. Robert Brassure and his wife Alice, Richard Poole, and Henry Jenkins (all of CV) exhibited that they know of no goods of the estate of Thomas Jackson (CV).

22 December. Anne Alvey (SM) widow of Pope Alvey was granted administration on his estate.

11:273 Appraisers: Thomas Lomax, James Pattison. Clement Hill to administer oath.

29 December. Sara Newton (DO) executrix of Samuell Prethett (DO) exhibited accounts.

1 January. Inventory of William Willson (CV) was exhibited, by appraisers William King and John Peerce.

11:274 Henry Exon (SMC) administrator of John Garnish (SMC) exhibited inventory, by appraisers Gerrett Vansweringen and John Baker.

2 January. John Askin (SM) was granted administration on estate of Philip Land (SM). Appraisers: Guilbert Turbervile, John Doxey. Thomas Keiton (SM) to administer oath.

11:275 3 January. Katherine Garnish (SM) rendered several goods she retained from Henry Exon administrator of John Garnish.

5 January. Isaac Winchester (KE) was granted administration on estate of his brother John Winchester (KE), for use of his orphan son. Appraisers: Morgan Williams, Francis Barnes. William Lawrence (g, KE) to administer oath.

11:276 Miles Gibson (BA) petitioned that Ellenor Jackson widow of Edward Jackson was granted administration on his estate 3/4 months ago, but cannot find security. Said Gibson was granted administration on said estate.

11:277 Appraisers: Peter Ellis, Robert Jones. George Wells (BA) to administer oath.

Henry Exon administrator of John Garnish
was granted continuance to exhibit an
additional inventory of goods
relinquished by Katherine Garnish.

11:278 John Robbins who married the mother of
Hugh Marnackoe (heir of Macom Thomas
(dec'd)) and chosen by said Marnackoe as
his guardian per SO Court exhibited that
he received goods from William Steevens
(Pocomoke, SO). Date: 30 September
1679. Signed: John Robins. Witnesses:
David Dale, William Smith.

11:279 6 January. Judith Parker (CV) widow of
William Parker (CV) was granted
administration on his estate.
Appraisers: George Parker (g), John
Hance (g). Capt. Samuell Bourne to
administer oath.

8 January. Henry Exon (SMC)
administrator of John Garnish exhibited
additional inventory, by appraisers John
Baker and Gerritt Vansweringen.

11:280 Alice Hinton relict and administratrix
of Francis Sourton (SM) exhibited
inventory, by appraisers Robert Graham
and John Walson.

James Murphey (TA) exhibited oath of
John Hunt and Alex. Laremore, appraisers
of Thomas Allen, sworn 14 October 1679.
Richard Lightwood (TA) administrator of
Thomas Allen (TA) exhibited inventory.

11:281 John Keirck (DO) administrator of
Francis Tassall (DO) petitioned that,
per court order, he paid the widow her
1/3rd and the youngest child's portion.
Said Keirck has been informed that said
widow retained several goods, that were
not part of the appraisal.
11:282 Sheriff (DO) to summon said relict of
Francis Tassall to render account of
said goods.

Capt. John Cobreath, age 48, deposed on
17 November 1678 that in 1658 or 1659,
the deponent carried letters from John
Billingsly (Cuchatuck, Nansamum Co. VA)

to his mother Agatha Billingsley
(Rotterdam, Holland). Said Agatha
mentioned a brother of said John
Billingsly. Bearer George Billingsley
is son of said John (VA). Witness: Sam.
Bourne.

11:283 John Troster, age 60, deposed on 17
November 1678 that John Billingsley
(Cuckatuck, Nansamum Co. VA) was son of
Agatha Billingsly (Rotterdam, Holland)
and George Billingsly is son of said
John. Said John came to VA on account
of Mr. James Dehem (merchant,
Rotterdam, Treasurer of Company of
Merchant Adventurers of Rotterdam).
Witness: Sam. Bourne.

9 January. Thomas Jessop (CV) was
granted administration on estate of
Robert Ryder (CV). Mentions: Robert
Ryder (son & heir
11:284 to dec'd). Appraisers: Samuell Goosey,
John Leach. Capt. Samuell Bourne to
administer oath.

12 January. Robert Henley (g, CH)
exhibited oath of Margarett Worrall
widow of Richard Ambrose. Also
exhibited were accounts.

Robert Henley (CH) exhibited bond of
Elin Bayne administratrix of Mathew Hill
(CH), with sureties: Humphrey Warren,
Thomas Clipsham.

11:285 Edward Cooke (DO) and John Richardson
(DO) overseers of will of Ezekiel Fogg
(DO) exhibited his will. John Brooke
(g) to prove said will. Said Cooke and
Richardson were granted administration,
on behalf of David Fogg (brother of
dec'd). Appraisers: William Steevens
(g), William Willoby. Said Brooke to
administer oath.

11:286 15 January. John Bird and Humphry Boone
appraisers of Ralph Hawkins were sworn
on 16 December 1679 by Richard Hill.
Flora Hawkins relict of said Ralph was
sworn on 8 October 1679. Said Flora
could not find security. Inventory was

exhibited. Date: 7 January 1679.
Signed: Richard Hill.

11:287 Capt. Richard Hill (AA) exhibited
inventory of Ralph Hawkins, by
appraisers John Bird and Humphry Boone.

17 January. James Phillips (BA)
administrator of Jacob Browning (BA)
exhibited accounts. Discharge was
granted.

James Phillips (BA) administrator of
John Stanford (BA) exhibited accounts.
11:288 Discharge was granted.

William Osbourne (BA) administrator of
John Gunn (BA) exhibited accounts.

Inventory of Thomas Notley, Esq. (Lt. of
the Province) was exhibited, by
appraisers Gerrard Sly (g) and John
Darnall (g), sworn by Capt. William
Diggs.
11:289 Said Notley made a will, constituting
"us" and Benjamin Rozer, Esq. executors.
Our son-in-law Nicholas Sewall, Esq. was
nominated in our stead.
11:290 Signed: dear uncle Philip Calvert, Esq.

19 January. George Parker (CV)
exhibited that Maudline Pascall is
dec'd. By petition of James Pascall,
George Pascall (p, AA) is runaway for 7
years, leaving behind a wife (an old
woman, lately dec'd) and no children.
He left an estate of 350 a. Said James
is said George's brother's son and next
heir-at-law.
11:291 Said James was granted administration on
estates of said George and Maudlin.
Appraisers: Mr. Robert Frankline,
Walter Carr. Maj. John Welsh (AA) to
administer oath.

23 January. John Carpenter (SMC)
exhibited oath of Gerritt Vansweringen
and John Baker, appraisers of John
Garnish, sworn on 9 January. Inventory
was exhibited.

11:292 Thomas Taylor exhibited oath of Abigall
        Turner widow of Henry Turner (DO), sworn
        on last day of October. Sureties:
        Benjamin Hunt, Richard Davil.
        Appraisers James Peterkin and John
        Salbury were sworn same day. Inventory
        was exhibited.

11:293 Will of Capt. Thomas Marsh (KE) was
        exhibited, proved.

        Nutthall vs. Bankes. Auditors: Mr.
        Bland, Mr. Dorsey. Signed (procurators
        for complainant and defendant): Robert
        Ridgely, Chr. Rousby.

11:294 24 January. William Hatton (g, SM)
        exhibited oath of John Wynn and John
        Evans, appraisers of Henry Jones (SM),
        sworn on 15 September 1679.

        William Hatton (g, SM) exhibited oath of
        Jacob Loetan and Robert Craine,
        appraisers of Thomas Evans (SM), sworn
        on 7 May 1679.

        Will of Silvanus Gilpin (CH) was
        exhibited, proved.

11:295 Benjamin Rozer petitioned that Edward
        Price (lately dec'd on account of fire)
        left a distracted widow and no children
        and a very inconsiderable estate. Said
        widow is not capable of administering
        the estate.
11:296 Thomas Hussey was granted administration
        on said estate. Appraisers: Marke
        Lanthorne, John Butcher. Col. Benjamin
        Rozer to administer oath. Said Rozer to
        examine Jane said widow.

11:297 26 January. Samuell Raspin (CH) was
        granted administration on estate of
        Henry Pratt (CH), who died a bachelor,
        with no relations in the Province, as
        principle creditor. Appraisers: Francis
        Wyne, John Courte. John Fanning (g) to
        administer oath.

11:298 Samuell Raspin (CH) was granted
        administration on estate of John
        Dudrick, who died a bachelor, with no

relations in the Province, as principle
creditor. Appraisers: Francis Wyne,
John Courte. John Fanning (g) to
administer oath.

11:299   Elisabeth orphan of George & Frances
Beckwith, her portion in the hands of
Thomas Banckes administrator. Robert
Ridgley procurator for Elias Nuthall
exhibited that said Elias married said
Elisabeth. Chr. Rousby (sick at this
time) procurator for said Banckes was
granted continuance.

11:300   31 January. John Griggs exhibited bond
of Ann Wilson administratrix of William
Wilson. Appraisers William King & John
Pearce were sworn on 8 December 1679.

9 February. Walter Kerby (KE)
administrator of Charles Banckes (KE)
petitioned for new appraisers: Alexander
Walters, Lewes Merredith. William
Lawrence (g) to administer oath.

10 February. John Bearecroft (SM)
administrator of Kazia White (SM)
exhibited accounts.

11:301   Henry Hosier (KE) exhibited accounts of
Thomas Parker and his wife Elisabeth on
their administration of Henry Gott (KE).

Henry Hosier (g, KE) exhibited accounts
of Hannah Gibson administratrix of John
White (KE).

Henry Hosier (g, KE) exhibited accounts
of Hannah Johnson administratrix of her
husband Jacob Johnson (KE).

11 February. Mary Anderson (CE) former
wife of William Bate
11:302   was granted administration on his
estate. Appraisers: Giles Porter, John
Gibbs. Joseph Hopkins (g) to administer
oath.

Mary Pether (KE) widow of Richard Pether
(KE) was granted administration on his
estate.
11:303   Appraisers: Alex. Waters, Henry Carter.

Court Session: 1679

William Lawrence (g) to administer oath.

11:304 Thomas Tolley (AA) executor of John Casson (AA) exhibited his will. Capt. Richard Hill (AA) to prove said will. Said Tolley was granted administration. Appraisers: Lawrence Draper, William Gamball. Said Hill to administer oath.

Richard Girling (TA) administrator of George Bayley (TA) exhibited accounts. Discharge was granted.

11:305 Kenelme Cheseldine attorney for John Bearcroft (SM) vs. Jane Williams widow & administratrix of William Williams. Exceptions to accounts exhibited. Mentions: bill of Gov. Nottley, bill of Mr. Turling.

11:306 12 February. John Larkin (AA) administrator of Enoch Bolton (AA) exhibited inventory, by appraisers Richard Tydens & Robert Wade. John Larking (AA) administrator of Enoch Bolton exhibited accounts.

Inventory of William Lawes (TA) was exhibited, by appraisers John Browne & Peter Dennis.

Edward Newton (DO) administrator of Thomas Newton (DO) exhibited accounts.

11:307 Col. Vincent Lowe, Esq. (TA) exhibited oath of Arthur Norwood (TA) administrator of John Eason, sworn on 19 July 1679. Surety: Robert Napp. Inventory was exhibited, by appraisers Robert Napp and Richard Gould. Ann Norwood exhibited her renunciation of administration of estate of her former husband John Eason, she being married to Arthur Norwood. Date: 9 July 1679.
11:308 Signed: Ann Eason. Witnesses: Richard Gould, John Whittinton.

Henry Haslewood (BA) exhibited bond of Lawrence Taylor administrator of Owen Williams (BA). Sureties: Edward Bedell, John Wallstone. Inventory was exhibited, by appraisers Peter Ellis and

Court Session: 1679

Robert Jones.

11:309   Jane widow of Edward Price is not of
sound memory. Thomas Hussey
administrator of Edward Price was sworn
3 February. Sureties: Edmund Dennis,
Marke Lampton. Signed: Benjamin Rozer.

Inventory of Richard Dod (CH) was
exhibited, by appraisers Thomas Backer
and Jaspin Cornell.

11:310   Commissioners of CH summoned Mary Ward
administratrix of Richard Fowke and
examined her accounts and took her oath.
Date: 11 November 1679. Signed:
Cleborne Lomax (subclerk).

Will of William Key (KE) was exhibited,
proved.

11:311   Will of Roger Shacocke (KE) was
exhibited, proved.

James Ringgold (g, KE) exhibited
accounts of William Bateman
administrator of Christopher Andrews
(KE).

John Welsh (g, AA) exhibited oath of
James Paschall administrator of Maudlin
Paschall, sworn on 2nd instant.
Sureties: Robert Franklin, John Walters.
Also exhibited was oath of appraisers
Robert Franklin and Walter Carr, sworn
same day.

11:312   Inventory was exhibited.

William Lawrence (g, KE) exhibited
accounts of Lewes Blangey and his wife
Mary on administration of Disborough
Bennett (KE).

Vincent Lowe exhibited oath of MM John
Rousby (g, TA) and Richard Peacock (g,
TA), appraisers of William Crosse (TA),
sworn on 14 November 1679.

11:313   Also exhibited was oath of Mr. Richard
Royston administrator of said Crosse,
sworn same day. Sureties: self, James
Murphey. Inventory was exhibited.

Richard Marsham and George Lingham (CV) executors of Charles Gosfreight (CV) exhibited accounts.

11:314 13 February. Mary DeRumple relict & administratrix of John Clements (TA) exhibited accounts, but cannot travel to Office. Anthony Mayle to examine & take oath.

Elisabeth Bardune (TA) widow of Charles Bardune (TA) was granted administration on his estate.

11:315 Appraisers: Henry Parker, Daniell Walker. Philemon Loyd (g, TA) to administer oath.

William Crommell (BA) administrator of Richard Mascall (BA) exhibited inventory, by appraisers William Ball & William Davis.

11:316 Martha Wells (KE) widow & executrix of John Wells (KE) exhibited his will. Joseph Wickes to prove said will. Said Martha was granted administration. Appraisers: Thomas Boone, Richard Lee. Said Wickes to administer oath.

11:317 Sara Foulk relict of Thomas Fisher (DO) was granted administration on his estate. Appraisers: John Kirke, Thomas Flowers. John Brooke (g) to administer oath.

Charles Boteler (CV) was granted administration on estate of Benjamin Hires (CV).

11:318 Appraisers: Christopher Baynes, John Brome. Roger Brookes (g) to administer oath.

Sara Thorton relict of John Woodas (BA) was granted administration on his estate. Appraisers: William Trevile, Stephen Hancocke. William Hopkins (AA) to administer oath.

11:319 14 February. Alice Ruxton (BA) widow of Nicholas Ruxton (BA) was granted administration on his estate. Appraisers: John Arden, Nicholas Corbin.

Court Session: 1679

John Borin (g, BA) to administer oath.

Jane Price (CH) widow & executrix of
Edward Price exhibited his will.
Benjamin Rozer, Esq. to prove said will.

11:320 16 February. William Harriss (KE)
administrator of Richard Mason (KE)
exhibited accounts.

William Ralls (KE) administrator of
Edward Coppidge (KE) exhibited accounts.

John Gray (Mogatta River, AA)
administrator of Thomas Jones (Mogatta
River, AA) was granted discharge.

11:321 Inventory of Gregory Rouse (SM) was
exhibited, by appraisers James Pattison
& Robert Drury.

William Ralls (KE) exhibited will of
Roger Shacocke, constituting William Key
executor. Said Key is dec'd before
completion of the estate. Said Ralls
was granted administration.

11:322 Appraisers: Philip Everitt, William
Harris. Maj. James Ringgold to
administer oath.

17 February. Inventory of Gerrard
Browne (CH) was exhibited, by appraisers
John Godshall and William Boyden.

Col. George Wells (BA) executor of John
Turpin (BA) exhibited accounts.

Thomas Allanson (CH) executor of Edward
Roberts (CH) exhibited accounts.

11:323 Thomas Alcocke (CH) one of executors of
David Tewell (CH) exhibited accounts.

18 February. Mary Ringgold (CE) relict
& administratrix of Edward Burton (KE)
was granted discharge.

20 February. Inventory of Samuel Jones
(SO) was exhibited, by appraisers Robert
Richardson and Thomas Poynter.

Col. William Coleborne (SO) was granted administration on estate of Thomas Feild (SO), who died a bachelor & without relations in the Province.

11:324 Appraisers: Nathaniell Dourghty, Benjamin Summer. Col. William Stevens (SO) to administer oath.

24 February. Arthur Emory (TA) administrator of John Wright exhibited accounts.

26 February. Bridgett Inglesby (CH) relict of Edward Philpott (CH)
11:325 was granted administration on his estate. Appraisers: John Coates, Sr., John Bracher. John Fanning (CH) to administer oath.

1 March. Henry Exon (SMC) administrator of John Garnish (SMC) exhibited accounts.

11:326 2 March. Inventory of Robert Rowland (CH) was exhibited, by appraisers Thomas Clipsham & John Fanning.

3 March. Thomas Taillor, Esq. (AA) was granted administration on estate of Edward Parish (AA). Nathaniell Heathcoate (AA) to take bond & widow's renunciation. Appraisers: Robert Lockwood, Will. Horne, Sen. Said Heathcoate to administer oath.

11:327 4 March. Thomas Clipsham (CH) administrator of Charles Gregory (CH) exhibited accounts.

Clement Hill (g, SM) exhibited bond of Anne Alvey on her administration of Pope Alvey, with sureties: James Pattyson, Daniel Hamond. Inventory was exhibited, by appraisers Thomas Lomax & James Pattyson.

11:328 5 March. Mary Brockas (CE) administratrix of William Brockas (CE) exhibited accounts.

James Halloway (CE) was granted administration on estate of Robert Cooke

(CE). Appraisers: William Price, Thomas Smith. Augustine Herman (g, CE) to administer oath.

11:329 10 March. Henry Dale (Poakamoke, SO) son of David Dale was granted administration on his estate. Appraisers: Marke Manlove, David Linsey. William Stevens, Esq. (SO) to administer oath.

11:330 15 March. Inventory of Henry Jones, by appraisers John Wynne & John Evans. John Michell (SM) administrator of said Jones exhibited accounts.

9 February. Elias Nutthall vs. Thomas Bankes administrator of George & Frances Beckwith. Answer by said Bankes.
11:331 Mentions: payment to John Miles,
11:332 Mr. Carvile, judgement by Millington vs. Beckwith,
11:333 ...
11:334 Signed: Chr. Rousby. Appearance of Thomas Bankes administrator of George & Frances Beckwith & his procurator Christopher Rousby & Elias Nuthall who married Elisabeth (one of daughters of dec'd) & his procurator Robert Ridgely. Ruling:
11:335 Said Bankes to pay said Nuthall at 1 penny per pound of tobacco.

19 March. John Johnson (TA) exhibited will of Adam Browne (TA). Col. Henry Coursey to prove said will.
11:336 Said Browne constituted Elisabeth Johnson (daughter of said John) as his sole executrix, and she is under age. Said John was granted administration, on behalf of his daughter. Appraisers: William Tilghman, John Ofley. Said Coursey to administer oath.

11:337 Martha Wells (KE) widow & executrix of John Wells (KE) exhibited that appraiser Richard Lee is very sick. New appraisers: William Bateman, Thomas Boone. Joseph Wickes to administer oath.

Court Session: 1679

22 March. George Gunnell (BA) & Thomas Russell (BA) were granted administration on estate of Edward Gunnell. Appraisers: William Osbourne, Edward Reeves.
11:338 Capt. John Waterton to administer oath.

John Thomas (BA) was granted administration on estates of Nicholas Ruxton & his wife Alice.
11:339 Appraisers: Francis Watkins, John Carrington. Anthony Demondidier (g, BA) to administer oath.

23 March. Inventory of William Thompson (CH) was exhibited, by appraisers Francis Wine & Robert Middleton.

24 March. Capt. Samuell Bourne (CV) exhibited accounts of Henry Jowles & his wife Sybell on estate of William Groome (CV).

11:340 Inventory of William Done in the hands of Capt. Richard Hill was exhibited, by appraisers Capt. Nicholas Greenbury & Robert Procter.

Court Session: 1680

12A:1 30 March. John Askin (SM) exhibited inventory of Philip Land, by appraisers Gilbert Turbervill and John Doxey.

5 April. Col. Benjamin Rozer (CH) exhibited will of Edward Price (CH), proved. Jane Price widow was granted administration, sworn by John Stone (g, CH).

12A:2 Thomas Wharton (CH) exhibited will of Edmund Gilpin (CH), which did not constitute an executor. Said Wharton was granted administration. Appraisers: Maj. John Wheeler, John Keeble. John Faning (g, CH) to administer oath.

12A:3 Anthony Mayle (g, TA) exhibited examination of accounts of Mary DeRumple administratrix of John Clements. Said Mayle cannot find the necessary

Page 145

12A:4 receipts. Mentions: Giles Blizard. Creditors should come to the house of James DeRumple to be paid. Date: 20 March 1679/80. Signed: Anthony Mayl.

6 April. William Lawrence (g, KE) exhibited bond of Isaac Winchester administrator of John Winchester (KE). Sureties: Morgan Williams, Francis Barnes.

7 April. Katherine Browne (KE) relict & executrix of Auther Wright exhibited accounts. Said Browne is unable to travel to Office.
12A:5 William Lawrence to examine & administer oath.

10 April. Christopher Rousby (CV) attorney for James DeRumple & Mary relict & administratrix of John Clements vs. Edward Pindar (DO) administrator of William Ford. Exceptions to accounts by said Pindar exhibited.
12A:6 ...
12A:7 Mentions: Maj. Thomas Taillor, Thomas Cooke, Humphry Hubbard, John Pope,
12A:8 John Kemball, Daniell Clark, Robert Ridgely (attorney), William Steevens, Henry Searcher,
12A:9 Benjamin Lawrence, John Sheppard, John Steevens, William Sharp, administrator of Arthur Wright, John Boult,
12A:10-11 ...
12A:12 Henry Turner.

12A:13 12 April. Col. William Burges (AA) exhibited inventory of James Ives (BA), by appraisers William Hollis & Peter Ellis.

14 April. Margarett Spinke (BA) widow of John Spinke (BA) exhibited her renunciation of administration. Date: 6 March 1679/80. Witnesses: Christo. Brownerige, William More.
12A:14 Robert Benjar (BA) was granted administration on his estate, as principle creditor. Appraisers: Thomas Pert, Henry Enlos. Maj. Thomas Long to administer oath.

12A:15 Robert Benjar (BA) exhibited will of
Thomas Browne (BA), proved by Thomas
Weapon. Said Benjar executor was
granted administration. Appraisers:
Thomas Weapon, John Carter. Maj.
Thomas Long to administer oath.

12A:16 Daniel Smith (CE) was granted
administration on estate of Daniel
Boulton (CE), as principle creditor.
Appraisers: John Rycroft, Hugh
Magregory. Augustine Herman to
administer oath.

12A:17 John Renols (Bohemia River, CE)
exhibited verbal will of Thomas Smith
(Bohemia River), who died suddenly on 25
March instant. Said will was made in
the presence of Morris Daniell & his
wife &* Richard Mapcary, devising to
John Renols & Daniel Boultane. Said
Boulton was sick & died the next day.
Augustine Herman to prove said will.

12A:18 15 April. Robert Benjar (BA) who
married relict & administratrix of John
Shadwell exhibited accounts.

Margarett Leekins (BA) widow of John
Leekins was granted administration on
his estate. Appraisers: David Jones,
John Arden. Lt. John Boring (BA) to
administer oath.

12A:19 John Brooke (g, DO) administrator of
William Worgan (DO) exhibited accounts.

John Brooke (g, DO) exhibited will of
Ezekiel Fogg (DO). Also exhibited was
oath of John Richardson & Edward Cooke
administrators of said estate, sworn 18
March 1679.

12A:20 Sureties: Bartho. Ennalls, Michael
Bassey, William Stephens, William
Willoby. John Brooke (DO) exhibited
oath of William Stephens & William
Willoby, appraisers of Ezekill Fogg,
sworn on 18 March 1679. Inventory was
exhibited.

12A:21 John Brooke (g, DO) exhibited oath of
Sara Foulkes (DO) administratrix of

Thomas Fisher, sworn 3 April 1680.
Sureties: Michael Bassey, John Walker.
Thomas Flowers & John Kirke, appraisers
of said estate, were sworn same day.
Inventory was exhibited.

12A:22 16 April. Stephen Murty (SM)
administrator of John Baily (SM)
exhibited accounts. Discharge was
granted.

20 April. John Kirke administrator of
Francis Tassall petitioned for new
appraisers: John Walker, Thomas Flowers.
John Brooke (g) to administer oath.

12A:23 Alice Furnes (CV) widow of Nicholas
Furnes exhibited his will, constituting
said Alice executrix. Capt. Samuell
Bourne to prove said will. Said Alice
was granted administration. Appraisers:
William Parker, John Hancocke. Said
Bourne to administer oath.

12A:24 22 April. John Askin (SM) exhibited
will of George Wright (SM), proved by
Anthony Evans & John Evans. Appraisers:
Anthony Evans, John Evans.

12A:25 Gerrard Slye (g, SM) administrator of
Richard Chillman exhibited accounts.

Inventory of John Inglish (CE) was
exhibited, by appraisers George Oldfeild
& Richard Edmonds. Edmond Cantwell (CE)
administrator of John Inglish (CE)
exhibited accounts.

12A:26 26 April. John Peaseley (p, AA)
administrator of Richard Moss (AA)
exhibited accounts.

29 April. Thomas Bankes (g, CV)
administrator of George & Frances
Beckwith (CV) exhibited additional
accounts.

Lewis Blangey (KE) administrator of
Disborough Bennet (KE) exhibited
additional inventory.
12A:27 Robert Carvile (g, SM) attorney for
Lewis Blangey (KE) administrator of

Disborough Bennett (KE) exhibited
additional accounts.

John Hance (g, CV) exhibited will of
John Staynes (g, CV), constituting
Charles Harford (Bristoll, ENG)
executor. Capt. Samuel Borne to prove
said will. Said Hance was granted
administration, on behalf of said
Harford.

12A:28 Appraisers: William Parker, William
Martin. Said Bourne to administer oath.

Simon Pickinor one of witness of will of
Nicholas Guither proved said will.

12A:29 1 May. William Gwither (SM) executor of
his brother Nicholas Gwither was granted
administration on his estate.
Appraisers: Thomas Courtney, William
Twisdell. Anthony Evans to administer
oath.

3 May. Thomas Hussey (CH) exhibited
inventory of Edward Price (CH).

12A:30 4 May. William Gwither (SM) executor of
Nicholas Gwither exhibited inventory, by
appraisers Thomas Courtney & William
Twisdell. Also exhibited were accounts.

5 May. Ann Fookes (KE) widow of John
Fookes (KE) exhibited her renunciation
of his estate.

12A:31 Date: 2 December 1679. Witnesses: John
Lewis, Robert Smith. Before: Sam. Tovy.
Date: 29 March 1680. Lewis Blangey (KE)
was granted administration on his
estate, as greatest creditor.
Appraisers: Thomas Osbourne, John
Steevens. William Lawrence to
administer oath.

12A:32 6 May. Col. Phylemon Loyd (TA)
exhibited will of widow Winclos. Mr.
Woolman is the only witness. Mentions:
James Downes

12A:33 father of James Downes (cited in will,
her sister's son) as heir-at-law. Said
Loyd relinquishes his right to
administer said estate.

Said Phylemon Loyd petitioned for Margaret widow of John Greene. Appraisers: Tristrum Thomas, Peter Sides. Maj. William Coursey to administer oath.

12A:34 Richard Woolman to prove will of Elisabeth Wincles. James Downes, Sr. was granted administration on said estate. Appraisers: Symon Steevens, Robert Noble.

12A:35 Margarett Greene (TA) widow of John Greene was granted administration on his estate. Appraisers: Tristrum Thomas, Peter Sides. Maj. William Coursey to administer oath.

12A:36 Clare Parrish (AA) widow of Edward Parish (AA) exhibited her renunciation of administration on his estate. Date: 17 April 1680. Nathaniel Heathcote (g, AA) exhibited oath of Robert Lockwood & William Horne, Sr., appraisers of Edward Parrish, sworn 23 April 1680. Col. Thomas Taylor administrator of said Parrish was sworn on 3 May 1680. Surety: Nicho. Gassaway. Inventory was exhibited.

12A:37 Kenelme Cheseldyne attorney for John Wynne vs. Jane Williams (SM) administratrix of William Williams. Exceptions exhibited.

12A:38 William Hopkins (g, AA) exhibited bond of Sara Thornton relict & administratrix of John Woodhous, with surety: William Trevell. Inventory of John Woodhouse was exhibited, by appraisers William Trevell & Stephen Hancock.

7 May. William Sinclar (CE) exhibited will of John Inglish (CE), constituting said Sinclar executor. James Frisby (g, CE) to prove said will.

12A:39 8 May. Edward Newton (DO) administrator of Thomas Newton (DO) was granted discharge.

Court Session: 1680

10 May. Col. William Burges (AA) administrator of William Jones (AA) exhibited accounts.

Hester Sutton (AA) widow of Thomas Besson exhibited accounts, but is unable to travel to Office. Thomas Francis (g, AA)

12A:40 to examine & administer oath.

Inventory of Edward Philpott (CH) was exhibited, by appraisers John Courte & John Bracher.

Augustine Herman exhibited bond of James Hollaway administrator of Robert Cooke. Sureties: William Price, Daniell Smith.

12A:41 Inventory was exhibited, by appraisers William Price & Daniell Smith.

Robert Carvile attorney for Col. William Burgess vs. Capt. Richard Hill administrator of Samuell Whithers. Exceptions to accounts exhibited.

12A:42 Mentions: Elisabeth Whithers, William Pennington,

12A:43 Thomas Pennington, (N) Glover, administrator of (N) Neale.

12A:44 ...

12A:45 11 May. Col. Phylemon Loyd (TA) exhibited oath of Elisabeth Bardune (TA) administratrix of Charles Bardune, sworn 16 March 1679/80.

12A:46 Sureties: John Cash, John Edmondson. Henry Parker & Daniel Walker, appraisers were sworn on 20 March 1679/80.

Col. Phylemon Loyd (TA) exhibited oath of Sara Lawes (TA) administratrix of William Lawes, sworn on 15 November 1679. Sureties: Edward Parrish, Mathias Hughes.

12A:47 Bridgett Inglesbie (CH) widow of Robert Inglesbie (CH) exhibited her renunciation of administrating his estate, recommending George Hodgson. Said Hodgson was granted administration, as principle creditor. Appraisers: Thomas Baker, Lawrence Young. Henry Adams (g, CH) to administer oath.

12A:48   John Thomas (BA) was granted administration on estate of John Woodfine (BA), as principle creditor. Appraisers: Nicholas Corbin, Thomas Marshall. Anthony Demondidier to administer oath.

12A:49   12 May. Mary Suttle widow of John Suttle (SM) exhibited his will. William Diggs, Esq. to prove said will.

Capt. Samuell Bourne (CV) exhibited oath of John Cobreath administrator of Thomas Jackson, sworn 3 December 1679. Surety: John Sunderland. Richard Stallings & John Sunderland, appraisers were sworn same day.

12A:50   Inventory was exhibited.

Capt. Samuell Bourne (CV) exhibited will of Nicholas Furness (CV), proved. Alice Furnes executrix was sworn 24 April 1680. William Parker & John Hance, appraisers were sworn same day.

12A:51   12 May. Joseph Hopkins (g, CE) exhibited oath of Mary Anderson administratrix of William Pate (CE), sworn 3 May 1680. Sureties: Guiles Porter, John Gibbs. Said Guiles & said Gibbs John appraisers were sworn same day. Inventory was exhibited.

12A:52   John Boring (g, BA) exhibited oath of David Jones & John Arden, appraisers of John Leekins, sworn 26 April 1680. Bond of Margarett Leekins administratrix of said John was exhibited. Sureties: John Arden, Thomas Durbin. Inventory was exhibited.

12A:53   Hester Nicholson relict & administratrix of William Gough (AA) exhibited accounts, but is unable to travel to Office. Col. Thomas Taillor, Esq. (AA) to examine & administer oath.

Inventory of John Wells (KE) was exhibited, by appraisers William Bateman & Thomas Boone.

12A:54   Col. George Wells (BA) exhibited oath of Miles Gibson (g, BA) administrator of Edward Jackson, sworn 11 March 1680. Sureties: Peter Ellis, Robert Jones. Peter Ellis & Robert Jones, appraisers were sworn 15 March 1679. Inventory was exhibited.

12A:55   13 May. Anthony Demondidier (g, BA) exhibited bond of John Thomas administrator of Nicho. Ruxton. Sureties: David Jones, John Wilmott. Inventory was exhibited, by appraisers John Carrington & Francis Watkins.

  William Bishopp (g, TA) administrator of Richard Sturme exhibited accounts, but is unable to travel to Office. Maj. William Coursey to examine
12A:56   & to administer oath.

  Walter Meekes (CE) was granted administration on estate of Richard Christopher (CE), as principle creditor. Appraisers: John Willis, Giles Porter. Capt. Joseph Hopkins to administer oath.

12A:57   Elisabeth Jones (CE) widow of Peter West was granted administration on his estate. Appraisers: John Hudson, Edward Blay. James Staveley to administer oath.

  William Harris (KE) administrator of Richard Mason (KE) was granted discharge.

12A:58   Edward Beck (CE) one of executors of John Dixon (CE) exhibited accounts.

  14 May. Peter Carwardin (SM) exhibited will of Richard Ring (SM), proved by William Wright. Said Carwardin was granted administration.

12A:59   Daniel Edge (AA) exhibited will of Jonathon Neales (AA). Capt. Richard Hill to prove said will.

  Revell vs. Jones. Randall Revell (SO) exhibited that his wife Katherine deserved 12,000# out of estate of James Jones & his wife, in the hands of Andrew Jones administrator.

12A:60 18 May. Additional inventory of Edward Price (CH) was exhibited.

Sheriff (SM) to summon Jane Williams administratrix of William Williams (SM) to answer exceptions by John Wynn.

12A:61 James Mills (BA) was granted administration on estate of Edward Curtis (BA), who left a very small estate.

21 May. Inventory of Thomas Marsh (KE) was exhibited, by appraisers John Edmondson, William Berry, & Thomas Taylor.

Inventory of Charles Burdon (TA) was exhibited, by appraisers Henry Parker & Daniel Walter.

12A:62 Rowland Williams (CE) exhibited will of Thomas Smith (CE). Augustine Herman to prove said will.

Elisabeth Clawson (CE) relict of Peter Lecroe exhibited his will. Augustine Herman to prove said will.

12A:63 24 May. George Powell (CV) was granted administration on estate of William Collins (CV), as principle creditor. Appraisers: Richard Gardner, Thomas Hall. Roger Brooke to administer oath.

25 May. John Wattson (SM) executor of John Cunningham (SM) exhibited accounts.

12A:64 31 May. William Digges (SM) exhibited will of John Suttle, proved by Thomas Carvill & John Gouldsmith.

12A:65 Comfort White (SO) widow of Ambrose White (SO) was granted administration on his estate. Appraisers: Edward Wale, John Emmett. William Steevens, Esq. (SO) to administer oath.

3 June. Jane Ladds (KE) exhibited will of William Ladds. Henry Hosier (g, KE) to prove said will.

12A:66 Roger Brooke (g, CV) executor of Edward Keene (CV) exhibited accounts.

Elisabeth Christison (TA) exhibited will of Wenlock Christison (TA), proved. Inventory was exhibited, by appraisers Bryan Omelia & William Southebe.

12A:67 10 June. Mary Suttle (SM) widow of John Suttle was granted administration on his estate. Appraisers: Thomas Carvile, Peter Mills. Clement Hill (g, SM) to administer oath.

11 June. Thomas Russell (BA) exhibited will of William Hollis (BA). Col. George Wells (BA) to prove said will.

12A:68 William Osbourne (BA) exhibited will of Thomas Troute (BA). Col. George Wells to prove said will. Said Osbourne was granted administration.

12 June. Capt. John Waterton (BA) exhibited oath of George Gunnell & Thomas Russell administrators of Edward Gunnell, sworn 12 June. Said Russell renounced administration.

12A:69 Witness: Robert Lee. Said George was granted administration. Appraisers: William Osborne, Edward Reeves. Capt. John Stanesby (high sheriff, BA) to administer oath.

12A:70 17 June. Elisabeth Griffith (DO) was granted administration on estate of her infant child Francis Tassall, who is lately dec'd. Appraisers: Alexander Fisher, John Walker. John Brooke (g, DO) to administer oath.

12A:71 19 June. Augustine Herman (g, CE) exhibited nuncupative will of Thomas Smith (CE), with testimony by Richard Mackarry & Maryan Daniell. Also exhibited was testimony by Thomas Sprye, relating to proof of said will by word of Maurice Daniel (who is sick in New

Castle on DE Bay) that on 23 March 1679/80 he was desired to fetch John Reynolls to write his will, but was late. Maryan his wife inquired of his heir & he replied John Reynolls & Daniel Boulton should have all, except his wife have her 1/3rds. Should Daniel Boulton (then sick) die, then

12A:72 his mate John to have all. Signed: Maurice O'Daniell. Witnesses: Steevens Griffeth, Tho. Sprye. Thomas Sprye swore in court at New Castle DE to the statement of Morris Daniell. Date: 4 May 1680, by Eph. Herman (clerk). Richard Mackarry deposed regarding the will of Thomas Smith, age 22, who was sick on 23 March at the house of the deponent's master Maurice Daniell,

12A:73 desiring his old mate John Reynolls to have 200 a. & Daniel Boulton to have 200 a. & his wife to have her 1/3rds. Maryan Daniell deposed

12A:74 that said Smith called for the deponent's husband. Maurice Daniell deposed the same.

12A:75 Ruling: nothing was given to John Reynollds or Daniel Boulton but land which could not pass without a written will. Therefore, said Thomas Smith died intestate.

12A:76 James Frisby (g, CE) exhibited will of John English (CE), proved.

22 June. Col. Thomas Taillor (AA) exhibited accounts of Hester Gough (AA) relict & administratrix of William Gough (CV).

Henry Coursey (g, TA) exhibited oath of William Bishopp administrator of John Bradbourne, sworn on 6 March 1679. Daniel Glover & Matthew Smith, appraisers were sworn same day.

12A:77 Inventory was exhibited.

25 June. John Wynn (chyrurgeon) vs. Jane Williams administratrix of William Williams (SM). Said Jane appeared.

12A:78 Ruling: plaintiff. Doctor's fees are to be paid first before any other debtor.

3 July. Susanna Wedge (KE) widow &
executrix of John Wedge (KE) exhibited
his will. Henry Hosier (g) to prove
said will. Appraisers: Thomas Boone,
William Bateman.

12A:79 Marian O'Daniell (CE) widow of Morris
O'Daniell exhibited his will. George
Oldfeild (g) to prove said will. Said
Marian was granted administration.

5 July. Francis Barnes & Matthew
Eareckson (KE) administrators of Thomas
Barnes exhibited accounts, but are
unable to travel to Office. Henry
Hosier (g, KE) to examine & administer
oath.

12A:80 Isaac Winchester (KE) exhibited
inventory of John Winchester (KE), by
appraisers Morgan Williams & Francis
Barnes.

7 July. Anne Dabridgecourt (SM) widow
of John Dabridgecourt was granted
administration on his estate. Richard
Gardner (g, SM) to administer oath.

12A:81 8 July. Rebecca Askins (SM) widow &
executrix of John Askins (SM) exhibited
his will, proved by Francis Pennington
(priest). James Pattison, the other
executor, exhibited his renunciation of
administration.

12 July. Mordeca Hunton (CV) was
granted administration on estate of
Thomas Cooke (CV), as principle
creditor.
12A:82 Appraisers: Charles Boteler, Symon
Wooton. Col. Henry Jowles to
administer oath.

Agnus Driver (SM) widow of David Driver
(SM) was granted administration on his
estate. Surety: Abraham Coombe.
Appraisers: Peter Mills, Abraham Coombe.
Clement Hill (g) to administer oath.

12A:83 Rebecca Askins (SM) widow & executrix of
John Askins (SM) was granted
administration on his estate.

Appraisers: Geritt Vansweringen, John Thompson.

Rebecca Askin (SM) exhibited that her husband John Askin has LoA on estate of Philip Land (SM). Said Rebecca was granted administration on said Land's estate.

12A:84 Sureties: Gerritt Vansweringen, John Thompson. Appraisers: said Vansweringen, said Thompson.

14 July. George Parker for Robert Rouse (CV) executor of Griffeth George (CV) exhibited his will. Samuell Bourne (g) to prove said will. Said Rouse was granted administration.

12A:85 Appraisers: William Needham, Thomas Hart. Said Bourne to administer oath.

Anthony Demondidier (g, BA) exhibited oath of John Thomas (BA) administrator of John Woodfine (BA), sworn 28 May 1680. Sureties: Francis Watkins, Hugh Jones. Also exhibited oath of Nich. Corbin & Thomas Marshall, appraisers sworn same day.

12A:86 Inventory was exhibited.

Thomas Francis (AA) exhibited accounts of Hester Sutton administratrix of her husband Thomas Besson.

Judith Painter (CV) relict & administratrix of William Parker (CV) exhibited inventory.

12A:87 19 July. Andrew Jones (SO) administrator of James & Sara Jones (SO) exhibited accounts.

20 July. Elisabeth Alvey (SM) widow & executrix of Joseph Alvey (SM) exhibited accounts.

Alice Hackitt (AA) relict & administratrix of Edward Skidmore (AA) exhibited accounts.

12A:88 Margaret Cole (SM) relict & executrix of Michaell Rochford (SM) exhibited accounts.

Court Session: 1680

Anne Crowly (CV) relict & administratrix
of William Willson (CV) exhibited
accounts.

21 July. John Faning (g, CH)
administrator of William Thompson (CH)
exhibited accounts.

12A:89 Thomas Clipsham (CH) administrator of
John Cage (CH) exhibited accounts.

Thomas Clipsham (CH) administrator of
Charles Gregory (CH) exhibited
additional accounts.

22 July. Clement Hill (g, SM) exhibited
oath of Abrah. Coombe & Peter Mills,
appraisers of David Driver (SM), sworn
19 July 1680.

12A:90 Clement Hill (SM) exhibited oath of
Thomas Carvill & Peter Mills, appraisers
of John Suttle (SM), sworn on 17 July
1680. Also exhibited was bond of Mary
Suttle administratrix of John Suttle,
with sureties: Thomas Carvill, Peter
Mills.

Alice Furnes (CV) executrix of Nicholas
Furnes (CV) exhibited inventory.

12A:91 John Hance (g, CV) administrator of John
Staines (CV) exhibited inventory.

John Faning (g, CH) exhibited oath of
Francis Wine (CH) & John Coates, Sr.
(CH), appraisers of Henry Pratt, sworn
20 <month not given> 1680.

Said Faning also exhibited oath of said
Wine and said Coates, appraisers of John
Dadick, sworn same day. Also exhibited
was oath of Samuell Raspin administrator
of said Dadick, with sureties: John
Martin, Hugh Jones.

12A:92 John Faning (CH) exhibited oath of John
Coates, Sr. & John Bracher, appraisers
of Edward Philpott, sworn 20 March.
Also exhibited was bond of Bridgett
Ingelesbie (CH) administratrix of said
Philpott, with sureties: William Ward,

Cleborne Lomax.

Said Faning also exhibited oath of Maj. John Wheeler & John Cable, appraisers of Sylvanus Gilpin, sworn by Col. Benjamin Rozer. Also exhibited was bond of Thomas Wharton administrator of said

12A:93 Gilpin, with sureties: John Davis, Richard Waklen.

Inventory of Matthew Hill (CH) was exhibited, by appraisers Thomas Clipsham & John Faning.

12A:94 John Thompson to examine accounts during absence of Philip Calvert. Date: 22 July 1680.

12A:95 24 July. George Parker (CV) attorney for Thomas Taillor, Esq. & Archibald Arthur (chyrurgeon) vs. James Balderstone administrator of John Disjordeine. Exceptions to accounts exhibited.

12A:96 ...
12A:97 Mentions: Maj. Ringold, widow of dec'd.
12A:98-99 ...
12A:100 27 June [sic]. Margarett Warren (CH) relict & administratrix of Richard Roelants (CH) exhibited accounts.

Peter Carwardine (SM) executor of Richard Ringe (SM) exhibited accounts.

28 July. Rebecca Askins (SM) widow & executrix of John Askins (SM) exhibited inventory, by appraisers G. Vansweringen & John Thompson.

12A:101 Rebecca Askins (SM) administratrix of Philip Land (SM) exhibited inventory, by appraisers G. Vansweringen & John Thompson.

31 July. John Beamon (AA) administrator of Francis Smith (AA) exhibited accounts.

Lydia Beetenson (AA) executrix of Thomas Watkins (AA) exhibited accounts.

Court Session: 1680

12A:102 Robert Carvile procurator for Randall
Revell (SO) & his wife Katherine vs.
Robert Ridgeley procurator for Andrew
Jones (SO). Petition by plaintiff for
satisfaction of his wife's attendance on
Sara Jones widow of James Jones. Said
Andrew is administrator of said James &
said Sarah.
12A:103 Ruling: for plaintiff.

1 August. Inventory of Charles Bankes
(KE) was exhibited, by appraisers
Alexander Walters & Lewes Meredith.

2 August. Inventory of John Suttle (SM)
was exhibited, by appraisers Thomas
Carvill & Peter Mills.

12A:104 3 August. William Coursey (g, TA)
exhibited oath of Margarett Green (TA)
administratrix of John Green (TA), sworn
16 June 1680. Sureties: Tristram
Thomas, Peter Sides. Tristram Thomas &
Peter Sides, appraisers were sworn same
day.
12A:105 Inventory was exhibited.

4 August. John Evans who married Sarah
(CV) relict & executrix of Guy White
(CV) exhibited accounts.

12A:106 George Hodgson (doctor, CH) was granted
administration on estate of Samuell
Raspin (g, CH), who died with no
relations in the Province, as greatest
creditor, on behalf of widow & orphans.
Appraisers: Thomas Carvile, John
Fanning. Henry Adams (g, CH) to
administer oath.
12A:107 The judge was informed that said Hodgson
was a debtor and not a creditor.
Therefore, LoA were revoked.

Cristopher Rousby procurator for James
Murphy who married sister & heir of
George Richardson petitioned for Tymothy
Guddrige (Giddridge) to render accounts.

12A:108 6 August. Peter Stoakes who married
Anne (DO) relict & executrix of Miles
Mason (DO) exhibited accounts.

7 August. Jane Prather (CV) widow of Jonathon Prather (CV) was granted administration on his estate. Appraisers: John Miles, Robert Clarke. Col. Henry Darnall (CV) to administer oath.

12A:109 Randall Revell & his wife Katherine vs. Andrew Jones. Itemization of costs presented. Mentions: Morgan Jones, John Evans, Robert Ridgeley. Ruling: costs allowed & to be paid by plaintiff.

12A:110 John Stanesby (BA) was granted administration on estate of Thomas Jones (BA).

9 August. William Steevens (SO) exhibited oath of Comfort White (SO) administratrix of Ambrose White, sworn on 1 July 1680. Sureties: Matthew Scarbrough, John Cropper. Also exhibited was oath of Edward Wale & John Emmett,
12A:111 appraisers sworn same day.

10 August. William Steevens (SO) exhibited oath of Henry Dale (SO) administrator of David Dale, sworn 5 May 1680. Sureties: William Manlove, John Ellis. Also exhibited was oath of Marke Manlove & David Lynsey, appraisers sworn on 6 May 1680.
12A:112 Inventory was exhibited.

Col. William Steevens (SO) exhibited oath of Col. William Coleborne (SO) administrator of Thomas Feild, sworn 7 May 1680. Sureties: John Winder, Thomas Dixon. Also exhibited was oath of Nathaniell Dourghty & Benjamin Summers, appraisers sworn 20 April 1680.

12A:113 Thomas Highway (SO) administrator of Nath. Parsons (SO) was granted continuance.

13 August. Jane Bond executrix of Stephen Bond (SO) exhibited accounts, but cannot travel to Office. Col. William Steevens (SO) to examine & administer oath.

12A:114 Matthew Earackson administrator of John
Earackson (KE) exhibited accounts.
There is a cause pending in Provincial
Court. Continuance was granted.

14 August. Capt. Richard Hill (AA)
exhibited will of John Casson (AA),
proved. Also exhibited was oath of
Thomas Tolley executor,
12A:115 sworn on 12 May 1680. Also exhibited
was oath of Lawrence Draper & William
Gamball, appraisers sworn same day.
Inventory was exhibited.

12A:116 Col. George Wells (BA) exhibited will
of Thomas Troute (BA), proved.

Col. George Wells (BA) exhibited
deposition of Miles Gibson regarding
will of William Hollis, made 14 July
1680. Said Gibson deposed that said
Hollis was speechless & senseless & not
capable of making his will. When the
deponent hold his wife, she said she
knew how he wished to dispose of his
goods & chattels. The deponent guided
12A:117 said Hollis' hand to make his mark.
Said Hollis recovered & was angry with
his wife for causing such a will.

Richard Gardner exhibited oath of Peter
Mills & William Shercliffe, appraisers
of John DabridgeCourt (SM), sworn 2
August 1680.
12A:118 Also exhibited was bond of Anne
DabridgeCourt (SM), with sureties: Peter
Mills, William Shercliffe.

16 August. Samuell Tovy (g, KE)
administrator of William Norman (KE)
exhibited accounts. Discharge was
granted.
12A:119 Samuell Tovy (g, KE) administrator of
Vincent Atchinson (KE) exhibited
accounts. Discharge was granted.

17 August. Inventory of Samuell Raspin
(g, CH) was exhibited, by appraisers
William Chandler & Edmond Dennis.
Mentions: orphans
12A:120 in ENG, Mr. Marshall.

12A:121 18 August. Lewis Blangey who married
Mary relict & administratrix of
Disborough Bennett (KE) was granted
discharge.

12A:122 19 August. Henry Jowles (g, CV)
exhibited oath of Mordeca Hunton (CV)
administrator of Thomas Crooke, sworn 20
July 1680. Surety: Symon Wooton. Also
exhibited was oath of Charles Boteler &
Symon Wooton, appraisers sworn same day.

20 August. Capt. Samuell Bourne (CV)
exhibited oath of Robert Rouse executor
of Griffeth George, sworn 3 July last.
Also exhibited was his will, proved.
12A:123 Also exhibited was oath of William
Needham & Thomas Hart, appraisers sworn
same day.

21 August. Leonard Coates who married
Martha relict & administratrix of
William Russell (AA) exhibited accounts,
but is unable to travel to Office.
Thomas Taillor to examine & administer
oath.

12A:124 George Parker for Elisabeth Howard (AA)
widow & executrix of Cornelius Howard
(AA) exhibited his will. Capt. Richard
Hill to prove said will. Said Elisabeth
was granted administration. Appraisers:
Lancelott Todd, John Dorsey. Said Hill
to administer oath.

12A:125 24 August. Will of Morris O'Daniel (CE)
was exhibited, proved.

Anne Wheeler (CE) relict of Richard Nash
(CE) exhibited his will. Augustine
Herman (g) to prove said will.

12A:126 John Reynolds (CE) was granted
administration on estate of Thomas Smith
(CE), as greatest creditor. Appraisers:
John Browning, Hugh Magregory.
Augustine Herman to administer oath.

12A:127 Barbara Witton (CE) was granted
administration on estate of Thomas
Witton (CE). Appraisers: John Cousins,
John Cockerell. George Oldfeild (g) to

administer oath.

12A:128 28 August. George Gunnell (BA) administrator of Edward Gunnell (BA) exhibited inventory, by appraisers William Osbourne & Edward Reeves. Also exhibited were accounts.

12A:129 Magdalen Bayley (SM) relict & administratrix of James Pean (SM) exhibited accounts.

1 September. Mary Rowland (DO) widow of John Rowland (DO) was granted administration on his estate, who died leaving a very small inconsiderable estate. Sureties: Henry Hooper, William Travers.

12A:130 Sarah Macknemara (DO) was granted administration on estate of Lewis Griffen (DO). Appraisers: Richard Meekings, Samuell Millington. Henry Hooper (g) to administer oath.

12A:131 2 September. Elisabeth Holt (SM) administratrix of David Holt (SM) exhibited accounts.

Kenelme Cheseldine (SM) executor of John Jones (SM) exhibited accounts.

Capt. Richard Hill (AA) exhibited will of Jonathon Neale (AA), proved.

12A:132 Inventory of John DabrideCourt (SM) was exhibited, by appraisers Peter Mills & William Shercliffe.

Inventory of Griffeth George (CV) was exhibited, by appraisers William Needham & Thomas Hart.

3 September. Thomas Evans (SM) executor of Gregory Rouse (SM) exhibited accounts.

12A:133 6 September. Charles James (CE) was granted administration on estate of Charles Howell (CE), as prime creditor. Appraisers: Nich. Shaw, John Ricketts. Joseph Hopkins (g, CE) to administer oath.

12A:134 10 September. Ninion Beall (CV) & James
Moore (CV) executors of Robert Lashley
(CV) exhibited his will. Samuell
Taillor (g) to prove said will. Said
executors were granted administration.
Appraisers: Arthur Ladford, Thomas
Ellis. Said Taillor to administer oath.

12A:135 George Yate (AA) administrator of Robert
Willson (BA) exhibited that there is a
cause pending in County Court. Col.
Thomas Taillor to examine & administer
oath.

13 September. Inventory of Henry
Elliott (SM) was exhibited, by
appraisers John Evans & Thomas Courtney.

12A:136 15 September. James Wheeler (CH) was
granted administration on estate of
James Jefferson (CH), as principle
creditor. Appraisers: George Godfrey,
Thomas Gibson. Henry Adams (g) to
administer oath.

12A:137 21 September. Robert Clarkson (AA) was
granted administration on estate of Evan
Tucker (AA), as principle creditor.
Appraisers: Jacob Harness, William
Bateman. Richard Hill (g) to administer
oath.

12A:138 John Butcher (CH) administrator of John
Woodward (CH) exhibited accounts.

26 September. William Coursey (g, TA)
exhibited accounts of William Bishopp
(g, TA) administrator of Richard Sturme
(TA).

Jochem Kirstede (CV) administrator of
Isaac Vantright exhibited accounts.

12A:139 Cornelius Comegys (g, KE) exhibited
accounts of Joane David (KE)
administratrix of John David (KE).

Joseph Manning (CH) administrator of
John Blackfan (CH) exhibited accounts.

29 September. Edmund Cantwell (DE) was granted discharge.

12A:140 30 September. Charles Co. Court. 28 August 1680. Regarding the estate of orphan of Samuell Raspin. Based on deference by said Raspin to Col. Rozer, the land remains with said Rozer. Signed: Henry Adams, John Stone, Robert Henley, Ignatius Causin, William Barton, Hum. Warren.

12A:141 4 October. Henry Hanslapp (AA) executor of William Hanson (AA) exhibited his will. Henry Stockett to prove said will.

James Coursey (g) for Jane Matthews (TA) widow of Henry Matthews (TA) was granted administration on his estate.
12A:142 Appraisers: Hugh Johnson, William Crompe. William Bishop (g) to administer oath.

5 October. Augustine Herman (g, CE) exhibited will of Richard Nash (CE), proved.

12A:143 Augustine Herman (g, CE) exhibited oath of John Reynolds (CE) administrator of Thomas Smith, sworn 11 September 1680. Sureties: John Browning, Hugh Makriger. Also exhibited was oath of John Browning & Hugh Makriger, appraisers sworn 1 September 1680.

Augustine Herman (g, CE) exhibited will of Peter Lecroe (CE), proved.

12A:144 Augustine Herman (g, CE) exhibited oath of John Reynolds & Richard Mackarry, as proof of nuncupative will of Daniel Boulton (CE), who deposed that on 25 March, Daniell Smith asked Daniell Boulton to whom his estate should go. Signed: John Reynolds, Richard Makary. Date: 10 May 1680. Daniell Smith (CE) administrator of Daniell Boulton (CE) exhibited inventory.
12A:145 Augustine Herman (g, CE) exhibited oath of Daniell Smith (CE) administrator of Daniell Boulton, sworn on 8 September

1680. Sureties: Hugh Makrigor, John Rycroft. Also exhibited was oath of Hugh Makrigor & John Rycroft, sworn on 12 May 1680.

Joseph Hopkins (g, CE) exhibited oath of Walter Meek (CE) administrator of Richard Christopher (CE), sworn 6 June 1680. Sureties: Giles Porter, John Willis. Also exhibited was oath of John Willis & Giles Porter, appraisers sworn same day.

12A:146 Walter Meekes (CE) exhibited inventory & accounts of Richard Christopher (CE).

Col. Thomas Taillor (AA) exhibited accounts of Leonard Coates & his wife Martha administrators of William Russell (AA).

12A:147 William Lawrence (g, KE) exhibited accounts of Katherine Browne (KE) administratrix of Arthur Wright (KE).

Bond of Mary Pather (KE) administratrix of Richard Pather (KE) was exhibited, with sureties: Charles Vaughan, Will. Vaughan. Also exhibited was inventory.

Bond of Lewis Blangey (KE) administrator of John Fowkes (KE) was exhibited, with sureties: Thomas Osbourne, John Steevens.

12A:148 Henry Hosier (g, KE) exhibited will of William Ladds (KE), proved.

Henry Hosier (g, KE) exhibited will of John Wedge (KE), proved. Also exhibited was oath of Susanna Wedge executrix, sworn 6 August 1680. Also exhibited was oath of Thomas Boone & William Bateman, appraisers sworn same day.

12A:149 Inventory was exhibited.

Samuell Bourne (g, CV) exhibited oath of Judith Parker (CV) administratrix of William Parker (CV), sworn 8 January 1679/80. Also exhibited was oath of George Parker & John Hance, appraisers sworn same day.

12A:150 Samuell Bourne (g, CV) exhibited will of John Staynes (g, CV), proved. Also exhibited was oath of John Hance administrator, on behalf of Charles Harfoord, sworn 3 May 1680. Also exhibited was oath of William Parker & William Martin, appraisers sworn same day.

12A:151 Sibella Broadribb (TA) widow & executrix of John Broadribb (TA) exhibited his will. William Bishopp (g, TA) to prove said will. Appraisers: Robert Ellis, Hugh Johnson. Said Bishopp to administer oath.

12A:152 Henry Constable (AA) was granted administration on estate of Richard Bennett (AA), as principle creditor. Capt. Richard Hill to prove said will. Appraisers: Francis Stockett, William Hawkins.

12A:153 John Hodson (DO) administrator of John Hodson (DO) exhibited accounts.

George Oldfeild (g, CE) exhibited oath of Barbara Whitton relict & administratrix of Thomas Whitton. Sureties: John Hyland, John Cockerell. Also exhibited was oath of John Cousins & John Cockerell, appraisers.
12A:154 Inventory was exhibited.

Henry Hooper (DO) exhibited bond of Richard Meekins (DO) administrator of Lewis Griffen (DO), with surety: Samuell Millington. Inventory was exhibited.

12A:155 John Waterton (g, BA) exhibited bond of George Gunnell (BA) administrator of Edward Gunnell (BA), with sureties: James Philips, Thomas Cannon.

6 October. Mordeca Hunton (CV) administrator of Thomas Crooke (CV) exhibited inventory.

Josias Langham (KE) surviving administrator of John Dejourdeine petitioned for new appraisers: William Bateman, Robert Parkes. Samuell Tovy

(g) to administer oath.

12A:156 Mary Hall (CH) widow of Richard Hall
(CH) was granted administration on his
estate. Appraisers: George Godfrey,
Michaell Menock. Henry Adams (g) to
administer oath.

12A:157 Isaac Winchester (KE) administrator of
John Winchester (KE) exhibited accounts,
but is unable to travel to Office, due
to great sickness. William Lawrence (g,
KE) to examine & administer oath.

Mary Pether (KE) administrator of
Jeremiah Pether (KE) exhibited accounts,
but is unable to travel to Office, due
to great sickness. Joseph Weekes (g) to
examine & administer oath.

12A:158 Walter Kerby (KE) administrator of
Charles Debanck (KE) exhibited accounts.
Henry Hosier (g, KE) to examine &
administer oath. Said Kerby is disabled
by great sickness.

Lewis Blangey (KE) administrator of John
Foulkes (KE) exhibited inventory.

12A:159 William Smith (CH) exhibited will of
John Thomas (Stafford Co. VA), attested
by Samuell Hayward (Stafford Co. VA
clerk). Said Smith was granted
administration, on behalf of John Waugh
executor.

12A:160 ...

12A:161 7 October. Thomas Hopkins (TA)
exhibited will of Hugh Dulin (TA). Col.
Vincent Lowe, Esq. to prove said will.

Thomas Hopkins (TA) exhibited will of
Jane Dulin (TA). Col. Vincent Lowe to
prove said will.

12A:162 11 October. Maryan O'Daniell (CE)
administratrix of Morris O'Daniell (CE)
petitioned for new appraisers: Daniel
Smith, James Hollaway. George Oldfeild
(g) to administer oath.

Nicholas Browne who married Anne (BA) relict of Dennis Inglish (BA) was granted administration on his estate.
12A:163 Appraisers: George Oldfeild, John Hyland. Henry Johnson (g, BA) to administer oath.

John Camell who married Anne (CE) relict of William Savin (CE) was granted administration on his estate. Appraisers: John Hyland, Edward Jones. George Oldfeild (g) to administer oath.

12A:164 12 October. Thomas Russell (BA) who married Elisabeth relict of William Hollis (BA) was granted administration on his estate. Appraisers: Peter Ellis, William Osbourne. Miles Gibson (g, BA) to administer oath.

12A:164½ Robert Ridgely & Robert Carvile procurators for William Sinclar & Joseph Sparnon (CE) exhibited will of John Inglish, proved by commission to James Frisby (g). LoA were formerly issued to Edmund Cantwell on suggestion of nuncupative will. Said will is declared null & void. Appraisers: Edward Jones, John Hyland. George Oldfeild (g) to administer oath.

12A:165 <does not exist>

12A:166 John Kirke (DO) administrator of Francis Tassall (DO) exhibited inventory.

13 October. Maj. Thomas Long (BA) exhibited oath of Thomas Pert & Henry Enlos, appraisers of John Spinke (BA). Also exhibited was bond of Robert Benjar (BA) administrator of said estate. Surety: Henry Kinlowes.

12A:167 Thomas Todd (BA) administrator of his father Thomas Todd exhibited additional inventory.

19 October. Clement Hely (SM) administrator of Edward Connary (SM) exhibited accounts.

21 October. Semelia Yeo (BA) relict & administratrix of Ruthen Garrettson (BA) exhibited accounts.

12A:168 Accounts of Elisabeth Haslewood executrix of Henry Haslewood executor of John Collett were exhibited. Col. Wells to depose. Mentions: debt from (N) Hawkins, orphans of Matthew Gouldsmith legatees of John Collett.

Will of Henry Haslewood (BA) was exhibited.

12A:169 Elisabeth Haslewood executrix was granted administration. Appraisers: George Wells (g, BA), Henry Johnson (g, BA). Miles Gibson (g) to administer oath.

12A:170 25 October. Samuell Taylor (g, CV) exhibited will of Robert Lashley (CV). Ninian Beall was granted administration on his estate. Appraisers: Arthur Ludford, Thomas Ellis.

12A:171 28 October. William Chandler (g, CH) was granted administration on estate of Roger Fowkes (lately arrived in ENG), as principle creditor.

12A:172 Owen Gwither (SM) was granted administration on estate of Mary Jones (SM). Surety: William Gwither. Appraisers: Elias Beach, Thomas Griffen. Said William Gwither to administer oath.

12A:173 2 November. Arthur Turner (CH) was granted administration on estate of John Ward (CH), as principle creditor. Appraisers: John Gough, John Fearson. Humphrey Warren (g, CV) to administer oath.

12A:174 William Reede (DO) was granted administration on estate of his brother John Reede, on behalf of widow & orphans. Appraisers: Thomas Harpin, William Hill. William Steevens (g, DO) to administer oath.

12A:175 Col. William Colebron (SO) administrator of Thomas Feild (SO)

exhibited inventory, by appraisers
Benjamin Summer & Nathaniell Dougherty.
Accounts were also exhibited.

James Philips (g, BA) exhibited that
George Gunnell was administrator of his
brother Edward Gunnell (BA), & said
Philips & Thomas Cannon were security to
said George.

12A:176 Said George exhibited accounts. Robert
Ridgely procurator for said Philips
examined the accounts. Said George is
runaway.

12A:177 Ruling: sureties to pay creditors &
dispense residue.

3 November. Isbell Harrison (TA) widow
& executrix of James Harrison (TA)
exhibited will of said Samuell. Edward
Mann to prove said will.

Mary Heigh (CV) widow & executrix of
Robert Heigh (CV) exhibited his will.

12A:178 Appraisers: James Mackall, Francis
Malden. Capt. Samuell Bourne to
administer oath.

24 November. Jane Nunne (TA) relict &
administratrix of Richard Richardson was
granted administration on his estate.
Appraisers: Henry Alexander, Thomas
Martin. Capt. George Cowley to
administer oath.

12A:179 George Cowley (g, TA) administrator of
John Slaughter (TA) exhibited accounts.

25 November. Elisabeth Browne (DO)
widow of Thomas Browne (DO) was granted
administration on his estate.
Appraisers: Richard Meekins, Richard
Tubbman. Maj. Thomas Taillor to
administer oath.

12A:180 Elisabeth Guilbert (DO) widow of Thomas
Guilbert (DO) was granted administration
on his estate. Appraisers: Richard
Meekins, Richard Tubbman. Maj. Thomas
Taillor to administer oath.

12A:181 Capt. Samuell Bourne (CV) exhibited
bond of Judith Painter relict &

administratrix of William Parker, with
sureties: Robert Franklin, William
Gwither.

John Reynolds (CE) administrator of
Thomas Smith (CE) exhibited inventory.

Maryan O'Daniell (CE) administratrix of
Morris O'Daniell (CE) exhibited
inventory.

12A:182 Vincent Lowe, Esq. (TA) exhibited will
of Hugh Dulin (TA), proved.

Vincent Lowe, Esq. (TA) exhibited will
of Jane Dulin (TA), proved.

Edward English (CE) exhibited will of
John Inglish (CE), proved.

12A:183 Edward English (CE) exhibited oath of
Edward Cantwell (New Yorke on Delaware
River) executor of John Inglish (CE).
Also exhibited was oath of George
Oldfeild & Richard Edmunds, appraisers.

William Vaughan, Robert Elliot, John
Hunking, & Jane Jouse (merchants, NE)
petitioned
12A:184 that Edward Gunnell (BA) was indebted to
the petitioners. George Gunnell
administrator absconded. Ruling: bond
of James Philips & Thomas Cannon
assigned to petitioners.

12A:185 Henry Johnson (g, BA) exhibited oath of
Nicholas Browne & his wife Anne relict &
administrators of Dennis Inglish, sworn
27 October 1680. Sureties: George
Oldfeild, John Hyland. Also exhibited
was oath of George Oldfeild & John
Hyland, appraisers sworn same day.
Inventory was exhibited.

12A:186 Henry Adams (g, CH) exhibited oath of
Mary Hall (CH) administratrix of Richard
Hall, sworn 18 October 1680. Sureties:
George Godfrey, Michaell Menock. Also
exhibited was oath of George Godfrey &
Mich. Menock, appraisers sworn same day.
Inventory was exhibited.

12A:187 Henry Adams (g, CH) exhibited oath of
Thomas Baker & Joseph Conwell,
appraisers of Thomas Dines (CH), sworn
on 12 December last. Also exhibited was
bond of Mary Dynes administratrix, with
sureties: Joseph Conwell, John Martin.
Mary Dines (CH) exhibited inventory.

Henry Adams (g, CH) exhibited oath of
Thomas Baker & Lawrence Young,
appraisers of Robert Inglesbie (CH).
12A:188 Also exhibited was bond of George
Hodgson administrator, with sureties:
Samuell Raspin, Lawrence Young.

Henry Adams (g, CH) exhibited oath of
George Godfrey & Thomas Gibson,
appraisers of James Jefferson (CH),
sworn on 27 September 1680. Also
exhibited was bond of James Wheeler,
with surety: George Godfrey.

12A:189 Capt. Richard Hill (AA) exhibited oath
of Henry Constable (AA) administrator of
Richard Bennett, sworn on 18 November
1680. Surety: James Rigbie. Also
exhibited was oath of Francis Stockett &
Edward Jones, appraisers sworn same day.

Richard Hill (g, AA) exhibited oath of
Robert Clarkson (AA) administrator of
Evan Tucker, sworn 10 November. Also
exhibited was oath of Jacob Harness &
William Bateman, appraisers sworn same
day.
12A:190 Also exhibited was bond of Robert
Clarkson administrator, with sureties:
Thomas Driffeild, John Beasely.
Inventory was also exhibited.

Richard Hill (g, AA) exhibited will of
Cornelius Howard (AA), proved.
12A:191 Also exhibited was oath of Elisabeth
Howard (AA) widow & executrix, sworn 15
October 1680. Also exhibited was oath
of John Dorsey & Lancelott Todd, sworn
14 October 1680. Inventory was
exhibited.

12A:192 Adam Boucher (CH) one of overseers of
will of William Love (CH) exhibited his
will, proved by William Theobalds. Said

Boucher & the other overseer Richard
Chandler were granted administration.
Appraisers: George Godfrey, James
Wheeler. Henry Adams (g) to administer
oath.

12A:193 William Chandler (CH) administrator of
Roger Fowkes (CH) petitioned for new
appraisers: George Godfrey, Michaell
Menock.

Jane Witton (CV) widow of John Witton
(CV) exhibited his will, constituting
her executrix. Col. Henry Jowles to
prove said will. Said Jane was granted
administration. Appraisers: William
Graves, Jonathon Goosey. Said Jowles to
administer oath.

12A:194 27 November. Cornelius Comagys (KE) was
granted administration on estate of Jane
Matthews (TA), on behalf of orphans.
Appraisers: Hugh Johnson, William
Crusape. William Bishopp to administer
oath.

Edward Pindar (DO) administrator of
William Ford (DO) exhibited accounts.

12A:195 29 November. On 12 October, Robert
Ridgely & Robert Carvile procurators for
Joseph Spernon & William Sincler
exhibited will of John Inglish (CE) &
petitioned that there was no nuncupative
will, because there is no proof that it
existed. Edmund Cantwell executor per
nuncupative will was granted
administration. Said nuncupative will
was proved. Ruling: said Spernon & said
Sincler to surcease all proceedings
until arguments made & final ruling.

12A:196 1 December. Henry Johnson who married
Elisabeth relict & administratrix of
Nathaniell Uty (BA) exhibited accounts,
but are unable to travel to Office.
Edward Beedle (g) to examine &
administer oath.

Peter Ellis (BA) administrator of
William Palmer (BA) was granted
discharge.

12A:197 2 December. Thomas Highway (SO)
         administrator of Nathaniell Parsons (SO)
         exhibited accounts.

         Col. William Steevens (SO) exhibited
         accounts of Samuell Jones (g)
         administrator of his father Samuell
         Jones (SO).

         Col. William Steevens (SO) exhibited
         accounts of Jane Bond widow & executrix
         of Stephen Bond.

12A:199 3 December. Robert Collier (SO)
         executor of John Hudson (SO) exhibited
         his will. Col. William Steevens to
         prove said will.

         Comfort White (SO) administratrix of
         Ambross White (SO) exhibited inventory,
         & a list of goods belonging to the
         orphans.

12A:199½ 20 December. Henry Constable (AA)
         administrator of Richard Bennett
         exhibited inventory.

         21 December. John Fitch (Gloster alias
         Cape Ann, NE) executor of his
         father-in-law William Steevens (Gloster
         alias Cape Ann, NE) exhibited his will,
         proved by John Haslewood & William
         Robson. Mentions: widow Mary.
12A:200 Said Fitch was granted administration.
         Appraisers: said Haslewood, said Robson.

         22 December. Cecil Bright (CE) widow of
         Thomas Bright
12A:201 was granted administration on his
         estate. Appraisers: Isaac Winchester,
         Thomas Osbourne. William Lawrence (g)
         to administer oath.

         Robert Mackline (TA) son of Robert
         Mackline (TA) exhibited his will, made
         in 1675.
12A:202 2 days after his death, said will was
         burned by Abigall Mattersey & Mary
         Chafe. On 17 December 1675, Col. Henry
         Coursey & his brother Maj. William
         Coursey were commissioned to examine the
         witnesses. Said Mattersey gave false

testimony & later became blind & died.
Ruling: said Mackline (the elder) died
intestate & Henry Ward (g, TA) & William
Bishopp (g, TA) were granted
administration during minority of
petitioner & his brother Richard
Macklin. Said Robert is now 18.

12A:203 Col. Henry Coursey to summon surviving
administrator said Bishopp to render
accounts. Col. Henry Coursey (TA)
exhibited his letter on behalf of Robert
Mackline (son of Robert Mackline).

12A:204 Mentions: Ralph Blackhall (who wrote the
will), an old woman, Mary Chafe,

12A:205 MM (N) Wickes & (N) Hynson (guardians of
the children). Date: 15 November 1680.
Said Robert Mackline deposed that he did
see his father's will, wherein the
plantation was to be divided between the
2 brothers.

12A:206 Robert Smith who married Ann (TA) relict
& executrix of Thomas Hynson (TA)
exhibited accounts.

23 December. On 25 November, LoA were
granted to Adam Boucher & Richard
Chandler administrators of William Love.
William Chandler renounced
administration, being sick & crazy.
Signed: Richard Chandler. Date: 20
December 1680.

12A:207 Said Boucher was granted administration.
Henry Adams (g, CH) to administer oath.

3 January. George Powell (CV)
administrator of William Collins (CV)
exhibited inventory, by appraisers
Richard Gardner & Thomas Hall.

Anne Alvey (SM) administratrix of Pope
Alvey (SM)

12A:208 was granted continuance.

6 January. Mathew Silley (AA) executor
of David Frye (AA) exhibited his will.
Nathaniell Heathcote (g, AA) to prove
said will.

13 January. Thomas Crowder (Clifts, CV)
exhibited will of William Kent (Clifts,
CV), with letter from John Cobreath,

John Hunt, & Richard Stallings
supporting themselves as executors.
12A:209 Said Crowder married one of the
daughters of said Kent. Date: 8
January. Will was written by an
illiterate Scotchman. Capt. Samuell
Bourne (Clifts) to prove said will.
12A:210 Said Crowder only was granted
administration. Appraisers: Marke
Clare, Abraham Clarke. Said Bourne to
administer oath.

22 January. William King (CV)
administrator of Ishmaell Wright (CV)
exhibited accounts.

28 January. Ursula Bagbie (CV) widow &
executrix of Amos Bagbie (CV) exhibited
his will, proved by John Willymot &
Daniel Taylor.
12A:211 Said Ursula was granted administration.
Appraisers: William Howes, Symon Wooton.
John Crycroft (g, CV) to administer
oath.

Ursula Bagbie (CV) executrix of Amos
Bagbie executor of his brother Michaell
Bagbie exhibited his will,
12A:212 proved by Samuell Bagbie. Said Ursula
was granted administration. Appraisers:
William Howes, Symon Wooton. John
Crycroft to administer oath.

12A:213 Margaret Stagg (CV) widow &
administratrix of Thomas Stagg (CV)
exhibited additional accounts.

31 January. John Fitch (Gloster at Cape
Anne, NE) executor of William Steevens
(Gloster at Cape Anne, NE) exhibited
inventory.

8 February. Anne Crauford (CV) relict &
executrix of John Clarke (CV) exhibited
his will. Roger Brooke to prove said
will.
12A:214 Said Crauford was granted
administration. Appraisers: George
Abbott, John Manning. Said Brooke to
administer oath.

9 February. James Wheeler (CH) administrator of James Jefferson (CH) exhibited inventory.

12A:215 Ninion Bell (CV) executor of Robert Lashley (CV) exhibited inventory, by appraisers Arthur Ludford & Thomas Ellis.

Thomas Russell (BA) who married Elisabeth relict & administratrix of William Hollis (BA) exhibited inventory.

William Chandler (CH) administrator of Roger Fowke (CH) exhibited inventory.

12A:216 Agnes Driver (SM) administratrix of David Driver (SM) exhibited inventory.

10 February. William Stephens (g, DO) exhibited oath of Thomas Harpin & William Hill, appraisers of John Reede (DO), sworn 6 January 1680. Also exhibited was oath of William Reede administrator of his brother John Reede, sworn 3 February. Inventory was exhibited.

12A:217 William Bishop (g, TA) exhibited accounts & oath of Robert Ellis executor of John Underwood. Date: 12 October 1679.

11 February. Edward Mann (TA) exhibited will of James Harrison (TA), proved.
12A:218 Isbell Harrison (TA) widow exhibited inventory, by appraisers Thomas Taylor, William Southebe, & John Edmondson.

12 February. Miles Gibson (g, BA) exhibited will of Henry Haslewood, proved.

Miles Gibson exhibited oath
12A:219 of Thomas & Elisabeth Russell administrators of William Hollis, sworn 10 January 1680. Also exhibited was oath of William Osborne & Peter Ellis, appraisers sworn same day.

Hum. Warren (g, CH) exhibited oath of Arthur Turner administrator of John

Court Session: 1680

Ward, sworn 29 November 1680. Surety:
James Turner. Also exhibited was oath
of John Gooch & John Farrson, appraisers
sworn same day

12A:220 Henry Stockett (g, AA) exhibited will of
William Hanson (AA), proved.

14 February. George Oldfeild exhibited
bond of John Camell (CE) administrator
of William Savin (CE). Sureties: Joseph
Spernon, William Price.

Elisabeth Haslewood (BA) widow &
executrix of Henry Haslewood (BA)
exhibited inventory.

12A:221 Commissioners (BA) exhibited accounts of
Elisabeth Haslewood executrix of John
Collett.

15 February. James Orrick (AA) who
married Mary relict & executrix of John
Ricks (AA) executor of William Slade
(AA) exhibited accounts of said Slade.
Commissioners (AA) to secure estate of
orphans of said Slade.
12A:222 Mentions: accounts of James Orrick who
married Mary relict of John Ricke (AA)
executor of William Slade.

William Cole (SM) who married Margaret
relict & executrix of Michaell Rochford
(SM) exhibited accounts.
12A:223 Said William & Margaret were married
immediately after death of dec'd.

16 February. Mary Hastings (BA) relict
of Thomas Biworth was granted
administration on his estate.
Appraisers: John Thomas,
12A:224 Nicholas Corbin. John Boreing (g) to
administer oath.

Robert Parks (KE) was granted
administration on estate of John Wyborow
(KE), as principle creditor.
12A:225 Appraisers: Robert Griffen, Bennett
Stares. Maj. James Ringgold to
administer oath.

Page 181

John Johnson (TA) executor of Thomas
Jones (TA) exhibited his will. William
Bishopp (g) to prove said will. Said
Johnson was granted administration.
Appraisers: Richard Jones, Daniell
Glover. Said Bishopp to administer
oath.

12A:226 17 February. Arthur Taylor (BA)
executor of John Taylor (BA) exhibited
additional accounts.

Timothy Macknemara (DO) who married
Sarah relict & administratrix of Lewis
Griffen (DO) exhibited accounts. Said
Timothy & Sarah were married immediately
after death of dec'd.

Edward Beck (CE) one of executors of
William Salsbury (CE) renounced
administration on his estate.
12A:227 Other executor is John Willis. Date: 31
January 1680. Witness: William Shaw.
John Willis exhibited his will. Joseph
Hopkins to prove said will. Said Willis
was granted administration. Appraisers:
richard Pullen, George Higginbotham.
Said Hopkins to administer oath.

12A:228 Ann Eagle (TA) widow of William Eagle
(TA) was granted administration on his
estate. Appraisers: John Stanlye, Roger
Sommers. Edward Man (g) to administer
oath.

18 February. Michaell Tawney for
Katherine Wynall (CV) widow of John
Wynall (CV)
12A:229 was granted administration on his
estate. Appraisers: Thomas Sedwicke,
James Gardner. Roger Brooke (g) to
administer oath.

Michaell Miller (high sheriff, KE) was
granted administration on estate of
Richard Lee (KE), as principle creditor.
12A:230 Appraisers: William Harris, Robert
Parke. Henry Hosier (g) to administer
oath.

19 February. Jane Walker (SO) widow &
executrix of Thomas Walker (SO)

Court Session: 1680

exhibited his will. Capt. David Browne
to prove said will. Said Jane was
granted administration. Appraisers:
Henry Smith, William Brereton.
12A:231 Said Browne to administer oath.

Mary Curtis (SO) widow & executrix of
Daniell Curtis (SO) exhibited his will.
Col. William Steevens to prove said
will. Said Mary was granted
administration. Appraisers: Charles
Hall, Thomas Tull. Said Steevens to
administer oath.

12A:232 George Parker (Clifts, CV) exhibited
that John Staines (Clifts, CV) made a
will in ENG, & appended a codicil. Said
codicil was proved on 29 April by
Samuell Bourne, witnessed by John
Boreham & Mary Barnes. John Hance
(Clifts) was granted administration, on
behalf of Charles Harford executor.
12A:233 Said will was proved in Court of
Canterbury. Petition for LoA to John
Hance be revoked & granted to said
Parker at attorney of executor. PoA by
Charles Harford (soapeboiler, Bristol)
executor of John Staines (merchant) to
George Parker (g).
12A:234 Date: 7 September 1680. Witnesses: John
Jones, Ralph Beames.
12A:235 Said Parker was granted administration.
LoA to said Hance was revoked.
12A:236 Letter from Rt. Rev. William Archbishop
of Canterbury.
12A:237 Will of John Staines (bound on voyage to
MD). Legatees: wife, Mary Holester
(unmarried, under age 21, daughter of
Philip Holester), Charles Harford (under
age 21, son of Charles Harford
(Bristol)). Residue:
12A:238 Charles Harford the elder (Bristol) to
be divided amongst the rest of his
children. Legatee: Edward Harford (son
of Charles Harford). Said Harford was
granted administration. Date: 17
October 1678. Witnesses: Symon Hurle,
George Lambert.
12A:239 Codicil: John Hance (Clifts, CV) to take
entire estate into his custody including
ship Sarah & Elisabeth to act for Mr.
Charles Harford (Bristol, executor in

Page 183

ENG). Legatee: Mr. John Hance, his wife Mrs. Sarah Hance, Basill Wareing, Mr. George Parker,

12A:240 Mr. William Parker, George Abott, Frances Cotton, servants of Mr. John Hance. Date: 17 April 1680. George Parker (Clifts, CV) to act for Charles Harford (soapeboiler, Bristol) executor.

12A:241 Said George Parker was granted administration.

12A:242 John Stansby (g, high sheriff, BA) was empowered to collect estate of Thomas Jones (Gunpowder River, BA) & exhibit inventory. Jones' plantation is in occupation of John Wright. Said land was first patented by William Yorke as "Yorke's Hope" 200 a. & sold to William Macanelly who died leaving a son to inherit & a wife who married said Thomas Jones. Said wife died leaving a son (infant, age 5/6) who died shortly afterwards.

12A:243 24 February. Anne Alvey administratrix of Pope Alvey (SM) exhibited accounts, but is unable to travel to Office. Clement Hill (g, SM) to examine & administer oath.

Robert Carvile procurator for William Sinclar (CE) & Joseph Spernon (CE) executors of John English vs. Edmund Cantwell. Said Cantwell summoned.

12A:244 25 February. James Philips (BA) & Thomas Cannon (BA) security for George Gunnell administrator of Edward Gunnell exhibited accounts. Said George has departed the Province.

12A:245 14 March. Thomas Marshall (milwright, CH) exhibited that he was employed by Samuell Raspin to repair the mill at head of Wicokomaco River. Said Marshall was granted administration on estate of said Raspin. Securities: Capt. Michaell Ashford, Francis Wyne (CH).

12A:246 Appraisers: John Courts, John Ward. Henry Adams (g) to administer oath.

18 March. Adam Boucher (CH)
administrator of William Love (CH)
exhibited inventory.

21 March. William Dixon (TA) executor
of Walter Dickenson (TA) exhibited his
will. William Combes (g, TA) to prove
said will.

12A:247 22 March. Elisabeth Muffitt (CV) widow
of William Muffitt was granted
administration on his estate.
12A:248 Appraisers: Symon Edwards, James Cobbs.
Roger Brooke (g) to administer oath.

24 March. Richard Harrison who married
Elisabeth relict & executrix of John
Benson (CV) exhibited accounts, but is
unable to travel to Office. George
Lingham to examine & administer oath.

12A:249 William Harris (CV) executor of John
Boureman (CV) exhibited his will. Capt.
Samuell Bourne to prove said will.

12A:250 Edward Talbott who married Elisabeth
(AA) relict & executrix of William Cole
was granted administration on his
estate. Appraisers: Nathaniell
Heathcoate (g), John Welch (g). Col.
Thomas Taillor to administer oath.
12A:251 Robert Macklin (TA) son & heir of Robert
Macklin exhibited that William Bishopp &
Matthew Ward were administrators of his
father's estate during his minority &
that of his brother Richard. Said
Robert is now 18. Said Robert was
granted administration on his father's
estate. Col. Henry Coursey to
administer oath.

12A:252 Robert Ridgely procurator for William
Sinclar (CE) & Joseph Spernon (CE)
executors of written will of John
Inglish vs. Edmond Cantwell (g, late
CE, now DE) executor of nuncupative will
of said Inglish.
12A:253 Said Inglish made will on 8 January
1678, witnessed by: William Price,
Thomas Shelton, John Rycroft. James
Frisby (g) proved said will.
12A:254 Said Inglish shortly afterwards went to

DE & died on 23 March at house of Dr. Thomas Sprye (New Castle). Said Cantwell exhibited nuncupative will of said Inglish, proved by Edward Inglish (g, CE).

12A:255 Appraisers: George Oldfeild, Richard Edmonds. Depositions by: Thomas Sprye, John Bricke, Peter Aldrick, Johannes Dehaes. Said Inglish has no relation in this country & appointed his countryman Capt. Edmond Cantwell his heir.

12A:256 Said Inglish did send for his brother-in-law Johannes Dehaes. He is a relation of a chief friend Capt. John Quigley (SM).

12A:257-261 ...

12A:262 Capt. Jonathon Sibrey summoned said Cantwell and Mr. John Moll (also John Mall, Delaway). Date: 10 March 1680.

Court Session: 1682

12B:1 25 March. John Fanning (CH) was granted administration on estate of Robert Cooper (taylor), who died at said Fanning's house, a single man without relation in these parts, as principle creditor. Appraisers: MM John Beane, Richard Beaumont. Capt. Humphrey Warren to administer oath.

Robert Carvile (SM) procurator for William Hopkins (p, AA) vs. John Bird administrator of Henry Lewis. Petition.

12B:2 Nathaniell Stinchcombe (AA) made his will on 11 June 1670 constituting his wife Thomasin executrix. Said Thomasin made her will on 13 August 1673, bequeathing to her 2 sons Nathaniell (under age 21) & John Stinchcombe (under age 21) & constituted Thomas Turner (AA) executor & guardian. Said Turner was "but a baze executor & not being free to take oath of executor" & gave bond with Mathew & Cornelius Howard. Not long after, said Turner died intestate. Said Howard petitioned for administration, which was put on hold until Paul Dorrell (heir to said Turner) should renounce or not administration on said Turner's estate. Said Dorrell renounced administration. Henry Lewis (AA) was granted administration on estate of said Turner, as principle creditor. It was then declared that the Stinchcombes were deceased intestate, &

12B:3 said Lewis was granted administration on their estates. Said Lewis gave bond with petitioner & John Ricks for both estates. Said Lewis exhibited inventory & accounts for both estates, leaving a residue for distribution to Stinchcombes' orphans.

12B:4 Henry Lewis made his will on 16 March 1678, constituting his wife Elisabeth executrix. Said Lewis' estate is considerable, with sufficient assets to pay Stinchcombes' orphans. Said Elisabeth married John Bird (AA) & exhibited inventory & accounts on said Lewis. Said Bird is about to leave the country.

12B:5 Said Bird is summoned.
12B:6 Exceptions to estate of Henry Lewis exhibited.
12B:7 Mentions: Joseph Connoway, William Cox, John Stinchcomb,
12B:8 John Williams (TA), Morris Cooper (KE), Francis Underwood (SO), John Boulton. (AA).

12B:9 Dr. John Wynn (SM) exhibited bill for services to William Williams (SM, dec'd). Jane Watson relict & administratrix of said Williams was ordered to pay said Dr. John Winn.

12B:10 William Calvert, Esq. (Principle Secretary) exhibited will of Constantine Hieft (SM), constituting said Calvert executor. Said will was declared void. Said Calvert was granted administration. Appraisers: Thomas Doxey, Daniell Divine. Capt. Henry Smith

28 March. Sarah Thompson (SM) widow of John Thompson was granted administration on his estate. Appraisers: John Doxey, Charles Priest.

12B:11 30 March. Henry Henley (SM) exhibited that Robert Cooper (CH, dec'd) discharged debt before Robert Taylor &

his wife, Thomas Carvile, Mary Cheshire. Said Cooper died at house of Mr. John Fanning. Said Fanning was granted administration on his estate, as greatest creditor. Before: William Diggs, Esq. Said Fanning to pay said Henley

12B:12 & Mr. Thomas Burford to keep bill.

31 March. James Philips (BA) exhibited will of William Hill (BA), constituting said Philips executor. Mr. Edward Bedle to prove said will. Appraisers: William Osborne, William Crowshen. Said Bedle to administer oath.

1 April. Thomas Davis (Choptico) who married one of daughters of Thomas Thomas (Newtowne Hundred, SM) exhibited his will, constituting Robert Perry executor & guardian to orphans. Said Thomas gave to Mary wife of said Davis her child's portion. Said Perry proved said will & was

12B:13 granted administration & died before William Thomas (son & heir) came to age 21. Said William took possession of the lands & chattels of his father & withholds legacy to said Mary. Said William summoned.

Henry Newton (TA) exhibited will of his brother John Newton (TA), constituting him executor. Insufficient witnesses were found. Therefore, will is void. Daniell Newton was granted administration, on behalf of orphans.

12B:14 Appraisers: John Stanley, Richard White. Mr. Edward Mann to administer oath.

Mr. William Combes (TA) exhibited will of Thomas Alexander, proved by John Price & Robert Fowler. The will is void in law, but recorded for benefit of orphans. Appraisers: George Robins, Samuell Abbot. Hannah Alexander executrix was sworn 7 March 1681/2. Inventory was exhibited.

12B:15 3 April. Amye Eagle (TA) widow of William Eagle (TA) exhibited that LoA were granted on 17 February 1680, with

appraisers John Stanly & Roger Sumers.
New LoA were granted, with new
appraisers: John Stanley, William
Caltrop Roger Sumers afsd was unable to
perform.

4 April. Martha Ridgely (SM) executrix
of Robert Ridgely (SM) was granted
continuance. Appraisers: MM John
Addisson, John Llewellin.

12B:16 Henry Stockett exhibited bond of Richard
Beard, Jr. administrator of Richard
Beard, Sr. (AA). Sureties: Thomas
Besson, John Gray. Inventory was
exhibited, by appraisers Thomas Besson &
John Gary.

Robert Henley (CH) exhibited oath of
Elisabeth Wyne executrix of Francis Wyne
(CH). Also exhibited was will, proved
by George Groves, Robert Price, &
Clebone Lomax. Also exhibited was oath
of Thomas Clipsham & John Fanning,
appraisers sworn 6 March 1681/2.

12B:17 Inventory of Thomas Coates (CH) was
exhibited, by appraisers Ralph Shaw &
John Martin.

John Carvile procurator for John
Salisbury nephew & heir of William
Salisbury (CE) petitioned that said
William's will be set aside & LoA
granted to John Willis be revoked. Said
John Salisbury is the son & heir of John
Salisbury (Nansemunne, VA, dec'd,
brother & heir of said William). Said
Willis was summoned.

Robert Carvile (SM) procurator for
William Wilkisson (p,
12B:18 BA) & his wife Elisabeth (daughter of
Abraham Clarke (dec'd)) vs. Miles
Gibson administrator of said Abraham
Clarke. Exceptions exhibited.
12B:19 ...
12B:20 Mentions: Maj. Long, (N) Allen, James
Armstrong, orphans of said Clarke,
12B:21 ...
12B:22 "Spring Neck". Said Clarke left Sarah
relict & 2 daughters (both infants under

age 21) Elisabeth & (N).

12B:23 Said Sarah died soon afterwards.

12B:24 Said Wilkisson petitions for guardianship of Elisabeth's sister.

12B:25 5 April. Robert Carvile (SM) procurator for John Salisbury (CE) vs. John Willis (CE) executor of William Salisbury (CE). Libel exhibited.

12B:26 Said John Salisbury (near age 20, p) is nephew of said William and represented by his guardian Thomas Whittle. Said William died c. 1 January 1680.

12B:27 Said John Salisbury was living in VA with his mother & elder brother George at the time of death of said William. Mentions: wife of said William who is also dec'd. Said John, his mother, & brother came to MD & since then said mother & brother both died.

12B:28-29 ...

12B:30 Richard Marsham & George Lingham (CV) executors of Charles Gosfright (CV) exhibited additional accounts. Thomas Tasker (CV) is empowered by George Gosfright (father of dec'd) to receive from the executors.

12B:31 15 April. Philip Davis (KE) who married Susanna Wedge widow & executrix of John Wedge (KE) exhibited accounts. Distribution: orphans.

Mich. Miller (KE) exhibited will of Francis Harmer (CE), constituting Ebenezar Blackiston executor. Capt. Joseph Hopkins to prove said will.

12B:32 Appraisers: Richard Powlen, Thomas Hawker. Said Hopkins to administer oath.

Additional inventory of William Key (KE) was exhibited, by appraisers Thomas Boone & William Bateman.

Mr. Henry Hosier (KE) exhibited oath of William Deane administrator of John Addison (KE), sworn 24 February 1681/2. Sureties: Thomas Warren, John Chandler. Also exhibited oath of John Bowles & Thomas Parker, appraisers sworn same day.

12B:33 Inventory was exhibited.

Mr. Edward English (CE) exhibited will of John Murwin (CE), written by a Frenchman. Barbara widow is also dec'd, leaving orphans. William Asbey who married one of the daughters was granted administration on behalf of his wife & rest of orphans. Said English to administer oath.

12B:34 Mr. Samuell Tovy (KE) exhibited will of John Neck (KE), proved by John Percifeild & Elisabeth Percifeild on 10 January 1681/2. Also exhibited was oath of William Bateman & Robert Parkes, appraisers sworn same day. Inventory was exhibited.

17 April. Clement Hill exhibited oath of William Rozewell & William Shercliffe, appraisers of Thomas Bassett, sworn 25 March 1682.

Mr. Thomas Gavan administrator of John Price (CH) exhibited his renunciation & petitioned for administration to be granted to Richard Gerforth (CH), as principle creditor.

12B:35 Said Gerforth was granted administration. Appraisers: John Godshall, John Wood. Mr. Henry Adams to administer oath.

18 April. Henry Henley (SM) exhibited affidavit of Richard Taylor & his wife Theresia & Mary Cheshire, as proof of bill from said Henley to Richard Cooper (SM, dec'd). Date: 27 March 1682.

12B:36 Said Cooper was sick at house of William Cheshire. Sworn on 6 April 1682 before William Diggs. Thomas Carvile testified

12B:37 that the dec'd said if he went for ENG or died in MD. Date: 3 April 1682. Signed: Thomas Carvile, Mary Carvile. Said Hinley also exhibited that John Fanning administrator of said Cooper was indebted to dec'd.

12B:38 19 April. Edward Sanders (CH) who married Sarah Braines widow &

administratrix of Henry Braynes
petitioned for new appraisers.
Appraisers that were appointed, Major
Wheeler & John LeMaire, are absent.

Thomas Cosden (inn holder, CV) exhibited
will of James Gardner (CV). Will ruled
"of none effect". Said Cosden was
granted administration on said estate in
name of Fredera Gardner.

12B:39 Appraisers: Thomas Sedgewick, John
Grover. Mr. George Brooke to
administer oath.

Thomas Davis (KI) for Mary Ashbery widow
of Francis Ashbery (KI) was granted
administration on his estate. Said
Francis accidentally drowned.
Appraisers: Isaack Winchester, Xopher
Goodhand. Capt. William Lawrence to
administer oath.

Col. Philemon Lloyd (TA) exhibited oath
of Alice Woolman administratrix of
Richard Woolman, sworn 29 December 1681.
Sureties: John Davis, Thomas Davis.

12B:40 Also exhibited was oath of Capt. Peter
Sayer & William Hemsley, appraisers
sworn same day.

Capt. Peter Sayer (TA) exhibited oath
of Mary Scot & James Scott executors of
James Scott, sworn 6 April 1682. Also
exhibited was oath of Thomas Collins &
John Kenniman, appraisers sworn same
day. Inventory was exhibited.

20 April. Maj. John Welsh (AA)
exhibited oath of John Hawkins
administrator of (N), sworn 12 February
1681. Sureties: Samuell Garland, Robert
Lockwood. Also exhibited oath of
Samuell Garland & Robert Lockwood,
appraisers sworn same day.

12B:41 Maj. John Welsh (AA) exhibited oath of
John Heathcoat administrator of
Nathaniell Heathcoat, sworn 20 February
1681/2. Sureties: John Lynan, Richard
Snowden, Edward Gawson. Also exhibited
was oath of Capt. Nicholas Gassoway &
John Gresham, appraisers sworn same day.

21 April. Sarah Michener widow of John Michener (CV) was granted administration on his estate. Said John is lately drowned. Said Sarah is sick & unable to travel to Office. Appraisers: James Nuthall, Robert Dove. Mr. Francis Hutchins to administer oath.

12B:42 Thomas Tasker attorney for George Gosfright (merchant, London) vs. Richard Marsham & George Lingham executors of Charles Gosfright (son to said George). Said Tasker given copy of accounts.
12B:43 Exceptions were exhibited.

22 April. Henry Coursey exhibited will of Henry Lambertson (TA), proved by James Ewstice & John Offley.

Capt. John Waterton (BA) exhibited oath of Henrietta Canon (BA) administratrix of Thomas Canon,
12B:44 sworn 14 March 1681/2. Sureties: Peter Ellis, Edward Reeves. Also exhibited was oath of Peter Ellis & George Hooper, appraisers sworn same day. Inventory was exhibited.

Capt. John Waterton (BA) exhibited oath of Henrietta Canon (BA) administratrix of Edward Swanson (BA), sworn 14 March 1681/2. Also exhibited was oath of Peter Ellis & George Hooper, appraisers sworn same day. Inventory was exhibited.

12B:45 Mr. Henry Hosier (KE) exhibited oath of Jane Cornelioson relict & executrix of William Ladds (KE), sworn 23 January 1681/2. Also exhibited was oath of John Bowles & Thomas Parker, appraisers sworn same day. Inventory was exhibited.

24 April. Mr. John Homewood for Providence Davidge (AA) widow of Robert Davidge (AA) exhibited his will, constituting said Providence executrix. Capt. Richard Hill to prove said will.

12B:46 Thomas Taylor petitioned for LoA on estate of Robert Williams, for NY.

Elisabeth Wyne (CH) executrix of Francis
Wyne (CH) petitioned for LoA to be sent
to ENG.

25 April. John Fanning exhibited bills
& books of Robert Cooper (taylor,
dec'd). Henry Henley was directed to
assist said Fanning. Inventory was
exhibited.

12B:47 Capt. Humphrey Warren (CH) exhibited
oath of John Fanning administrator of
Robert Cooper, sworn 30 March 1682.
Sureties: Richard Beamont, Thomas
Clipsham. Also exhibited was oath of
John Bayne & Richard Beamont, appraisers
sworn same day.

Maj. John Boaring (BA) exhibited oath
of Rowland Nance administrator of James
Wells (BA), sworn 20 February 1681/2.
Sureties: Christopher Gill, Henry Hall.
Also exhibited was oath of John Thomas &
Christopher Gill, appraisers sworn same
day. Inventory was exhibited.

12B:48 Mary Taylor (CV) exhibited will of
Robert Taylor (CV), constituting said
Mary & Samuell Taylor executors. Said
Samuell is since dec'd. Witnesses: John
Holloway, John Turner, Lidia Glover.
Said Glover is not present. Said will
was proved. Appraisers: James Beach,
Samuell Wynes. Capt. Richard Ladd to
administer oath.

Col. William Calvert (SM) exhibited
oath of
12B:49 Thomas Doxey & Edward Chester,
appraisers of William Asbeston, sworn 28
February 1681/2. Inventory was
exhibited.

Robert Carvile procurator for Sarah
Martin vs. John Pierce (SM) executor of
John Pierce, Sr. Answer was exhibited.
Said Sarah is one of daughters of
Abdiloe Martin (CV, dec'd), under
guardianship of Peter Mills.
12B:50 Mentions: another daughter. Said Sarah
claims 1/3rd part.
12B:51 Mentions: Emperor Smith, defendant's

12B:52 father was executor of said Abdiloe.
...

12B:53 29 April. Thomas Kingston (AA) for
Elisabeth Naylor relict of John Farr
(AA) was granted administration on his
estate. Appraisers: Thomas Kingston,
Robert Franklin. Maj. John Welsh to
administer oath.

Inventory of Thomas Bassett (Breton's
Bay, SM) was exhibited, by appraisers
William Rosewell & William Sherclife.

John Bird (AA) petitioned for Capt.
Richard Hill, Mr. John Homewood, and/or
Mr. Edward Dorsey to examine accounts
of

12B:54 Henry Lewis (AA) exhibited by said Bird,
to answer suit by William Hopkins on
behalf of orphans of said Lewis.

Robert Carvile (SM) procurator for
William Hopkins (AA) on behalf of
orphans of Dr. Henry Lewis (AA) vs.
John Bird (AA) who married widow &
executrix of said Lewis. Libel was
exhibited.

12B:55 John Fanning (CH) was granted
administration on estate of Robert
Cooper (taylor), who died at said
Fanning's house, a single man & has no
relations in these parts, as principle
creditor. Appraisers: MM John Pearte,
Richard Beaumont. Capt. Humphrey
Warren to administer oath.

Carvile for Hopkins vs. Bird. Libel
exhibited. Mentions: William Lewis &
Henry Lewis (children of Henry Lewis
(chirurgeon, AA), infants of very tender
years), said William Hopkins (p, AA) as
their grandfather & guardian, Elisabeth
wife of said Henry Lewis (dec'd),

12B:56 263 a. on south side of Petapscoe River
called "Lewis His Range", plantation
"Tannyard", 50 a. called "Cattle Neck",
bought of John Clarkson, 25 a. called
"Lewis' Addition".

12B:57 Indicates that said Bird is concealing
original inventory & created one in his

own handwriting, affixing appraisers signatures & seals, &

12B:58 said John Bird intends to depart the Province. Said John Bird & his wife Elisabeth are father-in-law & mother-in-law to orphans & mistreat them.

12B:59 Said Hopkins & his wife are grandparents.

12B:60-1 ...

12B:62 Robert Carvile (SM) procurator for William Hopkins (p, AA) vs. John Bird & his wife Elisabeth (AA) executrix of Henry Lewis (AA). Exceptions exhibited.

12B:63 Thomas Bruff (TA) administrator of James Barkehurst (TA) exhibited accounts.

1 May. Nicholas Painter (AA) was granted administration on estate of Robert Proctor (AA). Edward Morgan is cited as principle creditor. Appraisers: Andrew Norwood, Samuell Howard. Mr. Edward Dawsey to administer oath.

Robert Franklin (AA) exhibited will of Andrew Roberts (AA) constituting Jane Roberts executrix.

12B:64 Said Jane was granted administration. Capt. Thomas Francis to prove said will. Appraisers: Ferdinando Battey, John Gray.

Col. Jowles (CV) exhibited the will of Elisabeth Lashely (CV), constituting Mary Trueman executrix. Said Mary was granted administration. Mr. Thomas Brooke to prove said will. Appraisers: James Crutch, James Prart.

Walter Kerby (KI) exhibited accounts on estate of Charles Bankes, proved before Maj. Joseph Wickes.

12B:65 Mr. James Dasheil (SO) exhibited bond of Thomas Clarke administrator of Edward Davies (SO). Sureties: Stephen Cannon, John Bowne. Also exhibited was inventory of Edward Davyes, by appraisers Robert Collier & Andrew

Court Session: 1682

Jones.

Maj. James Ringold (KE) exhibited oath
of Robert Parke administrator of John
Wyborow (KE). Surety: Michaell Miller.
Also exhibited was oath of Bennett
Staires & Robert Griffin, appraisers.
Date: 4 March 1681/2.

12B:66   2 May. Maj. John Welsh (AA) exhibited
will of John Shrigley (AA), proved by
William Powell, John Swalwell, & Thomas
Meridale. Also exhibited was oath of
Robert Franklin & Robert Carr,
appraisers sworn 13 April 1682.

Maj. John Welsh exhibited oath of
Anthony Holland (AA) administrator of
Christopher Gardener (AA). Sureties:
Walter Car, Bryan Capell. Also
exhibited was oath of Robert Franklin &
Samuell Garland, appraisers sworn 20
March 1681/2.

12B:67   Also exhibited was inventory.

Col. Thomas Tailor (AA) exhibited will
of Maj. Samuell Lane (AA), proved by
John Hall, Thomas Merridale, & Arthur
Browne. Also exhibited was oath of
Capt. Thomas Francis & Dr. Fisher,
appraisers sworn 8 March 1681.

Col. Thomas Taylor (AA) exhibited oath
of John Larkin administrator of Edward
Ladd, sworn 4 February 1681. Surety:
Nicholas Nicholson.

12B:68   Cites that Nicholas Nicholson & George
Holland were first appointed as
appraisers. Also exhibited was oath of
Ferdinando Battey & Robert Watts,
appraisers sworn 6 February 1681. Also
exhibited was inventory.

Henry Stockett (AA) one of
administrators of Nathaniell Stiles (DE)
exhibited second additional accounts.

3 May. Capt. William Lawrence (KE)
exhibited oath of Mary Ashbery
administratrix of Francis Ashbery.
Surety: Thomas Davis. Also exhibited
was oath of Isaac Winchester &

Page 197

Christopher Goodhand, appraisers sworn
26 April 1682.

12B:69 Also exhibited was inventory.

5 May. Mathew Ereckson (KE)
administrator of John Ereckson (KE)
exhibited accounts, proved before Capt.
William Lawrence (KE) on 24 February
1681/2.

6 May. Mr. Thomas Burford for Cleborne
Lomax (CH) was granted administration on
estate of Mr. John Paris (CH), who died
having no relations in this country, as
principle creditor.

12B:70 Appraisers: John Courte, Sr., Merwell
Hulse. Mr. Henry Adams to administer
oath.

Miles Gibson (BA) exhibited additional
accounts on estate of Abraham & Sarah
Clarke.

8 May. Mr. George Parker (CV)
exhibited additional accounts on estate
of John Dott (CV), proved before Francis
Collier by Richard Eduards & Hannah
Eduards relict & executrix of said Dott.

Exhibited was inventory of Henry Simons
(Clifts, CV), by appraisers John
Cobradth & John Russell.

12B:71 William Wilkinson (p, BA) vs. Miles
Gibson (g, BA) administrator of Abraham
& Sarah Clarke. Answer exhibited.
Mentions: said Abraham left behind wife
Sarah & 2 daughters: Elisabeth (age 9),
Mary (age 3). Said Sarah was granted
administration. Before said Sarah and
said Gibson could marry, said Sarah fell
sick & committed the care of her 2
children to said Gibson.

12B:72 ...

12B:73 Mentions: debt due (N) Allen, James
Armstrong (who was killed by Indians
before death of said Sarah & left no
estate). Signed: Thomas Burford.

9 May. Miles Gibson (BA) administrator
of Abraham & Sarah Clarke

12B:74 (BA) exhibited his answer to William

Wilkinson & his wife Elisabeth (daughter of said Abraham & Sarah). Said William to have copies.

James Fugeet (BA) exhibited will of Anthony Watson (BA), constituting said Fugeet executor. Said Fugeet was granted administration. Appraisers: Robert Jones, Lawrence Tailor. Capt. Henry Johnson to administer oath.

12B:75 Thomas Vaughan (TA) was granted administration on estate of John Rawlings (TA). Appraisers: Richard Peacocke, Gurney Crow. William Combes to administer oath.

10 May. Mr. George Parker for Col. William Taylor petitioned for accounts of Margarett Lane executrix of Samuell Lane (AA) to be proved.

Eduard Swetnam (KE) was granted administration on estate of Eduard Rogers (KE). Appraisers: Samuell Tove, Nathaniell Eduard. James Ringold to administer oath.

12B:76 11 May. James Wheeler (CH) was granted administration on estate of Clement Theobalds (CH), who was killed by a horse, on behalf of said Clement's brother John Theobalds (age 16). Appraisers: Philip Hoskins, John Godson. Col. William Chandler to administer oath.

William Jones (SO) exhibited will of George Johnson (SO), proved by John Heath & Edmond Beauchamp. The other witness Thomas Price would not swear for opinion sake.

12 May. John Salisbury vs. John Willis (CE) executor of William Salisbury (CE). Answer exhibited.
12B:77 Mentions: Sarah widow of said William, defendant & Edward Beck (CE) executors of said William, said Beck refused administration.
12B:78 Signed: Thomas Burford procurator for John Willis.

Court Session: 1682

LoA issue to James Wheeler (CH) on
estate of Clement Theobalds (CH) were
recalled.

13 May. Exhibited was inventory of
William Evens (Clifts, CV), by
appraisers Thomas Clagget
12B:79 & Robert Dixon.

Elisabeth Dikinson widow of Edward
Dikinson (SO) was granted administration
on his estate. Appraisers: Walter
Powell, Richard Lewis. Col. William
Stevens to administer oath.

William Burden & Israell Skelton
executors of Thomas Cooke (BA) were
granted administration on his estate.
Capt. John Waterton (BA) to administer
oath.

12B:80 Miles Gibson (g, BA) administrator of
Eduard Jackson was granted discharge.

James Murphey (TA) exhibited will of
Robert Knap (TA), proved by Michaell
Turbut & John Swayn.

15 May. Hanse Rosomonson (KE) exhibited
will of Sarah Harrison (KE),
constituting her son Andrew Toulson (age
16) executor. Said Rosomonson was
granted administration, on behalf of
said Toulson.
12B:81 Capt. William Lawrence to prove said
will. Appraisers: John Dadd, William
Temple.

16 May. Robert Carvile (SM) exhibited
examination of accounts of Richard
Royston administrator of William Crosse
(TA), made on 17 June 1681. William
Dikeson executor of his father Walter
Dikeson sued said Royston in TA Court.
Said Carvile can find so such account.

12B:82 Elisabeth Harris relict & executrix of
Samuell Harris (SM) exhibited his will.
Said will is void, for want of proper
number of witnesses. Said Elisabeth was
granted administration. Appraisers:
Thomas Carvile, John Hilton. Capt.

Court Session: 1682

William Diggs to administer oath.

John Salisbury vs. John Willis.
Ruling: will of William Salisbury is
condemned. Defendant to prove accounts
&

12B:83   CE Court to examine said accounts with
regard to exceptions by said John
Salisbury. Appraisers: William O'Dary,
Ezekiel Jackson. Capt. Joseph Hopkins
to administer oath.

12B:84   ...
12B:85   <page torn>
12B:86   <page torn>
12B:87-88 ...
12B:89   Defendant was attorney for said William
Salisbury during his absence in ENG.

12B:90   ...
12B:91   Mentions: payment to Joseph Hopkins.

12B:92   22 May. Jeremiah Hooke (SO) exhibited
inventory of George Sutton (SO), by
appraisers Andrew Jones & Daniell Hast.

30 May. John O'Cane & John LeMaire (CH)
12B:93   vs. Adam Boucher (CH) guardian of
Thomas Love son & heir of William Love
(CH, dec'd). Libel exhibited.
12B:94   Plaintiffs were sureties to defendant.
12B:95   Said Boucher summoned to prove accounts.

Eduard Maddox who married Marjory relict
& executrix of Mathew Stone (CH)
exhibited accounts. Mentions: payment
to Col. Rozer. John Stone (g, CH) to
administer oath.

12B:96   John Wilkinson (CH) exhibited will of
Garrat Smott (CH). Said will is
declared void, for want of proper number
of witnesses. Ann Wilkinson (relict,
who has remarried) was granted
administration. Appraisers: John
Godson, Nicholas Bead. Col. William
Chandler to administer oath.

1 June. Exhibited was inventory of Col.
Benjamin Rozer (Portobacco, CH), by
appraisers Henry Adams & Thomas Hussey.

Col. William Chandler exhibited oath of
Maj. John Wheeler & John Lemaire (CH),

appraisers of Henry Brayne (CH). Also exhibited was oath of John Brayne, with sureties: John O'Cane, John Lemaire.

12B:97 Robert Henley (CH) exhibited oath of Richard Beaumont administrator of James Beaumont (CH). Also exhibited was oath of Capt. Humphrey Warren & Mr. Thomas Clipsham, appraisers.

Mr. Richard Hill (AA) exhibited will of Robert Davidge (AA), proved by Arthur Hide. Providence Davidge relict & executrix was granted administration. Appraisers: Richard Gwin, Theophilus Hackett. Said Hill to administer oath.

9 June. Elisabeth Calvert widow of Hon. William Calvert (Principle Secretary of Province) was granted administration on his estate.

12B:98 Sureties: John Stone (g, CH), Robert Doyne (g, CH). Appraisers: John Pattison (Crosse Mannor), Thomas Pinke (SM).

10 June. Capt. Ninian Beall (CV) exhibited will of William Smith, proved by Henry Jowles, Eduard Brooke, & Robert Norman. Also exhibited was inventory, by appraisers said Beall & James Moore.

Mr. Thomas Brooke exhibited oath of Mary Trueman executrix of

12B:99 Elisabeth Lashely, sworn 18 May 1682. Also exhibited was oath of James Keetch & James Pert, appraisers sworn same day. Said will was proved by John Burras, Thomas Trottman, & Thomas Trueman.

Lawrence Rowland (CV) who married Grace relict of James Williams (CV) was granted administration on his estate, for his wife. Appraisers: Capt. Ninian Beall, James Moore. Francis Collier to administer oath.

12B:100 12 June. William Osborne (BA) exhibited that Thomas Canon (BA, dec'd) committed an unworthy action against Col. Johnson (VA). Said Osborne was security for said Cannon. Henrietta Canon was

granted administration on estate of said
Canon. Caveat granted to said Osborne.

13 June. James Mills (BA) exhibited the
nuncupative will of John Dunston (alias
Nicholas Haskell, BA). Col. George
Wells (BA) to prove said will. James
Philips was granted administration.
12B:101 Appraisers: William Osborne, William
Crowshe. Said Wells to administer oath.

14 June. Archibald Wahop (CH) one of
the creditors of William Love (CH,
dec'd) exhibited that 12 months have
passed since Adam Boucher (CH) was
granted administration on estate of said
Love. As soon as he was granted
administration, said Boucher fled the
Province. Said Wahop is unpaid & the
orphans' estate is unsecured. Said
Wahop was granted administration de
bonis non.
12B:102 Appraisers: John Butcher, James Wheeler.
Col. William (N) to administer oath.

17 June. Exhibited was inventory of
Samuell Harris (SM), by appraisers
Thomas Carvil & John Hilton.

Exhibited was will of Andrew Roberts
(AA), proved before Col. Thomas Francis
by Catherine Larkins, Mary Farmar, &
Woolfan Hunt. Col. Thomas Francis
exhibited the oath of Ferdinando Battey
& John Gray, appraisers sworn 22 May
1682.

12B:103 20 June. Exhibited was inventory of
John Taylor (South River, AA), by
appraisers Edmund Beetenson & William
Mitchell.

Henry Stockett (AA) exhibited that Mr.
James Stavely (CE) was joint
administrator (with said Stockett) on
estates of (N) Styles & (N) Salmon &
petitioned
12B:104 to be summoned when any administration
be granted on estate of said Stavely.

Exhibited was inventory of Andrew
Roberts (AA).

Exhibited was inventory of Samuell Taylor (CV).

12B:105 Exhibited was inventory of James Beaumunt (CH).

21 June. Exhibited was will of John Taylor (AA), proved before William Burges (AA).

James Pattison (SM) & Thomas Spincke (SM) appraisers of estate of William Calvert, Esq. (Principle Secretary) were sworn.

12B:106 Exhibited was inventory of John Jourdain (AA), by appraisers Edmund Beetenson & John Gray. Said appraisers were sworn 29 November 1681 by Henry Ridgely.

ultimate June. William Theobalds (CH) petitioned that Penelope Morrice be granted administration on estate of Clement Theobalds (who was killed by a horse stroke). Appraisers: George Godshall, Philip Hopkins. Col. William Chandler to administer oath.

12B:107 John Martin (CH) exhibited his accounts on estate of Richard Hall.

Letter from Gerard Slye administrator of Richard Chilman to Judge of Court. Date: 12 March 1681/2 London.

12B:108 Accounts were dated 20 April 1680 & discharge was granted.

12B:109 Further accounts were dated 29 April 1681. Ruling: said further accounts disallowed.

12B:110 Said Slye indicated that he had not recovered from sickness.

Exhibited was inventory of John Thompson (SM), by appraisers John Doxey & Charles Prien.

12B:111 5 July. Frances Stavely (CE) widow of James Stavely (CE) & her son John Stavely were granted administration on his estate. Mr. Hopkins to administer oath & summon Henry Stockett.

12B:112 George Robotham exhibited will of John
Marks (TA), proved by William Kerwin &
John Baynard on 12 April 1682 & William
Freeland on 17 April. Mary Lane relict
was sworn 13 April. Also exhibited was
oath of Mr. George Robins & John
Stavely, appraisers sworn 25 April 1682.
12B:113 Also exhibited was inventory.

Exhibited was bond of Henry Newton (TA)
administrator of John Newton (TA).
Sureties: John Stavely, Thomas
Pendergrass. Also exhibited was
inventory, by appraisers John Stavely &
Richard White.

Exhibited was inventory of William Eagle
(TA), by appraisers John Stavely
12B:114 & William Kathrope.

Mr. John Rousby (TA) for Mr. Richard
Carter (now in ENG) petitioned that LoA
granted to Mr. Richard Woolman
administrator of Robert Hilton (TA),
dated 3 December 1679, be renewed for
said Carter. Said Woolman, Carter's
attorney, is dec'd. Peter Denny (TA)
now has PoA from said Carter, but cannot
recover any debt from estate of said
Hilton. Said Denny was granted
administration on estate of said Hilton.

12B:115 Richard Holland (TA) was granted
administration on estate of William
Kelley (TA, killed by a fall from a
horse). Appraisers: William Combes (g),
Samuell Abbot. Mr. Eduard Man to
administer oath.

John Rousby (g, TA) exhibited that
Samuell Abbot (TA) administrator of (N)
Padeley has several suits pending
against him in County Court.
Continuance was granted.

12B:116 11 July. Samuell Withers (AA) son &
heir of Samuell Withers (AA) exhibited
that he is age 20 & was granted
administration on said estate.
Administrators Col. William Burges &
Richard Hill were summoned to render
accounts & deliver the estate.

Court Session: 1682

12B:117 13 July. Exhibited was will of William Granger (KE). Ruling: said will was not allowed since no executor was named nor proof by 3 witnesses. Grace Granger widow was granted administration on said estate. Appraisers: Walter Kerby, Anthony Workman. Philip Connor to administer oath. Mentions: son & heir at law; said Grace cannot travel to the Office.

Eduard Swetnam (g, KE) petitioned for
12B:118 new appraisers: Cornelius Comegys, William Laurence. Mentions former appraisers: Samuell Tove (infirm), Nathaniell Evens (illiterate).

James Cullens (g, SM) exhibited inventory of Col. William Calvert (Principle Secretary), by appraisers Thomas Spinke & James Pattison.

14 July. Col. William Chandler (CH) exhibited
12B:119 oath of Peneloppy Morrice, sworn 6 July 1682. He also exhibited oath of John Godshall & Philip Hopkins, appraisers sworn same day. He also exhibited bond of Penelopy Morrice. Sureties: Richard Morrice, William Theobalds.

Col. William Chandler exhibited oath of Arch. Waahup, sworn 20 June 1682. He also exhibited oath of James Wheeler & John Boutcher, appraisers sworn same day.
12B:120 He also exhibited bond of said Waahop administrator of William Love (CH). Sureties: John O'Cane, John Lemaire.

Col. William Chandler exhibited oath of James Wheeler administrator of Clement Theobalds (CH), sworn 2 days after administration was granted.

Samuell Bourne (g, CV) exhibited oath of Henry Symons, Jr. administrator of Henry Symons, Sr., sworn 2 December 1681. Also exhibited was oath of John Cobreath & John Russell, appraisers.
12B:121 Also exhibited was bond of said Symons Jr. Surety: Thomas Crowder.

Exhibited was will of Robert Taylor
(Patuxent River, CV), proved before
Capt. Richard Ladd by Lydia Glover &
formerly by John Holloway & John Turner.
Also exhibited was oath of James Beach &
Samuell Vynes, appraisers sworn 27 May
1682.

15 July. James Collyer & William Yorke
(BA) exhibited will of John Waterton
(BA), to be proved by Miles Gibson (g),
constituting Thomas Reede &
12B:122 Thomas Ridge his 2 nephews executors.
Said Reede & Ridge are presently in ENG.
Said Collyer & Yorke overseers were
granted administration, on behalf of
said executors. Appraisers: James
Thompson, John Tylliards. Said Gibson
to administer oath.

17 July. Eduard Dorsey (g, AA)
exhibited oath of Robert Proctor
administrator of Eduard Morgan. Surety:
Robert Francklin.
12B:123 Also exhibited was inventory, by
appraisers Andrew Norwood & Samuell
Howard.

Exhibited was will of Sarah Harrison
(KI), proved by Patrick Sexton, William
Heather, & Sarah Full. The other 2
witnesses are dec'd. William Laurence
(g, KE) exhibited bond of Hanse
Rosomonson administrator of said
Harrison. Sureties: John Dobbs, William
Temple. Also exhibited was inventory,
12B:124 by appraisers John Dobbs & William
Temple. Said Laurence exhibited bond of
said Rosomonson, sworn 6 July 1682.

18 July. Henrietta Canon (BA) relict &
administratrix of Thomas Canon (BA)
exhibited accounts. Said Henrietta
12B:125 is also administratrix of Eduard Swanson
her 1st husband. Since she cannot
travel to the Office, Miles Gibson (g)
to examine both & take oath.

Hannah Gray (BA) was granted
administration on estate of John Gray
(BA). Miles Gibson (G) to administer
oath.

Exhibited was inventory of Thomas Cooke (BA), by appraisers Mich. Judd & Robert Love.

12B:126 Raymond Staplefort (g, DO) creditor vs. Timothy McNemara & his wife Sarah relict & administratrix of Lewis Griffith. Exceptions cited.

12B:127 Mentions: Henry Hooper assignee of John Offley,

12B:128 ...

12B:129 Said Macknemarra. Signed: Robert Carvile. Ruling: sufficient assets exist to pay the plaintiff.

17 July. Mary Evans (Poplar Hill Hundred) relict of Anthony Lamb (Poplar Hill Hundred) exhibited

12B:130 her renunciation. Witnesses: E. Turin, Jacob Looton.

27 July. Robert Carvile (SM) vs. Gerard Slye (g) administrator of Richard Chilman. Exceptions cited.

12B:131 Robert Carvile filed for self & as attorney for William Cole & his wife Margaret executrix of Michaell Rochfort, Philip Swerett (merchant), Marmaduck Simms, & Miles Gray creditors. Mentions: Robert Carvile, William Cole & his wife, Philip Swerett, Marmaduke Sems, Miles Gray,

12B:132 John Roberts,

12B:133 Dr. Mollins

12B:134 (also Dr. Molines), (N) Martindale,

12B:135 Bridgett Jones, Nathaniell Fisher, (N) Cheseldyn, (N) Ellis,

12B:136 (N) Lomax,

12B:137 John Manely (court clerk, SM),

12B:138 ...

12B:139 Mr. Lomax, (N) Vansweringen, (N) Mudd, (N) Ratclife, (N) Wynne, (N) Fox, (N) & Carvile (N) Lemaire,

12B:140 Mr. Rousby,

12B:141 (N) Miller,

12B:142 (N) Bonner, (N) Ridgely,

12B:143 (N) Oliver, (N) Mason. Ruling: for plaintiff.

12B:144 Mentions: (N) Rousby, (N) Miller, (N) Anderson, (N) Sems, (N) Exon, (N) Mills, (N) Fanning, (N) Ward, (N) Ramsey, (N) Pile, (N) Rozer, (N) Batson, (N) Feild,

(N) Barecroft, (N) Barson, (N) Ellis,
(N) Jones, (N) Anderson, (N) Doxey,
Thomas Mudd,

12B:145 Mich. Miller, orphans, Morgan Jones,
William Novell (CE), Capt. Wyndall, Mrs.
Cordea, Joseph Edloe, John Rawlings
(DO),

12B:146 James Crew (carpenter), John Lewis,
Francis Lunton, Thomas Suell (DO),
Robert Ellis for Jasper Howley, Thomas
Patison (DO), Edward Jones (SO), Salomon
Jones (SM), Thomas Spinke attorney for
Stephen Davis, Thomas Pritchard (SM),
Rich. Higinbothom (SO),

12B:147 Henry Lawrence who married relict of
Henry Hyde, William Dare (CV), Jasper
Howley, Mr. Richard Smith (CV) attorney
for James Serscife, Edward Husbands, Mr.
Tenhill (CV), William Crosse (TA),
Richard Edmonds, (CE), John Browning
(CE), John Hinson (KE), Henry Ward (CE),
Samuell Debanck (AA), Miles Gibson (BA),

12B:148 Henry Parker (TA), John King (CH), John
Ereckson (KE), Walter Lane (SO), John
Hussey Thomas (CH), Mary Paper (CH),
Thomas Smithson (TA), Allen Oare (SM),
John Price (TA), Thomas Poole (SO), Dr.
John Brooke (DO), Mr. Cheseldyn for John
Jones (dec'd), Samuell Hatton (TA),
Eduard Newton (DO), Joseph Edloe (SM),
Joseph O'Cane,

12B:149 Eduard Penn (formerly at Henry Exon, now
CE), William Gosvell (AA), George
Grumwell (BA), John Browning (CE), John
Hollins (TA), Thomas Browne, Col.
Colebourne (SO), John Edmunson (TA),
Anthony Andrewes (SM), Rich. Swetnam (TA
& KE), William Guyther for his brother
Nich. Guyther (dec'd), Thomas Jones
(sloopman, SO),

12B:150 Henry Potter (SM & now SO), John
Blomfeild (SM), Thomas Griffin (SO),
George Thompson (SM), John Bell (TA),
Edmund Bennett (SM), William Rozewell
(SM), Maj. Thomas Long (BA), Besse
Potter for Thomas Potter (SM, now
dec'd), Rich. Keen (CV), Eduard Man
(TA), Randall Revell (SO), Thomas Tasker
(CV), Stephen Morty (SM), Robert
Pudoughton (SM & now BA), William Thomas
(SM),

12B:151 Henry Howard (AA), James Collam (SM),

John Hamlton (CH), John Wells (KE),
Thomas Wauhab (SM), Robert Thompson
(CH), Thomas Window (SM), William Harper
(SM), William Hemsley (TA), Thomas Gant
(CV), James Notwell (CV), Roger Brooke
(CV), William Hill (DO), Eduard Dorsey
(AA), Thomas Greenfeild (CV), John Evans
Taylor (SM), John Hamilton (CH), George
Parker (CV), Eduard English (CE),
Charles Priest (SM),

12B:152 George Carley (TA), Capt. Henry Darnall
(CV), George Yates (AA), Henry Mitchell
(CV), Capt. Sawyer (TA), Joseph Dorsey
(AA), William Stephens (SO), Clement
Hill (SM), Eduard Swetnam (KE), Richard
Fenwick (CV), Nich. Hatch (Accomack, had
estate in (N) Vansweringen's hands),
Henry Fox (SM, now TA), Nathaniell
Fisher (CV), John Wade (SM),

12B:153 Eduard Morgan (SM), Raphaell Hayward
(CV), Hugh Manning (SM), (N), Boareman,

12B:154 (N) Lomax, (N) Grunwin,

12B:155 Thomas Turpin. Signed: Ro. Carvile.

12B:156 28 July. Jacob Looton (SM) was granted
administration on estate of George Fenck
(St. George's Hundred), as principle
creditor. Appraisers: John Evans,
Philip Levin. William Hatton (g, St.
George's Hundred) to administer oath.

29 July. Eduard Fishwick for his wife
Margarett relict of Thomas Basset
exhibited accounts. Continuance was
granted.

12B:157 31 July. Exhibited was inventory of
John Price (CH), by appraisers John
Godshall & John Wood.

1 August. Thomas Wharton (CH) exhibited
inventory of Sylvanus Gilpin (CH), by
appraisers John Cable & John Wheeler.
Also exhibited were accounts. Estate is
overpaid. Discharge was granted.

12B:158 2 August. James Pattison (Crosse
Mannor, SM) administrator of his wife
Margarett & administrator of Walter Hall
was granted continuance.

Court Session: 1682

3 August. Anthony Underwood for Martha
Ridgely (SM) widow of Robert Ridgely
administrator of Nich. Badcock was
granted continuance.

4 August. Col. William Chandler (CH)
administrator of Roger Fowke (CH)
12B:159 exhibited accounts.

Thomas Hussy (CH) administrator of
Eduard Price (CH) was granted
continuance. Said Hussy is unable to
travel by reason of an imposthume of his
knee.

10 August. Richard Edelen (SM)
exhibited that he & Edmund Dennis were
instructed to take inventory of Samuell
Raspin (CH).
12B:160 Petition for payment. Ruling:
administrator is to pay.

Robert Carvile attorney for Lewis
Cloyther (TA) who married Susan sole
daughter & heir of Robert Knap (TA)
exhibited that said Knap, departing for
ENG, deeded in June 1681 said Lewis all
of his 5 servants. Elisabeth Knapp
(widow)
12B:161 has retained same. Said Elisabeth has
married James Ward & they are embezzling
the estate. Mentions: one of the
witnesses to the will is a legatee.
Said Susan is daughter of said Knap by a
former wife.
12B:162 Ruling: widow Knapp summoned.

11 August. Thomas Jessup (CV)
administrator of Robert Rider (CV)
exhibited accounts. Estate is overpaid.
Discharge was granted.

16 August. James Fugeett (BA) executor
of Anthony Watson (BA) petitioned that
some chattel remains in the hands of
Col. Wells who refuses to deliver same.
12B:163 Continuance was granted.

18 August. Philip Conner (KE) exhibited
oath of Walter Kerby & Anthony Workman
appraisers of estate of William Granger
(KE), sworn 4 August last. Also

Page 211

exhibited was bond of Christopher
Granger administrator. Surety: Thomas
Cooper.

12B:164 Bryan Daley (SM) who married Rebecca
relict & administratrix of Philip Land
(SM) was granted continuance.

Owen Guyther (SM) administrator of Mary
Jones was granted continuance.

Mordecai Hunton (CV) administrator of
Thomas Crooke (CV) exhibited accounts &
12B:165 a general release from Daniell Pensare
(mariner, London) attorney for Thomas
Crooke (citizen, plasterer, London)
father & executor of dec'd. PoA proved
before Thomas Taylor, Esq. (AA).
12B:166 ...
12B:167 Date: 6 March 1682. Witnesses: Thomas
Taylor, Charles Boteler.

12B:168 John Grover (CV) who married relict of
John Wynnall (CV) exhibited accounts.
Distribution: orphans.

19 August. William Sharpe (TA)
exhibited renunciation of William Dixon
& his wife Elisabeth (TA)
12B:169 on estate of "our brother" John Geery
(CV), to "our brother" William Sharpe
(TA).
12B:170 Date: 19 January 1681. Witnesses: Hugh
Hutchins, John Phelen. Also the
renunciation of Stephen Geery (DO)
kinsman of John Geery (CV), to William
Sharpe (TA)
12B:171 brother of said John Geery. Mentions:
renunciation of William Dixon & his wife
Elisabeth sister & heir of said John
Geery. Date: 5 August 1682. Witnesses:
Thomas Bondell, Griff. Jones.

Miles Gibson (g, BA) exhibited oath of
12B:172 William Osborne & Peter Ellis,
appraisers of Thomas Russell sworn 28
March 1682. Also exhibited was oath of
Elisabeth Russell administratrix sworn
15 May 1682. Sureties: William Crashaw,
William Osborne. Also exhibited was
inventory.

Court Session: 1682

21 August. Richard Attwood (SM)
executor of William Asbeston (SM)
12B:173 exhibited accounts.

22 August. Simon Wilmer (TA) exhibited
that Thomas Barnes made a will.
Mentions: LoA granted to Frances Barnes
& Mathew Ereckson.
12B:174 Col. Henry Coursey to summon
administrators to produce the real will.

24 August. Jane Prather (CV) widow &
administratrix of Jonathon Prather (CV)
exhibited inventory.

12B:175 Elisabeth Ward (TA) relict & executrix
of Robert Knapp (TA) exhibited validity
of said Knapp's will.

12B:176 Exhibited was inventory of Frances Wynn
(CH), by appraisers Thomas Clipsham (g)
& John Fanning (g).

25 August. (N) Rouse (CV) exhibited
accounts of estate of Griffith George
(CV).

Edward Maddox (CH) who married Marjery
relict & administratrix of Mathew Stone
(CH) exhibited accounts, proved before
John Stone.

12B:177 28 August. Elisabeth Ward (TA) relict
of Robert Knapp (TA) waived said will &
was granted administration on his
estate. Appraisers: James Murphy, (N).
Col. Vincent Low (TA) to administer
oath.

James Downes (TA) exhibited accounts of
estate of Elisabeth Winckles (TA).

12B:178 Philip Hopkins exhibited accounts of
estate of Nehemia Covington (TA).

William Clayton (TA) who married
Margarett relict & administratrix of
John Greene (TA) exhibited accounts.

Anthony Underwood (g, SM) exhibited
inventory of estate of Robert Ridgely
(SM), on his plantation on Wicocomoco

Page 213

River (SO).

12B:179 Also exhibited was oath of Andrew Jones & Daniell Hast, appraisers for SO.

29 August. Robert Carvile procurator for William Hopkins (AA) petitioned for summons to John Bird & his wife Elisabeth to receive judgement on the auditor's report regarding the suit of the orphans of Henry Lewis & said Bird & his wife.

Ann Crawford (CV) executrix of John Clarke (CV)
12B:180 responded to summons. Ruling: dismissal.

30 August. Anthony Underwood (g, SM) exhibited that Sarah Ballard (SO) administratrix of Charles Ballard (SO) had LoA on 28 April 1681, & petitioned for new LoA.
12B:181 Appraisers: David Browne, Roger Woolford. Capt. Henry Smith to administer oath.

Col. Lloyd (TA) for Alice Woolman (TA) administratrix of Richard Woolman (TA) was granted continuance.

Martha Wells (KE) executrix of John Wells (KE)
12B:182 was granted continuance.

Richard Hill (AA) exhibited oath of Providence Davidge executrix of Robert Davidge (AA), sworn 3 July 1682. Also exhibited was oath of Richard Gwin & Theophilus Hackett, appraisers sworn same day.

12B:183 4 September. Maj. Thomas Taylor (DO) exhibited inventory of John Quigley (DO), by appraisers Eduard Pindar & William Smithson. "Said inventory is confused and not in a form to be well understood."

Sarah Yates (TA) administratrix of Eduard Roper (TA) exhibited his will, which is not sufficiently proved. Said Yates was granted administration.

Appraisers: John Stanely, Thomas Long.
Mr. Eduard Mann to administer oath.

12B:184 John Nunn who married Jane Richardson
(TA) administratrix of Richard
Richardson (TA) exhibited accounts.
Said Jane is unable to travel to Office.
Mr. Eduard Mann to examine & take oath.

7 September. George Parker (CV) & John
Hans administrators of John Staines (CV)
exhibited accounts.

12B:185 George Parker (CV) petitioned for Capt.
Samuel Bourne to examine the following &
administer oath:
• Alice Durham executrix of Nicholas
Furnes.
• William Harris executor of John
Boreman.
• Richard Pelley who married Sarah
administratrix of Henry Harrison.
• Henry Simons administrator of Henry
Simons.

George Parker petitioned for Col.
Thomas Taylor (AA) to examine accounts
of Hester Nicholson administratrix of
William Gough (AA).

8 September. Cornelius Comagys (KE) was
summoned to render accounts on estate of
Jane Mathewes. The clerk searched
12B:186 for an inventory, by appraisers Hugh
Johnson & Thomas Crompe. Since none was
found, said Comagys could not exhibit
accounts.

Thomas Bruffe (TA) administrator of
James Barkhurst was granted discharge.

John Johnson (TA) executor of Thomas
Jones (TA) exhibited second accounts.

Eduard James (KE) exhibited the
nuncupative will of Humphrey Limbrey
(KE),
12B:187 bequeathing all to said James. Philip
Conners (KE) to prove said will.

Providence Davidge (AA) executrix of
Robert Davidge (AA) was granted

Court Session: 1682

continuance.

12B:188 George Parker (CV) exhibited list of debts of John Staines (CV).

Exhibited was bond of Grace Rowland (CV) administratrix of James Williams. Sureties: Francis Swinfer, James Nuthall. Also exhibited was inventory, by appraisers Ninian Beall & James Moore.

12B:189 Francis Jenkins (SO) exhibited will of David Lyndsey (SO), proved. Also exhibited was bond of Walter Taylor who married Sarah relict & executrix. Sureties: Daniell Quillaine, John Taylor. Also exhibited was oath of Sarah Taylor executrix. Also exhibited was oath of Josias Seward & Walter Powell, appraisers.
12B:190 Also exhibited was inventory.

9 September. Exhibited was inventory of William Grange (KE), by appraisers Anthony Workeman & Walter Kerby.

Joseph Sudler (KE) who married Ciccily administratrix of Thomas Bright (KE) exhibited accounts.

William House, Jr. (CV) who married Ursula executrix of
12B:191 Amos Bagby (CV) exhibited accounts.

11 September. Henry Ward (CE) exhibited that Joseph Spernon & William Synklers administrators of William Porter (CE) cannot find security. Date: 16 July 1682. CE County to provide blank bond.

12B:192 Eduard Inglish (CE) exhibited that William Asbey administrator of John Murvin (CE) is a very unfit man & cannot find security. CE County to provide blank bond.

Jacob Looton (SM) administrator of George Fenwick (SM) exhibited inventory.

12B:193 12 September. Maj. Thomas Taylor (DO) exhibited inventory of John Quigley

(DO), by appraisers Eduard Pindar & William Smithson.

Agnes Driver (SM) widow & administratrix of David Driver (SM) exhibited accounts.

12B:194 Eduard Swetnam administrator of Eduard Rogers (KE) exhibited inventory, by appraisers Cornelius Comegys & William Laurence.

14 September. Sarah Simpers (CV) administratrix of Henry Barnes (CV) petitioned for new LoA.

12B:195 James Paschall (AA) administrator of Maudline Paschall (AA) exhibited accounts.

Anthony Holland (AA) administrator of Christopher Gardner (AA) exhibited accounts.
12B:196 County Court to secure residue for orphans.

Ruth Martindale (SM) relict & administrator of Thomas Vaughan (SM) exhibited accounts.

19 September. Elisabeth Croshow (BA) relict & administratrix of Thomas Russell (BA) exhibited accounts.

12B:197 20 September. Richard Jaxson, Jr. (TA, elder son & heir apparent of Richard Jaxson (TA)) exhibited his renunciation on his father's estate, recommending Richard Mirax & Thomas Thompson.
12B:198 Date: 8 September 1682. Witness: Ja. Coursey. Richard Mirax (TA) & Thomas Thompson (TA) exhibited will of Richard Jaxson (TA), constituting them as executors. Said Mirax & Thompson were granted administration. Appraisers: Richard Jones, John Offley. Col. Philemon Lloyd to administer oath.

12B:199 Mich. Miller (KE) petitioned for him to examine accounts & administer oath to Hans Hanson who married Martha executrix of John Wells (KE).

Mich. Miller (KE) petitioned for him to administer oath to Robert Parks (KE) administrator of John Wiborow (KE).

12B:200 Col. Thomas Taylor exhibited will of John Hillen (AA). Said Taylor to prove said will. Johanna Hillen widow & executrix was granted administration. Appraisers: Maj. John Welsh, Wolfram Hunt. Said Taylor to administer oath.

12B:201 22 September. William Dikenson (TA) executor of Walter Dikenson (TA) was summoned to render accounts. Said William is a Quaker & cannot take an oath. Nor is there any inventory.

12B:202 26 September. Gervais Lacells (BA) was granted administration on estate of Robert Connyworth (BA) as principle creditor. Appraisers: John Ardin, Thomas Morrice. Maj. Thomas Long (BA) to administer oath.

12B:203 28 September. Henry Constable (AA) who married Katherine relict & executrix of James Rigby (AA) exhibited accounts.

12B:204 Henry Constable (AA) exhibited will of John Homewood (AA), constituting his wife Sarah as executrix. Richard Hill (g, AA) to prove said will.

12B:205 Letter from George Parker (g, CV): he is procurator for John Bird & his wife Elisabeth executrix of Henry Lewis regarding the suit between William Hopkins guardian of orphans of said Lewis & said Birds. Said Parker cannot attend because he is not well. Date: 26 September 1682. Robert Carvile (SM) procurator

12B:206 for William Hopkins was granted continuance.

12B:207 30 September. Miles Gibson (g, BA) exhibited oath of James Collyer & William Yorke administrators/executors of John Waterton (BA) on behalf of Francis Reede

& Thomas Ridge executors, both being in
ENG. Sureties: James Thompson, John
Tilliard. Also exhibited was oath of
James Thompson & John Tilliard,
appraisers.
12B:208 Also exhibited was inventory.

Miles Gibson (g, BA) exhibited oath of
Hannah Gray administratrix of John Gray
(BA). Sureties: Israell Skelton,
Michael Judd.
12B:209 Also exhibited was inventory.

Henry Johnson (g, BA) exhibited will of
Anthony Wattson (BA).
12B:210 Also exhibited was oath of Robert Jones,
Sr. & Laurence Taylor, appraisers.

Sarah Claw (SM) administratrix of
William Claw executor of John Reynolds
(SM) exhibited additional accounts on
estate of said Reynolds.

Martha Ridgely (SM) widow & executrix of
Robert Ridgely (SM) administrator of
Nicholas Badcock (SM) was granted
administration de bonis non on estate of
said Badcock.
12B:211 Surety: John Llewellen (g, SMC).

2 October. Miles Gibson (BA)
administrator of Abraham & Sarah Clarke
(BA) exhibited suit of William Wilkinson
& his wife Elisabeth (one of daughters
of said Clarkes)
12B:212 in BA Court. Date: 1 August 1682.
Present: Col. George Wells, Maj.
Thomas Long, Capt. Henry Johnson,
Edward Bedell. Mentions: Philip Pitsto,
12B:213 Lewis Barton, Johanna Barton, John
Arden.
12B:214 Ruling: said Gibson to pay said
Elisabeth her child's portion.
12B:215 ...

12B:216 William Hopkins (AA) guardian to Henry
Lewis & William Lewis orphans of Henry
Lewis (AA) to reserve judgement. George
Parker attorney for defendants is unable
to attend. Said Hopkins exhibited that
said John Bird has absconded with his
wife & family & runaway & left no one to

look after the plantation.

12B:217 Sheriff (AA) to collect estate of said Henry Lewis (dec'd).

12B:218 Richard Hill (g), John Homewood (g), & Edward Dorsey (g) to examine defendants.

12B:219-221 ...

12B:222 7 October. William Crowder (Clifts, CV) executor of William Kent (CV) exhibited accounts.

John Bird (AA) exhibited that he went to SO where a portion of estate of said Henry Lewis resided. Said Lewis married Elisabeth relict of Henry Boston (SO). After he said Bird arrived in SO, he fell sick so that he could not attend Court.

12B:223 Said Bird brought certificate from Col. William Steevens (SO). Robert Carvile procurator for William Hopkins guardian for orphans of said Lewis

12B:224 was summoned.

9 October. John Bird who married Elisabeth relict & executrix of Henry Lewis (AA) petitioned.

12B:225 ...

12B:226 Letter to AA Commissioners: to set aside order to collect estate of Henry Lewis.

12B:227 Col. William Coulborne (SO) administrator of Thomas Feild (SO) exhibited inventory, by appraisers Benjamin Sumers & Nathaniell Dougherty. Also exhibited were accounts.

12B:228 Eduard Jones who married Mary (CE) relict & administratrix of William Broakhurst (CE) exhibited accounts.

Exhibited was inventory of John Inglish (CE), by appraisers Eduard Jones & John Hiland.

John Reynolds (p, CE) executor of Thomas Smith (CE) exhibited accounts.

12B:229 James Holloway (CE) administrator of Robert Cooke (CE) exhibited accounts, but cannot travel to Court.

12B:230 John Thompson (g, CE) to examine said

Court Session: 1682

accounts & administer oath.

John Camell who married Elisabeth relict
& administratrix of William Savin (CE)
12B:231 exhibited accounts, but cannot travel to
Court. John Thompson (g, CE) to examine
said accounts & administer oath.

12B:232 10 October. Accounts of Eduard Jones
who married Mary relict & administratrix
of William Broakhurst (CE) were
examined. Distribution: widow (1/3rd).
Residue: 2 daughters.

Thomas Evans (KE) exhibited
12B:233 who lately married relict of Richard
Pether (KE) petitioned that his wife has
not appeared to render accounts by
reason of disability & weakness of body.
She is very ancient. Petition for Capt.
Laurence or Mr. Philip Conner to
examine accounts & administer oath.
Date: 4 September 1682 at KI.
12B:234 Said Conner to examine.

12 October. Henry Hanslap (AA)
petitioned for Col. William Burges to
swear Joseph Williams & his wife Mary
relict & administratrix of John
Robinson. [Said Williams was not
sworn.]

12B:235 John Clarke (CH) executor of Thomas
Coates exhibited accounts.

Letter from John Willis (CE) executor of
William Salisbury (CE) exhibited that
said Willis delivered goods to John
Salisbury administrator of William
Salisbury
12B:236 & mentions Mr. Charles James attorney
of said John Salisbury.
12B:237 Date: 14 September 1682.

Mary Jones wife of Eduard Jones & relict
of William Broakhurst exhibited
accounts.
12B:238 Orphans to be care for by their mother.

John Shankes (SM) petitioned
12B:239 that orphans of William Watts (St.
Clement's Hundred, SM, d. 1678) are 3

sons: Charles (eldest), William, Eduard. They are children by his wife Emma (she predeceased said William) who is a daughter of petitioner. Said William Watts (father) left a will

12B:240 constituting Capt. Gerrard Slye as executor. Said Shankes deposed.

12B:241-242 ...

12B:243 ...
- Richard Craine deposed concerning the eldest son (age 10) 2 years ago. Mentions: John Sheppeard (cooper). The next son is age 9.

12B:244 ...
- Henry Poulter deposed.

12B:245 ...
- John Dotting (ship's master) deposed.
- Emma Rosewell deposed

12B:246 ...
that she gave a Negro girl to her goddaughter Emma Watts.
- Arthur Thompson deposed.

12B:247 ...
- William Rozewell deposed.

12B:248
- William Taylor deposed.
- John Hoskins (p, SM), age 40, deposed.

12B:249 Date: 27 July 1682. Signed: William Diggs (clerk).
- Capt. Justinian Gerrard deposed on 1 August 1682.
- Vincent Mansfield deposed.

12B:250 ...
- Colline Makensie deposed.
Signed: Thomas Grunwin (clerk). Ruling: (1) no tutor appointed for the 3 children.

12B:251 ...

12B:252 (2) John Shanks (grandfather, protestant of Church of ENG, next of kin) is fit guardian.

12B:253 ...

12B:254 James Bowling (SM) exhibited inventory of Thomas Speake (SM), by appraisers Robert Gwinn & Francis Grave.

12B:255 John Bowling (SM) executor of Thomas Speake exhibited accounts.

Joseph Hopkins (CE) exhibited bond on estate of William Salisbury, which is inconsiderable to the whole estate, for John Willis (former administrator) & John Salisbury (last administrator) cannot comply.

12B:256 Date: 5 October 1682. Sureties: Nich. Shaw, Ezekiell Jackson, Nathaniell Hellen. Also exhibited was oath of William Odery & Ezekiell Jackson, appraisers sworn 18 June 1682. Also exhibited was inventory.

12B:257 Exhibited was will of Francis Harmor (CE), proved. Joseph Hopkins (CE) exhibited oath of Richard Pullen and Thomas Hawker, appraisers sworn 21 June 1682.

Joseph Hopkins (CE) exhibited oath of Frances Stavely & John Stavely (CE) administrators of James Stavely (CE), sworn 12 August 1682.

12B:258 Sureties: Ebenezar Blakiston, James Wroth. Also exhibited was oath of Joseph Langley & Eduard Blais, appraisers sworn 12 August 1682. Also exhibited was inventory.

12B:259 Exhibited was letter from Sibella Broadrib (TA) executrix of John Broadrib. Date: 7 October 1682. Continuance was granted.

Exhibited was letter from Charles James (CE). Date: 3 October 1682.

12B:260 Said James is very sick. Continuance was granted.

12B:261 John Welsh (AA) exhibited bond of Joseph Naylor (AA) administrator of John Farr (AA). Surety: Abraham Naylor. Also exhibited was inventory, by appraisers Robert Franklin & Thomas Knighton.

Roger Brooke (g, CV) exhibited bond of Anne Robinson (CV) administratrix of James Garner (CV). Sureties: Thomas Sedgewick James Garner.

12B:262 Exhibited was inventory of John Farr (AA), by appraisers Thomas Sedgewick &

Court Session: 1682

John Grover.

Exhibited was bond of Katherine Wynnall (CV) administratrix of John Wynall (CV). Sureties: Thomas Sedgewick, James Garner.

Exhibited was bond of Elisabeth Muffett (CV) administratrix of William Muffett (CV).
12B:263 Sureties: Christopher Baines, Simon Eduards.

13 October. Henry Hawkins (CH) who married Elisabeth relict & executrix of Dr. Francis Wyne (CH) exhibited accounts.

Col. Thomas Taylor (AA) exhibited accounts of Margarett Lane executrix of Samuell Lane (AA) & accounts of estate of George Simons.

12B:264 Charles Carter (CH) was granted administration on estate of Patrick Venstone (CH), as principle creditor. Appraisers: Alexander Smith, John Coates. Capt. William Barton (CH) to administer oath.

William Reade (DO) administrator of John Reade (DO) exhibited accounts.

12B:265 Exhibited was inventory of William Love (CH), by appraisers John Butcher & James Wheler.

Henry Hanslap (AA) executor of William Hanson (AA) exhibited list of goods & accounts.

12B:266 Col. Thomas Taylor (AA) exhibited will of Thomas Forde (AA), constituting Thomas Lunn (AA) executor. Said Taylor to prove said will. Appraisers: Major Welsh, Walter Carr. Said Col. Taillor to administer oath.

Col. Thomas Taylor exhibited will of Henry Stockett (AA).
12B:267 Said Taylor to prove said will.

Court Session: 1682

Col. William Burges & Samuell Withers
(AA) son, heir & executor of Samuell
Withers (AA) vs. Richard Hill (AA).
Complaint filed.

14 October. Col. Philemon Lloyd (TA)
exhibited accounts of Alice Woolman
administratrix of Richard Woolman (TA).
Said Alice is unable to travel to
Office.
12B:268 Said Lloyd to examine accounts &
administer oath.

Exhibited was inventory of Thomas
Hallings (TA), by appraisers Daniell
Glover & Mathew Smith.

Exhibited was inventory of John Bennett
(TA), by appraisers Roger Wedill & John
Jaxson.

James Murphey (TA) administrator of
12B:269 Henry Cloy Stockfish (TA) exhibited
accounts.

Richard Harrington (TA) administrator of
Robert Page (TA) exhibited accounts.

16 October. Marjory Mines (CV) relict &
administratrix of Patrick Dive (CV)
exhibited accounts, sworn by George
Lingham.
12B:270 Discharge was granted.

George Parker for Elisabeth Plott (AA)
relict & executrix of Robert Parnafee
(AA) exhibited accounts. Capt. Richard
Hill (AA) to administer oath.

Exhibited was inventory of Maj. Samuell
Lane (AA), by appraisers Thomas Francis
& William Fisher.

12B:271 Hester Nicholson relict & administratrix
of William Gouh (AA) exhibited accounts,
sworn before Col. Thomas Taylor (AA).

Alice Durham executrix of Nicholas
Furnace (CV) exhibited accounts, proved
before Samuell Bourne (CV).

Court Session: 1682

Exhibited was inventory of John Shrigley
(AA), by appraisers Robert Francklin &
Walter Carr.

12B:272 William Jones who married Elisabeth
relict & administratrix of Peter Wast
(CE) petitioned that several actions are
pending in County Court.
12B:273 Continuance was granted.

Richard Edmonds who married Elisabeth
relict & executrix of Henry Haslewood
(g, BA) petitioned that several actions
are pending in County Court.
12B:274 Continuance was granted.

17 October. Thomas Patisson (DO)
petitioned that Elisabeth Dukes be
granted administration on estate of
Robert Dukes (DO). William Steevens
(DO) to administer oath. Appraisers:
Alexander Fisher, Eduard Pindar.

12B:275 Eduard Cooke (DO) executor of Ezekell
Fogg (DO) exhibited accounts. Said
Cooke is joint executor with John
Richardson. Said Richardson was
summoned.

19 October. Eduard Man (TA) exhibited
oath of William Combes & Samuel Abbot,
appraisers os William Kellye (TA). Also
exhibited was bond of Richard Holland,
administrator. Surety: Samuell Abbot.
12B:276 Also exhibited was inventory & accounts.

Richard Holland (TA) who married Hannah
relict & executrix of Thomas Alexander
(TA) exhibited that his wife cannot
travel to Office. Mr. Eduard Man to
administer oath.

12B:277 28 October. Sarah Francklin (AA) widow
of Robert Francklin (AA) exhibited her
renunciation, recommending as
administrator Col. William Burges,
principle creditor. Date: 21 October
1682. Witnesses: John Meriton, Walter
Car.
12B:278 Said Burges was granted administration.
Appraisers: Henry Hanslap, Nicholas
Painter.

Exhibited was inventory of Robert Taylor (CV), by appraisers James Veitch & Samuell Vomes.

Exhibited was inventory of Clement Theobalds (CH), by appraisers John Godshall & Philip Hoskins.

12B:279 Charles Boteler (CV) administrator of Benjamin Aires (CV) exhibited accounts.

Exhibited was bond of Jacob Looton (SM) administrator of George Fenwick. Sureties: John Evans, Philip Lewin. Appraisers were sworn by William Hatton (g).

Exhibited was will of John Homewood (AA), proved before Richard Hill (g, AA).

12B:280 Exhibited was will of Henry Stockett (AA), proved before Col. Thomas Taylor (g, AA).

Exhibited was will of John Waterton (BA), proved before Miles Gibson (g, BA).

Elisabeth Howard (AA) executrix of Cornelius Howard (AA) was granted continuance.

Samuell Abbott (TA) exhibited several action in TA Court regarding estate of (N) Badley. Continuance was granted.

12B:281 Michaell Judd (BA) vs. James Philips administrator of Robert Taylor (BA). Caveat exhibited.

Capt. Thomas Francis (AA) administrator of John Shaw (AA) exhibited accounts. Distribution: orphans. Discharge was granted.

30 October. Mr. Henry Adams (CH) exhibited oath of Richard Garforth (CH) administrator of John Price (CH). Sureties: John Wood, John Godshall.
12B:282 Also exhibited was oath of John Godshall & John Wood, appraisers sworn by said

Adams.

George Hodgeson (SM) administrator of
Robert Inglesby (SM) exhibited that
papers and receipts for said estate are
in the hands of Thomas Marshall (CH).

John Hall (BA) administrator of Robert
Peca (BA) exhibited accounts.

2 November. Col. Thomas Taylor (AA)
administrator of Eduard Parish (AA)
exhibited accounts, proved before
Nicholas Gassaway (AA).

12B:283 Col. Thomas Taylor (AA) for Katherine
Stockett widow of Henry Stockett (AA) &
her son Francis Stockett executors of
said Henry petitioned that said Taylor
administer oath to said Katherine &
Francis. Appraisers: Capt. Nicholas
Gassaway, Capt. Thomas Francis. Said
Taylor to administer oath.

Exhibited was will of Adam Browne (TA),
proved before Col. Henry Coursey (TA)
on 20 April 1680 by George Philips &
Mary Withed. Also exhibited was
inventory,
12B:284 by appraisers William Tilchman & John
Offley.

Robert Thompson (CH) was granted
administration on estate of William
Wright (CH), who accidentally drowned on
Saturday last, leaving neither wife nor
children, as next of blood. Appraisers:
Thomas Crackson, John Wood. John Stone
(CH) to administer oath.

3 November. William Dane (KE)
administrator of John Adison (KE)
exhibited accounts.

12B:285 4 November. Thomas Hopkins (TA)
executor of Hugh Dulin (TA) exhibited
accounts. Said Dulin died very poor &
much indebted to several persons.

John Dyne (TA) administrator of Venlock
Christison (TA) exhibited that he had no
accounts on said estate, only what was

due him.

6 November. Col. William Burges (AA) &
Samuell Withers (AA) son & heir &
executor of Samuell Withers (AA) vs.
Richard Hill (g, AA). Said Hill
appeared.

12B:286 Miles Gibson (g, BA) exhibited accounts
of Henrietta Canon (alias Henrietta
Reeves, BA) administratrix of Eduard
Swanson (BA).

8 November. Exhibited was inventory of
Robert Davidge (AA), by appraisers
Richard Gwinn & Thomas Hackett.

9 November. Maj. Peter Sayer (TA)
exhibited oath of Mary Scott & James
Scott executors of James Scott (TA).
Will was proved by Andrew Ambleton.
Other witness is in ENG.

12B:287 10 November. John Thompson (CE)
exhibited accounts of James Halloway
administrator of Robert Cooke (CE), with
oath.

Said Thompson exhibited accounts of
Elisabeth Camell relict & administratrix
of William Savin (BA), with oath.

14 November. Michaell Hastings (BA)
administrator of Thomas Byworth
exhibited accounts. Said Hastings was
summoned to exhibit inventory.

12B:288 15 November. Col. Steevens (SO)
exhibited bond of Elisabeth Dickeson
administratrix of Eduard Dickeson (SO).
Sureties: Oliver Berry, Thomas
Cottingham. Also exhibited was
inventory, by appraisers Walter Powell &
Richard Lewis.

Robert Macklin (TA) administrator of
Robert Macklin, Sr. (TA) exhibited that
he could not exhibited accounts because
he has not received the estate from his
guardian.

16 November. Col. William Steevens
(SO) exhibited that Mary Curtis (SO)
executrix of Daniell Curtis (SO) cannot
travel to Office.

12B:289 Said Steevens to administer oath.

Col. William Steevens (SO) exhibited
will of Robert Richardson (SO). Said
Steevens to prove said will.
Appraisers: Capt. John Osborne, William
Walton. Said Steevens to administer
oath.

Col. William Steevens (SO) exhibited
that Katherine Johnson (SO)
administratrix of (N) is a Quaker & has
not exhibited an inventory nor accounts.

12B:290 Appraisers: William Planner, Thomas
Tovy. Said Steevens to administer oath.

17 November. Capt. Richard Hill (AA)
for widow Meeke was granted
administration on estate of Guy Meeke
(AA). Appraisers: Richard Warefeild,
Philip Howard. Said Hill to administer
oath.

12B:291 20 November. Eduard Day (g, SO)
executor of Capt. Thomas Walker (SO) on
behalf of his wife Jane the relict, was
granted continuance.

23 November. William Barton (g, CH)
exhibited oath of Charles Carter
administrator of Patrick Venstone. Also
exhibited was oath of Alexander Smith &
John Curtis, appraisers. Date: 12
November 1682.

12B:292 Sureties: Thomas Marshall, John Turner.

Exhibited was inventory of Robert Cooper
(CH), by appraisers John Baynes &
Richard Beaumont.

18 December. Maj. John Welsh (AA)
exhibited will of Mathew Silley (AA),
proved. Also exhibited was oath of
Nicholas Painter & Walter Carr,
appraisers.

12B:293 William Sharpe (TA) exhibited will of
William Hemstead (TA). William Combes

(g) to prove said will.

Eduard Bedell (g) exhibited will of
William Hill, proved. Also exhibited
was oath of James Philips (BA) executor.
Also exhibited was oath of William
Croshaw & William Osborne, appraisers.
Also exhibited was inventory.

12B:294 Colline Mackensie (SM) was granted
administration on estate of Richard
Crane (SM). Appraisers: John Bulock,
Joseph Fowler. Clement Hill (g, SM) to
administer oath.

20 December. Anne Randall (KE) widow of
Benjamin Randall exhibited his will,
made 3 years ago. Said will was neither
dated nor witnessed. Said Anne was
granted administration. Henry Hosier
(KE) to administer oath.

12B:295 James Mills (BA) was granted
administration on estate of John Gills
(SM). Estate is inconsiderable.
Appraiser: John Blomfeild.

22 December. Henry Newton (TA)
administrator of John Newton (TA)
exhibited accounts.

Henry Newton (TA) was granted
administration on estate of Thomas
Pindergrasse (TA), as principle
creditor. Appraisers: John Stanly,
Francis Chapplin.
12B:296 Eduard Man (TA) to administer oath.

29 December. Sarah Claw (SM) exhibited
that she has overpaid the accounts of
John Reynolds (Fresh Pond Neck, SM).
William Calvert, Esq. (Secretary) bought
the land & said Claw is as yet unpaid.
Elisabeth administratrix of said Calvert
to pay said Claw.

2 January. Exhibited was inventory of
Robert Ridgly (SM),
12B:297 by appraisers Garrett Vansweringhen &
Daniell Clocker.

3 January. James Bodkins (merchant, Galloway, IRE) one of executors of Dominick Bodkin fitzJames (merchant, Galloway, IRE) exhibited that on 4 October 1677 Benjamin Rozer (g) exhibited PoA from Richard Foote (merchant, London) attorney for executors & was granted administration on said estate. Said Rozer is since dec'd. Former LoA

12B:298 are declared void. James Bodkin one of the executors was granted administration. Mentions: will of said Bodkin proved before William Archbishop of Canterbury on 10 November 1681. On 5 May 1681 before

12B:299 Richard Lloyd knight, doctor of laws & Leolin Jenkins knight, doctor of laws, master keeper of Prerogative Court of Canterbury said will was proved. Legatees: Benedictin Dames of Dunkirke, English Clares of same place, Father Parsons,

12B:300 Augustines of Galloway, Franciscans, Dominicans, mother. Executors (all of Galloway): Mr. Peter Kerwan (brother-in-law), Mr. Francis Blake (brother-in-law), James Bodkin (nephew). Legatees: James Bodkin (nephew), my wife & 2 children. Date: 9 October 1674 at Dunkirke.

12B:301 Witnesses: Richard Goodwin, Jeane Francis, Daniell Palmer, Francis Henford. Mentions: Schiper Francis Vanderkerkhorne (ship's carpenter), Aaron (Englishman), Charles (seaman), Mr. Benjamin Salley (my attorney in VA), Father Massey (VA), my sister Massey (Princes Hoef in Bruges Weching), bill of lading to Mr. Blacke from Berye Norway,

12B:302 Mr. Ralph Grant & James Bodkin, Mr. Benjamin Salley (MD), Father Henry Warren,

12B:303 Mr. John Owner, Jacq. Lebac, Francis Herford.

12B:304 Said James was granted administration.

John Massey & his wife (VA) exhibited that William Cane (SM) died while said Massey's wife was in ENG. Said Cane made will, constituting Joseph Edloe

(SM) executor. Residue: Massey's wife's child.

12B:305 Massey's wife is relict of said Cane. Said child is since dec'd. Said Edloe has filed accounts on said estate.

4 January. Col. Thomas Taylor (AA) exhibited will of Henry Stockett (AA), proved by Jacob Harris, Joseph Owen, & Nathaniell Smith. Also exhibited was oath of Katherine Stockett & her son Francis Stockett

12B:306 executors, sworn 22 December 1682. Also exhibited was oath of Maj. Nicholas Gassaway & Capt. Thomas Francis, sworn same day.

5 January. John Massey who married relict of William Cane (SM) vs. Joseph Edloe executor of said Cane. Exceptions cited. Mentions: Mich. Rochford.

12B:307-308 ...
12B:309 Signed: George Thompson.

8 January. John Massey vs. Joseph Edloe. Continuance was granted, since the judge was called abroad.

10 January. Richard Gardiner (g, SM) exhibited the nuncupative will of Colline Mackensie (SM), made in presence of Peter Mills, Richard Walker, James French, & Hugh Benson.

12B:310 Clement Hill (g, SM) to prove said will.

13 January. John Massey vs. Joseph Edloe. Continuance was granted, since the judge is very ill.

18 January. William Belfore (TA) exhibited will of George Reade (TA), constituting said Belfore executor. William Combes (g, TA) to prove said will. Appraisers: Samuell Abbot, Thomas Martin. Said Combes to administer oath.

12B:311 Exhibited was nuncupative will of Colline Mackensie (SM), proved before Clement Hill (g, SM). Said will is held, since the judge is now dec'd.

Court Session: 1682

25 January. Justinian Tennison (SM)
exhibited will of John Tennison (SM),
constituting his brother Absalom
Tennison executor. Said Absalom is
under age 17. Col. William Digges (SM)
to prove said will. Said Justinian was
granted administration. Appraisers:
Capt. John Cood, Vincent Mansell. Said
Digges to administer oath.

GENERAL INDEX

(N) 227
Bagbie
    Amos 179
    Michaell 179
    Samuell 179
    Ursula 179
Bagby
    Amos 216
Baily
    John 148
Baines
    Christopher 224
Baker
    John 93, 117, 127,
        133, 134, 136
    Joseph 20
    Thomas 56, 71, 75,
        132, 151, 175
    William 110
Balderston
    James 67, 69, 120,
        122
Balderstone
    James 85, 160
Balford
    William 32
Ball
    Richard 1, 2
    William 1, 119,
        121, 141
Ballard
    Charles 214
    Sarah 214
Balley
    John 13, 71
Baltemore
    C. 130
Banckes
    Charles 132, 138
    Thomas 129, 130,
        132, 138
Bankes
    Charles 161, 196
    Thomas 79, 86, 91,
        109, 118, 128,
        144, 148
Barbery
    Susanna 4, 5
    Thomas 4, 5
Barbier
    Conniers 4
Bardune
    Charles 141, 151
    Elisabeth 141, 151

Barecroft
    (N) 209
Barkehurst
    James 196
Barkhurst
    James 215
Barnell
    Francis 8
Barnes
    Frances 213
    Francis 133, 146,
        157
    Henry 1, 111, 217
    John 15, 74, 75,
        127, 130
    Mary 183
    Sarah 48, 75
    Thomas 124, 157,
        213
Barnwell
    Francis 16
Barsett
    Thomas 60
Barson
    (N) 209
Bartlet
    George 18
Barton
    Johanna 219
    Lewis 219
    William 167, 224,
        230
Basey
    Michaell 17
Basse
    Michaell 99
Basset
    Thomas 35, 210
Bassett
    Thomas 191, 195
Bassey
    Michael 147, 148
Batch
    Philip 88
Bate
    William 138
Bateman
    William 5, 6, 8,
        10, 26, 28, 40,
        58, 69, 98, 122,
        123, 140, 144,
        152, 157, 166,
        168, 169, 175,
        190, 191

Batson
(N) 208
Battey
Ferdinando 196,
197, 203
Baxter
Thomas 2
Bayley
Charles 67, 84
George 96, 106, 139
John 97, 101, 109
Magdalen 165
Mary 67
Bayly
John 108
Baynard
John 205
Bayne
Christopher 44
Elenor 121
Elin 135
John 194
Baynes
Christopher 141
John 230
Beach
Elias 112, 172
James 194, 207
Sara 112
Bead
Nicholas 201
Beale
Daniel 31
John 9
Ninian 1, 19
Beall
Ninian 172, 202,
216
Ninion 166
Beames
Ralph 183
Beamon
John 78, 79, 90,
160
Beamont
Mr. 77
Richard 194
Beane
John 186
Bearcroft
John 139
Beard
Elisabeth 48, 61
Hester 87, 102

John 48, 61, 81,
87, 102, 116
Richard 1, 189
Bearecroft
John 92, 138
Beasely
John 175
Beauchamp
Edmond 199
Sam. 78
Beaumont
James 202
Richard 186, 195,
202, 230
Beaumunt
James 204
Beck
Edward 83, 104,
153, 182, 199
Elisabeth 23, 47,
51, 60
Jonathon 32
Lewis 23
Mary 32
Richard 23, 47, 51,
60
Beckwith
Barbara 79, 109
Charles 79, 109
Elisabeth 53, 79,
118, 138
Frances 118, 128,
129, 130, 132,
138, 144, 148
Francis 86
George 79, 86, 91,
109, 118, 119,
128, 129, 130,
132, 138, 144,
148
Margaret 109
Margarett 79
Bedell
Eduard 231
Edward 110, 139,
219
Bedle
Edward 124, 188
Edwarde 91
Bedworth
Richard 20
Beedle
Edward 176
Sophia 42

Richard 35, 53
Boullay
James 131
Boulley
James 127
Boult
John 146
Boultane
Daniel 147
Boulton
Daniel 147, 156, 167
Daniell 167
Elisabeth 83
Enoch 83, 89
George 90
John 187
Boureman
John 185
Bourne
Sam. 135
Samuel 53, 68, 74, 75, 111, 215
Samuell 4, 17, 20, 22, 37, 46, 111, 117, 128, 130, 134, 135, 145, 148, 152, 158, 164, 168, 169, 173, 179, 183, 185, 206, 225
Boutcher
John 206
Bowing
Jonas 115, 121
Bowles
John 4, 190, 193
Bowling
James 222
John 222
Bowne
John 196
Boyden
William 15, 142
Bracher
John 143, 151, 159
Bradborne
Eleanor 93
Elenor 93
John 93, 132
Bradbourne
John 87, 125, 156
Bradford
George 129

Bradle
Henry 16, 17, 41, 42
Bradley
Henry 54, 99, 113
Mary 99, 116
Bradly
Henry 116
Braines
Sarah 191
Brams
Benjamin 32
Brashire
John 130
Brassure
Alice 130, 132, 133
Robert 130, 132
Brayne
Henry 202
John 202
Braynes
Henry 192
Bread
Jane 15
Breames
Christopher 72, 116
Breereton
William 84
Brereton
William 60, 69, 70, 87, 112, 116, 183
Brewerton
William 30, 52
Brewton
William 68
Brian
Robert 83
Bricke
John 186
Bridges
Francis 83
Bright
Cecil 177
Thomas 100, 177, 216
Broadrib
John 69, 223
Sibella 223
Broadribb
John 100, 125, 169
Sibella 169
Broakhurst
William 220, 221

Burton
   Edward 142
Busse
   George 75
   Henry 75
   Jane 75
   Michaell 113
Bussy
   Michaell 116
Butcher
   John 78, 81, 90,
      137, 166, 203,
      224
Butten
   John 104
Button
   John 90
Buttrum
   Nicholas 93
Byworth
   Thomas 229

Cable
   John 39, 160, 210
Cage
   John 71, 159
Cager
   Robert 46, 130
   Thomas 27
Caltrop
   William 189
Calvert
   Charles 35
   Elisabeth 202, 231
   Philip 130, 136,
      160
   William 22, 63,
      187, 194, 202,
      204, 206, 231
Cambell
   John 49
Camell
   Anne 171
   Elisabeth 221, 229
   John 171, 181, 221
Cammell
   John 51
Campher
   Anne 22
   Thomas 22
Cane
   William 232, 233
Cannon

Stephen 196
Thomas 169, 173,
   174, 184
Cannons
   William 25
Canon
   Henrietta 193, 202,
      207, 229
   Thomas 193, 202,
      207
Cantwell
   Edmond 104, 148,
      185, 186
   Edmund 12, 39, 167,
      171, 176, 184
   Edward 174
Capell
   Bryan 197
Car
   Walter 197, 226
Carew
   Henry 7, 85
Carewe
   Henry 61, 62, 64,
      65, 67
   Mr. 64
Carleton
   Arthur 18
   Thomas 18
Carley
   George 210
Carlile
   Thomas 45
Carpenter
   John 136
Carr
   John 28, 32
   Nicholas 48
   Robert 197
   Walter 84, 136,
      140, 224, 226,
      230
   William 33
Carre
   William 68
Carrington
   John 145, 153
Carter
   Charles 224, 230
   Edward 32
   Henry 138
   John 147
   Richard 131, 205
Cartwright

Demetrius 44
Mathew 60
Matthew 35
Carty
Charles 74
Carvil
John 32
Thomas 203
Carvile
(N) & 208
John 189
Mary 191
Mr. 80, 144
Ro. 46, 77, 210
Robert 48, 56, 67,
77, 80, 84, 93,
94, 97, 98, 109,
112, 114, 116,
117, 125, 148,
151, 161, 171,
176, 184, 186,
189, 190, 194,
195, 196, 200,
208, 211, 214,
218, 220
Thomas 155, 161,
188, 191, 200
Carvill
Thomas 154, 159,
161
Carwardin
Peter 153
Carwardine
Peter 160
Cash
John 151
Cassocke
John 21
Casson
John 139, 163
Castleston
May 60
Robert 60
Castleton
(N) 47
Mary 47
Robert 23, 47, 51
Cattle Neck 195
Causin
Ignatius 167
Ceely
George 42, 52, 53
Robert 40
Thomas 5

Chadborne
John 54
Chadbourne
William 69, 117
Chadwell
John 30
Chafe
John 124, 132
Mary 177, 178
Chamberlain
Mary 32
William 32
Chandler
John 190
Mary 62
Richard 37, 126,
176, 178
Thomas 5, 117
William 37, 62, 69,
85, 126, 163,
172, 176, 178,
180, 199, 201,
204, 206, 211
Chaney
John 76
Chaplin
Francis 33
Chapman
Richard 16
Robert 43
Chapplin
Francis 231
Charlcraft
James 105
Charlesworth
George 18
Cheir
John 110
Cheseldine
Kenelme 107, 118,
127, 139, 165
Cheseldyn
(N) 208
Mr. 209
Cheseldyne
Kenelme 49, 125,
150
Cheshire
Mary 188, 191
William 191
Chesledyne
Kenelme 57, 125
Chester
Edward 194

Morris 187
Richard 191
Robert 186, 187,
   194, 195, 230
Samuell 127
Thomas 212
Coopper
  Samuel 75
Coppedge
  Edward 2, 37
Coppidge
  Edward 87, 101,
   108, 142
Corbin
  Nich. 158
  Nicholas 141, 152,
   181
Cordea
  Mrs. 209
Corker
  Thomas 5, 52
Corkes
  Thomas 53
Cornel
  Joseph 71
Cornelioson
  Jane 193
Cornell
  Jaspin 140
  Joseph 75
Cornewallis
  William 77
Cornish
  John 23, 67
  Richard 23, 67
Cornwaleys
  William 67
Cornwalleys
  William 41, 47
Cosden
  Thomas 91, 105, 192
Cosford
  Thomas 3
Cottingham
  Thomas 229
Cottle
  Marcus 35, 39, 44
Cotton
  Frances 184
Coulborne
  William 220
Coursey
  Henry 25, 67, 69,
   82, 132, 144,

   156, 177, 178,
   185, 193, 213,
   228
  Ja. 93, 217
  James 92, 93, 99,
   167
  William 7, 24, 42,
   93, 103, 124,
   150, 153, 161,
   166, 177
Courte
  John 103, 137, 138,
   151, 198
Courtney
  Thomas 16, 80, 127,
   131, 149, 166
Courts
  John 184
Cousins
  John 28, 164, 169
Coventon
  John 28, 30, 54
  Nehemia 54
  Nehemiah 68
Covill
  Richard 67
Covington
  (N) 87
  Nehemia 213
Cowley
  George 24, 47, 59,
   96, 106, 173
Cox
  James 81, 88
  William 187
Coxe
  James 88
Crackeson
  Thomas 78
Crackson
  Thomas 228
Craine
  Richard 222
  Robert 137
Cran
  Robert 107
Crane
  Richard 231
Cranford
  James 130
Crashaw
  William 212
Crauford
  Anne 179

Crauley
  Michaell 103
Crawford
  Ann 214
Crawley
  Michaell 92
Craxon
  Thomas 90
Credwell
  George 53, 114
Cressey
  Samuell 3
Crew
  James 209
Crocket
  Richard 21
Crockett
  Richard 55, 66, 117
Cromewell
  William 99
Crommell
  William 119, 141
Crompe
  Thomas 215
  William 167
Cromwell
  William 83, 121
Crooke
  Thomas 164, 169,
    212
Cropper
  John 162
Croshaw
  William 231
Croshow
  Elisabeth 217
Crosse
  Thomas 93
  William 1, 19, 56,
    128, 129, 140,
    200, 209
Crouch
  (N) 46
  Jane 46
Crouche
  John 7
Crow
  Gurney 199
Crowder
  Thomas 178, 206
  William 220
Crowly
  Anne 159
Crowshe

William 203
Crowshen
  William 188
Crusape
  William 176
Crutch
  James 196
Crycroft
  John 179
Cubnall
  Symon 77
Cuffyn
  Anne 41
  David 41
Cullens
  James 206
Cunningham
  John 45, 154
Curtice
  Daniell 66
Curtis
  Daniel 78
  Daniell 183, 230
  Edward 154
  John 230
  Mary 183, 230

Dabanck
  Samuel 77
DabrideCourt
  John 165
Dabridgcourt
  Ann 108
  John 106, 108
Dabridgecourt
  Anne 157, 163
  John 157, 163
Dadd
  John 200
Dadick
  John 159
Dale
  David 134, 144, 162
  Henry 144, 162
Daley
  Bryan 212
  Rebecca 212
Dalton
  John 96
  Richard 54, 61, 62,
    64
Danbridge
  John 91

Dane
   William 228
Daniel
   Maurice 155
   Thomas 54
Daniell
   Constant 110
   Constantine 22, 38
   Love 22, 38
   Maryan 155, 156
   Maurice 156
   Morris 147, 156
   Thomas 21, 41, 48,
      54, 55, 72, 94,
      95
Dare
   William 18, 209
Darnall
   Elisabeth 103
   Henry 79, 86, 89,
      91, 93, 94, 100,
      101, 123, 162,
      210
   John 68, 79, 88,
      91, 103, 136
Darwall
   Elisabeth 127
   John 127
Darwell
   Elisabeth 119, 131
   John 119, 131
Dash
   Elisabeth 9, 10
Dasheil
   James 196
Dashiele
   James 70
Dashiell
   James 55
Dauzey
   Martha 20
David
   Joane 166
   John 23, 123, 166
   Jone 123
Davidg
   Robert 112
Davidge
   Providence 193,
      202, 214, 215
   Robert 105, 112,
      193, 202, 214,
      215, 229
Davies

Edward 196
Elisabeth 17
Joane 28, 39
John 17, 18, 28,
   39, 96
Rebecca 9
Thomas 42
William 23
Davil
   Richard 137
Davis
   John 119, 160, 192
   Jonas 58
   Mary 127, 188
   Philip 190
   Robert 8
   Stephen 209
   Thomas 12, 31, 192,
      197
   Walter 127
   William 55, 79, 91,
      119, 121, 122,
      141
Davyes
   Edward 196
Dawbridge
   John 101
Dawe
   Tho. 39
Dawsey
   Edward 196
Dawson
   Abraham 116
   Anne 116
   Philip 55
   Ralph 63
Day
   Edward 230
   Jane 230
de la Roche
   Mrs. 77
de Rumple
   James 93
   Mary 93, 99, 101
Deale
   Mary 38
   Thomas 38
Deane
   Sara 108, 121
   William 23, 55, 58,
      190
Deavor
   Richard 103
Deavors

Jane 170, 174
Dunch
    Barnaby 67
Dunkerton
    William 38
Dunne
    Robert 108
Dunston
    John 203
Durbin
    Thomas 152
Durham
    Alice 215, 225
Dushile
    James 9, 21
Dyne
    John 228
Dynes
    Mary 70, 175

Eagle
    Amye 188
    Ann 182
    William 182, 188,
        205
Earackson
    John 163
    Matthew 163
Eareckson
    John 100, 118
    Mathew 100
    Matthew 157
Earle
    Ann 59
    Michael 33
    Thomas 13, 59
    widow 13
Eason
    Ann 139
    John 106, 139
    Lownes 4
Eaton
    Jeremiah 122
Ebden
    Jane 27, 49, 62
    John 104
    William 27, 49, 62,
        70
Edbden
    Jane 70
Edelen
    Richard 211
Edelin

Richard 3
Edge
    Daniel 153
Edleñ
    Richard 71
Edloe
    Joseph 9, 209, 232,
        233
Edmonds
    (N) 45
    Elisabeth 226
    Richard 104, 148,
        186, 209, 226
    Tho. 46
Edmondson
    John 105, 151, 154,
        180
Edmunds
    Richard 174
Edmundson
    John 13, 23, 90
Edmunson
    John 209
Eduard
    Nathaniell 199
Eduards
    Hannah 198
    Richard 198
    Simon 224
Edward
    John 65
Edwards
    James 129
    John 31, 55, 85,
        90, 116
    Simon 96, 111
    Symon 110, 111, 185
Elliot
    Edward 22
    Henry 108
    Jane 108
    Robert 174
Elliott
    Henry 127, 131, 166
    Jane 30, 127
    John 69
Ellis
    (N) 208, 209
    James 96
    John 162
    Peter 111, 119,
        120, 122, 124,
        133, 139, 146,
        153, 171, 176,

180, 193, 212
Robert 111, 169,
180, 209
Thomas 166, 172,
180
Ellys
Robert 30, 35
Elmer
William 104
Elmes
Jane 7
William 7
Elms
William 78
Elston
Ralph 102
Elves
Thomas 120
Emmett
John 154, 162
Emory
Arthur 143
English
E. 46
Eduard 210
Edward 17, 41, 54,
60, 76, 78, 83,
97, 104, 115,
174, 191
John 104, 156, 184
Enlos
Henry 146, 171
Ennall
Bartholomew 99
Ennalls
Bartho. 147
Bartholomew 17, 35,
41, 54, 107,
113, 114, 116,
118, 121
Ennis
Hester 8
William 8
Erackson
John 87
Ereckson
John 198, 209
Mathew 198, 213
Erickson
Elisabeth 13, 25
John 13, 25
Eure
Peter 8, 16
Evans

Anne 90
Anthony 74, 148,
149
John 21, 35, 48,
55, 66, 69, 93,
95, 109, 112,
113, 117, 124,
127, 131, 137,
144, 148, 161,
162, 166, 210,
227
Mary 66, 69, 70,
87, 95, 208
Richard 4
Sarah 6, 161
Thomas 26, 90, 107,
130, 137, 165,
221
Evens
Nathaniell 206
William 200
Everitt
Philip 142
Everton 120
Ewstice
James 193
Exon
(N) 208
Henry 3, 75, 77,
126, 127, 130,
133, 134, 143,
209

Faning
John 145, 159, 160
Fanning
(N) 208
John 53, 70, 81,
82, 122, 137,
138, 143, 161,
186, 188, 189,
191, 194, 195,
213
Farmar
Mary 203
Farr
John 76, 195, 223
Farrar
Joanna 62, 76
Robert 62, 76
Farrer
Robert 63
Farrson

Godfrey
George 13, 53, 166,
170, 174, 175,
176
Godhall
John 60
Godshall
George 204
John 142, 191, 206,
210, 227
Godson
John 47, 51, 199,
201
Sarah 1
Godwin
Anne 25
William 22, 25, 101
Goffe
Hester 50
Mary 3
Stephen 3
William 50
Goland
Robert 42
Gold
Richard 25, 65
Golde
Richard 106
Golding
Edward 77
Goldsmith
George 119
Johanna 36
John 103
Samuell 36
Goldson
Daniell 110
Goldstone
Daniell 4
Gooch
John 181
Good
Edward 40, 52
Margery 40, 52, 78
Thomas 78
Goodhand
Christopher 198
Xopher 192
Goodwin
Richard 232
Goosey
Jonathon 176
Samuel 76
Samuell 93, 110,

111, 113, 135
Goozey
Samuell 4
Gordon
Johanna 91
Patrick 71, 91
Gosfreight
Charles 114, 141
Gosfright
Charles 70, 80,
131, 190, 193
George 190, 193
Gosvell
William 209
Gott
Henry 138
Gough
Hester 67, 156
John 172
William 67, 152,
156, 215
Gouh
William 225
Gould
Edward 84
Richard 63, 139
Gouldsmith
John 154
Matthew 172
Gouldson
Alice 75, 111
Daniel 75, 111
Daniell 111
Gourden
Johanna 76
Patricke 76
Gourdon
Johannah 118
Patrick 118
Graham
Robert 9, 49, 127,
134
Gramer
John 55
Grammar
Elisabeth 41
John 41
Grammer
John 52, 97, 100,
106
Grange
John 2, 57, 83, 96,
103, 106, 117
William 216

Granger
 Christopher 212
 Grace 206
 John 125
 William 206, 211
Grant
 Ralph 232
Grave
 Francis 222
Graves
 Alice 44
 Samuel 53, 66, 67
 Samuell 111
 William 176
Gray
 Hannah 207, 219
 Jane 49
 John 14, 122, 142,
  189, 196, 203,
  204, 207, 219
 Miles 208
Graye
 John 105
Greaer
 John 93
Green
 John 102, 161
 Margarett 161
Greenberry
 Nicholas 118
Greenbury
 Nicholas 130, 145
Greene
 (N) 46
 Anne 39
 Elisabeth 45, 46
 John 150, 213
 Leonard 7
 Luke 39
 Margaret 150
 Margarett 150
 William 109, 114
Greenfeild
 Thomas 210
Gregory
 Charles 143, 159
Gresham
 John 31, 192
Grey
 John 86, 102
Griffen
 Lewis 165, 169, 182
 Robert 181
 Thomas 172

Griffeth
 Steevens 156
Griffin
 Robert 197
 Thomas 8, 16, 74,
  84, 209
Griffith
 David 116, 121
 Elisabeth 155
 Lewis 208
 Owen 112
Griggs
 John 109, 131, 138
Grigs
 John 124
Grodtwell
 George 52
Groome
 William 117, 145
Gross
 Elisabeth 96
 Roger 53
Grosse
 Roger 96
Grover
 John 192, 212, 224
Groves
 George 189
Grumwell
 George 209
Grunwin
 (N) 210
 Thomas 222
Guddrige
 Tymothy 161
Gugat
 Alice 53
 John 53
Guibert
 Joshua 92
Guilbert
 Elisabeth 173
 Thomas 173
Guin
 Richard 106
Guither
 Nicholas 149
Gun
 John 88
Gundary
 Gideon 97
Gundery
 Gideon 97
Gundry

Benjamin 81, 104
Gideon 104
Gunn
John 92, 136
Gunne
John 88
Gunnell
Edward 37, 38, 81,
99, 145, 155,
165, 169, 173,
174, 184
George 107, 108,
122, 145, 155,
165, 169, 173,
174, 184
Jane 97, 110
Gunnery
Benjamin 69
Gupton
Stephen 17, 20
William 17
Guyat
Alice 111
John 111
Guyatt
John 67
Guyn
Richard 83
Guyther
Nich. 209
Nicholas 16
Owen 17, 212
William 16, 18, 209
Gwin
Richard 90, 103,
130, 202, 214
Gwinn
Richard 229
Robert 222
Gwinne
Susanna 14
Gwither
Nicholas 149
Owen 172
William 149, 172,
174
Gylick
Mr. 32

Hacker
Thomas 83
Hacket
Theophilus 57

Hackett
Nicholas 83
Theophilus 202, 214
Thomas 229
Hackitt
Alice 158
Haffort
George 75
Haile
Oliver 89, 120
Hale
Robert 12
Hales
John 7
Haley
Mary 7
Halfehead
Jane 16
John 9, 16, 30, 108
Hall
Charles 183
Christopher 35
Henry 54, 194
John 197, 228
Jos. 32
Margaret 80
Margarett 86
Mary 65, 170, 174
Patrick 65, 75
Richard 170, 174,
204
Robert 78
Thomas 154, 178
Walter 7, 80, 86,
210
Hallee
John 89
Hallings
Thomas 225
Halloway
James 143, 229
Halls
John 118, 119
Hallyfeild
John 118
Hallyfield
John 35
Hambleton
Sarah 22
William 22, 39, 115
Hamillton
Jon. 39
Hamilton
John 210

Hamlton
    John 210
Hammet
    Martha 43
Hammon
    John 73
Hammond
    Elinor 18
    John 113
    Mary 113, 120
Hamond
    Daniel 143
Hampsted
    Nicholas 88
Hance
    John 37, 53, 134,
        149, 152, 159,
        168, 169, 183,
        184
    Sarah 184
Hancock
    Benjamin 2
    Stephen 150
Hancocke
    John 148
    Stephen 141
Handaker
    Anthony 113, 121
Handslipp
    Henry 77
Hans
    John 215
Hanslap
    Henry 221, 224, 226
Hanslapp
    Henry 167
Hanson
    Hans 217
    John 69, 121
    Martha 217
    Randolph 49, 59
    William 167, 181,
        224
Harbud
    Mary 91
    Sarah 91
    William 91
Harbut
    Sarah 105
    William 105
Hardacre
    Anthony 131
Hardy
    Ann 116

Hardye
    Ann 112
    Robert 112, 116
Harfoord
    Charles 169
Harford
    Charles 149, 183,
        184
    Edward 183
Harlings
    Thomas 92
Harmer
    Francis 190
    Timothy 46
Harmor
    Francis 223
Harnes
    Isaac 66, 76
Harness
    Elisabeth 65
    Isaac 8, 42
    Jacob 20, 65, 166,
        175
    Susanna 21, 65
    William 21, 65
Harnesse
    Susanna 86
Harney
    Isaac 69
Harnies
    Susanna 102
Harning
    (N) 32
Harnise
    Isaac 104
    Susanna 82
Harniss
    Elisabeth 86
    Jacob 86, 100
Harnisse
    Jacob 120
Harper
    William 210
Harpin
    Thomas 172, 180
Harrington
    Charles 5
    John 17, 18
    Mary 5
    Richard 225
Harris
    Elisabeth 200
    Henry 40
    Jackelina 2, 3

Husbands
    Edward 209
Hussey
    Thomas 78, 90, 137,
        140, 149, 201
Hussy
    Thomas 211
Hutching
    Francis 75
Hutchings
    Charles 54, 84
    Francis 110, 111
    Richard 130
Hutchins
    Charles 41, 48, 72
    Francis 70, 193
    Hugh 212
    Richard 75, 130
Hutchinson
    Samuell 132
Hyde
    Henry 209
Hyland
    John 106, 169, 171,
        174
Hynson
    (N) 178
    Ann 110
    John 33
    Richard 32
    Thomas 79, 82, 110,
        125, 178

Illingsworth
    Sarah 24, 47
Inclock
    Henry 72
Ingelesbie
    Bridgett 159
Inglesbie
    Bridgett 151
    Robert 151, 175
Inglesby
    Bridgett 143
    Robert 228
Inglish
    Dennis 171, 174
    Ed. 33
    Eduard 216
    Edward 7, 8, 24,
        28, 33, 42, 43,
        44, 45, 46, 69,
        97, 186

    John 148, 150, 171,
        174, 176, 185,
        220
Ingram
    John 54
Innes
    Thomas 15
Insley
    Andrew 6
Ireland
    John 55, 71, 91
Iron
    Symon 83
Irons
    Simon 48
    Symon 61
Ives
    James 55, 91, 120,
        146
    Martha 120

Jackson
    Eduard 200
    Edward 124, 133,
        153
    Elinor 124
    Ellenor 133
    Ezekiel 201
    Ezekiell 223
    John 73
    Mary 43
    Thomas 91, 130,
        132, 133, 152
James
    Abell 118
    Anne 99
    Charles 165, 221,
        223
    Eduard 215
    John 38
Jarboe
    John 3
Jardins
    Jean 67
Jaward
    John 32
Jaxson
    John 225
    Richard 217
Jeff
    Thomas 10
Jeffe
    Thomas 58, 119

Page 265

219
Salomon 209
Samuel 54, 142
Samuell 177
Sanders 54
Sara 95, 125, 158,
    161
Sarah 11, 12, 21,
    48, 56, 57, 87,
    94, 98
Thomas 14, 49, 122,
    142, 162, 182,
    184, 209, 215
William 6, 14, 21,
    22, 44, 57, 66,
    67, 73, 74, 81,
    98, 115, 122,
    124, 126, 151,
    199, 226
Jourdain
    John 35, 117, 204
    Thomas 16, 24
Jourdaine
    John 50
Jourdein
    John 117
Jourdins
    Jean Des 67
Jouse
    Jane 174
Jowles
    Col. 196
    Henry 1, 3, 4, 19,
    23, 68, 145,
    128, 131, 157,
    164, 176, 202
    Sybell 145
Judd
    Mich. 208
    Michael 219
    Michaell 227
Junis
    Thomas 62
Jynifer
    Jacob 121

Kaine
    William 9
Kathrope
    William 205
Keeble
    John 145
Keech

    James 32
Keefe
    Constant 22
Keely
    John 73
Keen
    Rich. 209
Keene
    Edward 77, 85, 155
    Francis 37, 73, 126
    Richard 109
    William 112, 116
Keetch
    James 202
Keirck
    John 134
Keirke
    John 105
Keiton
    Thomas 133
Kelley
    William 205
Kellye
    William 226
Kemball
    John 146
Kenneday
    James 123
Kenniday
    James 6, 40
    Mary 6, 40
Kenniman
    John 192
Kent
    William 4, 17, 22,
    178, 220
Kerby
    Walter 2, 138, 170,
    196, 206, 211,
    216
Kerwan
    Peter 232
Kerwin
    William 205
Keryon
    J. 44
Keverne
    Ann 101
Kewellyn
    John 39
Key
    William 84, 85, 98,
    108, 122, 140,
    142, 190

King
  Allexander 60
  Johanna 21
  John 209
  Thomas 21, 71
  William 109, 113,
    124, 131, 133,
    138, 179
Kingston
  Thomas 195
Kinlowes
  Henry 171
Kirby
  Walter 132
Kirested
  Jochem 79
Kirke
  John 17, 84, 107,
    114, 116, 119,
    141, 148, 171
Kirkum
  WIlliam 24
Kirstede
  Jochem 166
Knap
  Robert 200, 211
Knapp
  Elisabeth 211
  Robert 213
  widow 211
Knighton
  Thomas 75, 223
Knott
  Capt. 46

Lacells
  Gervais 218
Ladd
  Edward 197
  Richard 40, 41, 42,
    44, 52, 53, 68,
    74, 79, 82, 89,
    96, 111, 194,
    207
  Rozamond 42
Ladde
  Richard 67
Ladds
  Jane 155
  William 155, 168,
    193
Ladford
  Arthur 166

Laine
  Samuel 81
Lamb
  Anthony 208
Lambert
  Ann 31
  George 183
Lambertson
  Henry 193
Lampton
  Marke 140
Land
  Philip 133, 145,
    158, 160, 212
  Phylip 127
Lane
  Margaret 100, 105
  Margarett 199, 224
  Mary 205
  Samuel 70, 74, 78
  Samuell 20, 91, 92,
    99, 100, 105,
    197, 199, 224,
    225
  Walter 209
Langham
  Josias 122, 169
Langley
  George 20, 68
  Joseph 223
  Robert 120
Langworth
  William 97, 108
Lanham
  Josias 67, 69, 84,
    98
Lanthorne
  Marke 137
Lanworth
  William 101
Laremore
  Alex. 134
  Alexander 119
  Allexander 102
Large
  Robert 7, 81, 131
Larimore
  Alexander 63, 65,
    115
Larkey
  Nicholas 115
Larkie
  Mary 65
  Nicholas 65

Page 271

Meekings
    Richard 128, 165
Meekins
    Richard 169, 173
Melem
    John 38
Menock
    Mich. 174
    Michaell 170, 174,
      176
Mercury
    Richard 32
Meredith
    Lewes 161
    William 39
Meridale
    Thomas 197
Meriton
    John 226
Merredeth
    Lewis 132
Merredith
    Lewes 138
Merrekin
    Hugh 90
Merridale
    Thomas 197
Merriken
    Christian 62
    Hugh 61, 62
    John 62
Merrikin
    Hugh 77, 101
Miccell
    John 65
Miceell
    John 85
Michell
    Jame 79
    John 144
    William 73
Michener
    John 92, 193
    Sarah 193
Middleton
    Robert 145
Midgely
    Richard 121
Midgley
    Richard 69
Midleton
    Robert 53, 70
Miles
    Francis 30

Henry 66, 78
James 91
John 79, 91, 93,
    144, 162
Miller
    (N) 208
    Mich. 190, 209,
      217, 218
    Michael 82
    Michaell 11, 26,
      28, 36, 56, 58,
      71, 83, 84, 85,
      97, 98, 108,
      182, 197
    Michell 82
    Miles 11
Millington
    Samuell 165, 169
Mills
    (N) 208
    James 55, 56, 58,
      68, 124, 154,
      203, 231
    John 79
    Peter 155, 157,
      159, 161, 163,
      165, 194, 233
    William 53
Mines
    Marjory 225
Ming
    Edward 72, 116
Mirax
    Richard 217
Mitchell
    Henry 210
    John 82
    William 10, 203
Mitchill
    John 117
Molines
    Dr. 208
Moll
    John 186
Mollins
    Dr. 208
Mondidier
    Anthony de 57
Moore
    James 1, 2, 3, 19,
      166, 202, 216
    Mary 26
    Richard 87, 101,
      108, 118

Mooretun
  John 111
Moorton
  John 110
More
  William 146
Moretun
  John 96
Morgan
  Eduard 207, 210
  Edward 196
  Thomas 20
  William 12
Morlin
  Francis 41
Morrice
  Penelope 204
  Peneloppy 206
  Penelopy 206
  Richard 206
  Thomas 218
Morris
  James 96, 110, 111
  Katharine 27
  Robert 27
  Thomas 20, 127
Morty
  Stephen 209
Moss
  Richard 148
Motts
  Joseph 129
Mould
  John 102, 114
Mounford
  John 31
Mountague
  Henry 123
  William 7, 24
Moy
  Elisabeth 116
Mudd
  (N) 208
  Thomas 209
Muffett
  Elisabeth 224
  William 224
Muffitt
  Elisabeth 185
  William 185
Munkiastor
  Elisabeth 116
Munkister
  James 116

Munn
  John 15, 103
Muns
  John 126
Murfey
  John 60
Murphey
  James 25, 48, 61,
    134, 140, 200,
    225
Murphy
  James 81, 119, 161,
    213
Murty
  Stephen 13, 14, 71,
    109, 148
Murvin
  John 216
Murwin
  Barbara 191
  John 191
Muschamp
  Geo. 31
Musgrove
  Cuthbeard 72

Nance
  Rowland 57, 81,
    101, 194
Napp
  Robert 106, 139
Nappe
  Robert 24
Nash
  Richard 82, 164,
    167
Naylor
  Abraham 223
  Elisabeth 195
  Joseph 223
Neale
  (N) 151
  Elisabeth 32
  Jonathon 165
  Rebecca 74
  Samuel 74
  William 14, 32
Neales
  Jonathon 153
Neck
  John 191
Needham
  William 158, 164,

O'Kaine
   Martha 16, 44
   Rickart 16, 24, 44
   widow 24
O'Rurrke
   James 78
Oare
   Allen 209
Odery
   William 223
Offley
   John 6, 193, 208,
     217, 228
Ofley
   John 144
Ogden
   Sarah 43
Ogdine
   Sarah 44
Ogdon
   James 36
Oldfeild
   George 104, 148,
     157, 164, 169,
     170, 171, 174,
     181, 186
Oldfield
   George 38
   Peternella 28
Oliver
   (N) 208
   James 22
   Thomas 16, 24
Omelia
   Bryan 155
Ope
   Thomas 88
Orrick
   James 181
   Mary 181
Orronck
   James 79
Orrouck
   James 90
Orruck
   James 77
Orrurcke
   James 34
   Mary 34
Orrurke
   James 27
Orson
   Elisabeth 37
Osborne

John 230
Thomas 2
William 87, 88, 92,
   155, 180, 188,
   202, 203, 212,
   231
Osbourne
   Thomas 51, 100,
     118, 149, 168,
     177
   William 88, 92,
     136, 145, 155,
     165, 171
Oulson
   Peter 44
Overton
   Thomas 97, 107,
     108, 110, 122
Owen
   John 29, 51, 66
   Joseph 233
Owner
   John 232
Oxman
   John 83

Pack
   Edward 112
Padeley
   (N) 205
Page
   Robert 225
Paget
   Elisabeth 17
   Thomas 17, 22
Pagett
   Thomas 55
Paine
   Jane 47
   Matthew 27
Painter
   Judith 158, 173
   Nic. 74
   Nicholas 61, 62,
     63, 64, 196,
     226, 230
Palmer
   Daniell 232
   William 111, 122,
     176
Paper
   Mary 209
Paramore

John 126
Paris
  John 198
Parish
  Eduard 228
  Edward 89, 143, 150
Park
  Robert 104
Parke
  Robert 182, 197
Parker
  (N) 46
  Elisabeth 138
  George 4, 17, 27,
    28, 33, 34, 37,
    42, 43, 44, 45,
    46, 53, 66, 71,
    77, 83, 92, 99,
    100, 111, 117,
    130, 134, 136,
    158, 160, 164,
    168, 183, 184,
    198, 199, 210,
    215, 216, 218,
    219, 225
  Henry 141, 151,
    154, 209
  John 18
  Judith 134, 168
  Mr. 71
  Thomas 138, 190,
    193
  William 5, 37, 53,
    68, 134, 148,
    149, 152, 158,
    168, 169, 174,
    184
Parkes
  Robert 169, 191
Parks
  Robert 181, 218
Parnafee
  Robert 225
Parrish
  Clare 150
  Edward 77, 150, 151
Parsons
  Father 232
  Nath. 162
  Nathaniel 75
  Nathaniell 127, 177
Parvinge
  Michaell 103
Pascall

George 136
James 136
Maudline 136
Paschall
  James 140, 217
  Maudlin 140
  Maudline 217
Pate
  William 152
Pather
  Mary 168
  Richard 168
Patison
  Thomas 209
Patisson
  Thomas 226
Patricks
  Anne 54
Pattison
  James 130, 131,
    133, 142, 157,
    204, 206, 210
  John 113, 202
  Margarett 210
Pattyson
  James 143
Paul
  Porten 33, 120
Pawson
  Henry 112
  John 112
Paxston
  Hugh 54
Paxton
  Hugh 32
Peacock
  Richard 140
Peacocke
  Richard 129, 199
Pean
  James 101, 106, 165
Pearce
  John 138
Pearle
  Henry 100, 125
  Thomas 121
Pearly
  William 66
Pearte
  John 195
Peaseley
  John 148
Peasley
  Joseph 60

widow 27
Rider
    Robert 75, 211
Ridge
    Thomas 207, 219
Ridgeley
    Robert 57, 95, 161,
        162
Ridgely
    (N) 46, 208
    Charles 31
    Henry 10, 100, 120,
        204
    Martha 189, 211,
        219
    Robert 18, 61, 65,
        87, 98, 112,
        117, 125, 128,
        129, 137, 144,
        146, 171, 173,
        176, 185, 189,
        211, 213, 219
Ridgley
    Robert 138
Ridgly
    Robert 231
Rigbie
    James 73, 175
Rigby
    James 52, 61, 62,
        68, 77, 218
Rigeley
    Mr. 77
Rigg
    Geo. 32
Right
    Richard 28
Ring
    Richard 153
Ringe
    Richard 160
Ringgold
    James 23, 26, 28,
        44, 97, 108,
        123, 140, 142,
        181
    Mary 142
Ringold
    James 58, 85, 197,
        199
    Maj. 160
Rix
    John 44
    Mary 44

Roades
    Abraham 67
    Frances 67
Robbins
    John 134
Roberson
    John 102
    Mary 102
    Robert 79
Roberts
    Andrew 196, 203
    Edward 12, 15, 18,
        142
    Jane 196
    John 208
    Katherine 60
    William 31
Robins
    George 23, 188, 205
    John 134
    Rob. 65
    Robert 21, 71, 126
Robinson
    Anne 223
    John 221
    Thomas 32
Robotham
    George 205
Robson
    William 177
Robynson
    John 86
    Mary 86
Roche
    Mrs. de la 77
Rochford
    Mich. 233
    Michael 13
    Michaell 14, 65,
        94, 158, 181
Rochfort
    Michaell 208
Rodaway
    John 4
Rodoway
    John 3
Roe
    Edward 12
    Mary 12
Roelands
    Robert 71
Roelants
    Margery 82
    Richard 160

Sacker
　Edward 56
Salbury
　John 137
　William 97
Salisbury
　George 190
　John 189, 190, 199,
　　201, 221, 223
　Sarah 199
　William 189, 190,
　　199, 201, 221,
　　223
Salley
　Benjamin 232
Salmon
　(N) 71, 76, 203
　Thomas 72
Salsbury
　William 38, 182
Sanders
　Edward 191
　John 73
Saunders
　James 21, 87, 102
　John 37, 126
Sauvage
　Edward 35, 47
Savin
　William 171, 181,
　　221, 229
Sawyer
　Capt. 210
Sayer
　Peter 192, 229
Sayles
　Clement 24
Scarbrough
　Matthew 162
Scorey
　Guil. 129
　William 120
Scot
　Mary 192
Scott
　Cuthbert 117
　James 98, 115, 124,
　　192, 229
　John 93
　Mary 229
Searcher
　Henry 146
Seares
　Joseph 81

Sedgewick
　Thomas 192, 223,
　　224
Sedwicke
　Thomas 182
Seeres
　Joseph 37, 38
Semme
　Marmaduke 58, 118
Sems
　(N) 208
　Marmaduke 208
Serscife
　James 209
Seth
　Barbara 132
　Jacob 132
Sewall
　John 14
　Nic. 88
　Nicholas 136
　Thomas 42
Seward
　Josias 216
Sewell
　Thomas 16
Sexton
　Patrick 207
Shacock
　Roger 85, 122
Shacocke
　Roger 140, 142
Shadwell
　John 147
Shanke
　Thomas 95
Shankes
　John 221
Shanks
　John 222
Sharp
　William 74, 146
Sharpe
　William 90, 105,
　　212, 230
Shaw
　Gervis 129
　John 227
　Nich. 165, 223
　Ralph 189
　William 182
Shawe
　Gervas 76
　Gervase 80

Ann 178
Daniel 147, 170
Daniell 151, 167
Emperor 194
Francis 78, 79, 90,
    160
George 91
Henry 183, 187, 214
Margarett 78
Margrett 78
Mathew 132, 225
Matthew 132, 156
Nathan 12, 20, 47,
    100
Nathaniell 233
Richard 97, 98,
    100, 127, 209
Rob. 90
Robert 32, 82, 99,
    100, 149, 178
Thomas 144, 147,
    154, 155, 156,
    164, 167, 174,
    220
William 49, 51,
    134, 170, 202
Smithson
    Thomas 209
    William 214, 217
Smoote
    Richard 127
Smott
    Garrat 201
Snell
    Thomas 23, 67
Snow
    Marmaduke 27
Snowden
    Richard 192
Sockwell
    Thomas 32
Sollers
    John 92, 99, 100
Solomon
    Robert 40
Sommers
    Roger 182
Sotherne
    Valentine 118
Sourton
    Francis 134
Southebe
    William 155, 180
Southerne

Valentine 2, 51,
    100
Sparkes
    (N) 44
Sparnon
    Joseph 171
Speake
    Thomas 107, 222
Spence
    Ann 93, 116
    David 93, 116
Spencer
    Francis 27, 68
    Mary 27, 68
    Walter 4
Spernon
    Joseph 176, 181,
        184, 185, 216
Spincke
    Thomas 47, 204
Spinke
    John 146, 171
    Margarett 146
    Thomas 206, 209
Sprigg
    Hester 8
    Thomas 101, 119
Sprigge
    Thomas 94
Spring Neck 189
Spry
    Henry 108
    Johanna 14
    Mary 7
    Thomas 104
Sprye
    Christopher 81, 131
    Henry 57
    Tho. 156
    Thomas 155, 156,
        186
Stafford
    Sarah 68, 73
    William 68, 73, 77
Stagg
    Margaret 97, 179
    Margarett 89, 93,
        132
    Thomas 91, 93, 132,
        179
Stagge
    Margarett 79, 86
    Thomas 79
Staines

John 159, 183, 215, 216

Staires
Bennett 197

Stallings
Richard 130, 152, 179

Standle
Elisabeth 74
William 74

Standley
William 82

Standly
William 111

Staneley
John 106

Stanely
John 215

Stanesby
John 14, 99, 107, 110, 155, 162
Mary 14

Stanford
John 86, 92, 136

Stanley
John 23, 25, 188, 189
Mary 6
William 6, 10, 40

Stanly
John 189, 231

Stanlye
John 182

Stansby
John 107, 184

Staplefort
Raymond 208

Stares
Bennett 181

Starling
Thomas 109, 128

Staveley
James 153

Stavely
Frances 204, 223
James 70, 71, 72, 97, 98, 203, 204, 223
John 204, 205, 223
Mr. 76

Staynes
John 149, 169

Steevens
Charles 2

Col. 229
Edward 55, 107
Giles 89, 120
Guiles 121
Henry 7
John 24, 146, 149, 168
Mary 177
Mr. 95
Sarah 89, 120
Symon 150
William 9, 10, 12, 21, 48, 54, 55, 61, 66, 75, 78, 85, 87, 123, 134, 135, 146, 154, 162, 172, 177, 179, 183, 220, 226, 230

Steevenson
Anne 98, 124
Edward 58
John 91
Philip 54, 56, 98, 124

Steeventon
John 106

Stennart
(N) 45
Cornelius 46

Stephens
John 20
William 54, 116, 147, 180, 210

Sterling
Thomas 68, 75, 130

Stevens
Symon 98
William 99, 143, 144, 200

Steventon
John 101

Steward
David 32

Stiles
(N) 71, 76
Nath. 72
Nathaniell 97, 197

Stimson
Rachaell 1, 41

Stinchcomb
John 187

Stinchcombe
(N) 35

John 186
Nathaniell 14, 186
Thomas 14
Thomasin 186
Thomazin 14
Stoakes
Anne 161
Peter 161
Stocket
Henry 41
Stockett
Fr. 77
Francis 74, 81,
169, 175, 228,
233
Henry 76, 167, 181,
189, 197, 203,
204, 224, 227,
228, 233
Katherine 228, 233
Stockfish
Henry Cloy 225
Stockley
James 5
Stone
John 37, 65, 73,
76, 103, 116,
126, 145, 167,
201, 202, 213,
228
Margery 73
Mathew 201, 213
William 41, 44
Stookes
Peter 90
Streete
Francis 113
Strong
Capt. 46
Elisabeth 111
Sturme
Rachell 73
Richard 73, 99,
125, 153, 166
Styles
(N) 203
Sudler
Ciccily 216
Joseph 216
Suell
Thomas 209
Sugden
Thomas 112
Sulberry

John 123
Sulevant
Patrick 82
Sulivant
Patrick 110
Sumers
Benjamin 220
Roger 189
Summer
Benjamin 143, 173
Summers
Benjamin 162
Sunderbee
Thomas 18
Sunderland
John 75, 110, 130,
152
Surton
Alice 127
Francis 127
Suttle
John 103, 119, 152,
154, 155, 159,
161
Mary 152, 155, 159
Sutton
George 201
Hester 151, 158
Phillip 13
Swalwell
John 197
Swanson
Eduard 229
Edward 193
Swayn
John 200
Swerett
Philip 208
Swetnam
Eduard 199, 206,
210, 217
Rich. 209
Swinfer
Francis 216
Swiny
John 8
Sybrey
Jonathon 50
Sydes
Peter 56
Sykes
Ann 32
Symons
Henry 206

Synklers
    William 216
Synnot
    Garret 51

Taillor
    Col. 75, 224
    Lawrence 124
    Robert 44
    Samuell 166
    Thomas 35, 65, 67,
        74, 76, 77, 78,
        79, 81, 85, 123,
        124, 143, 146,
        152, 156, 160,
        164, 166, 168,
        173, 185
Tailor
    Lawrence 199
    Thomas 197
Talbott
    Edward 185
    Elisabeth 185
Tall
    Anthony 55, 65, 85
    Elisabeth 55, 65,
        85
    Philip 85
Taney
    Mich. 44
    Michaell 70
Tanney
    William 74
Tannyard 195
Tant
    James 32
Tasker
    Thomas 91, 105,
        190, 193, 209
Tassall
    Elisabeth 84, 107,
        114
    Francis 84, 105,
        107, 114, 116,
        119, 134, 148,
        155, 171
Tate
    John 89
Tattersell
    Lawrence 32
Tawney
    Michaell 36, 44,
        52, 182

Taylor
    Arthur 29, 182
    Batt. 105
    Daniel 179
    Daniell 1
    Grace 13
    Henry 18, 32
    John 13, 182, 203,
        204, 216
    John Evans 210
    Joseph 74
    Katharine 18
    Laurence 219
    Lawrence 139
    Mary 4, 194
    Morgan 35
    Richard 191
    Robert 4, 36, 44,
        53, 66, 67, 187,
        194, 207, 227
    Samuell 172, 194,
        204
    Sarah 216
    Theresia 191
    Thomas 24, 35, 50,
        71, 77, 90, 105,
        137, 150, 154,
        180, 193, 197,
        212, 214, 215,
        216, 218, 224,
        225, 227, 228,
        233
    Walter 216
    William 199, 222
Teagle
    Nathaniell 24
Temple
    William 200, 207
Tench
    Francis 58
    Mary 58
Tenhill
    Mr. 209
Tennahill
    Andrew 72
Tennison
    Absalom 234
    John 234
    Justinian 234
Tewell
    David 142
Teye
    John 55
Teyne

Francis 72
Theobald
    Clement 5
Theobalds
    Clement 199, 200,
        204, 206, 227
    John 199
    William 175, 204,
        206
Therrell
    Margaret 37
Therrill
    Margaret 30
Thomas
    John 101, 145, 152,
        153, 158, 170,
        181, 194
    John Hussey 209
    Macom 60, 134
    Rice 95
    Thomas 188
    Tristram 161
    Tristrum 150
    widow 10
    William 35, 47,
        188, 209
Thompson
    Arthur 222
    George 209, 233
    James 80, 93, 109,
        114, 207, 219
    John 117, 130, 131,
        158, 160, 187,
        204, 220, 221,
        229
    Robert 210, 228
    Sarah 187
    Thomas 217
    William 70, 81,
        145, 159
Thomson
    James 77
Thorley
    Edward 65, 78, 89,
        99
    Mary 78, 89
Thornborough
    Rowland 38
Thornton
    Sara 150
Thorpe
    (N) 46
    Hannah 43, 44
    Hester 43

Joseph 43
Martha 43
Mary 43
Newton 46
Roger 8, 17, 28,
    33, 42, 43, 45,
    46, 111
Sarah 43
Thorton
    Sara 141
Tilchman
    William 228
Tiler
    Robert 14
Tilghman
    Mary 110
    Richard 110
    William 144
Tilliard
    John 219
Tillison
    John 54
Tison
    William 8
Todd
    John 19, 34, 68
    Lancellot 19, 20,
        34, 73
    Lancellott 68
    Lancelott 164, 175
    Thomas 34, 57, 68,
        73, 171
Todde
    Lancellott 68
Tolley
    Thomas 139, 163
Tolson
    An 104
Tomkins
    Gilles 79
Tooll
    David 33
Toulson
    Andrew 200
    Anne 60
    William 123
Tove
    Samuell 199, 206
Tovy
    Sam. 149
    Samuel 98
    Samuell 7, 10, 23,
        26, 36, 40, 105,
        117, 163, 169,

Wallstone
  John 92, 139
Walson
  John 134
Walston
  John 80, 87
Walstone
  John 88, 92
Walter
  Daniel 154
Walters
  Alexander 138, 161
  John 140
Walton
  William 230
Ward
  (N) 208
  Elisabeth 213
  Henry 109, 112,
    114, 178, 209,
    216
  James 211
  John 172, 181, 184
  Mary 71, 72, 82,
    114, 124, 140
  Mathew 82
  Matthew 124, 185
  William 72, 114,
    159
Warde
  Mary 23, 25, 38, 52
  Mathew 99
  Matthew 23, 25, 38,
    48
  William 52
Ware
  John 80
  Mary 15
Warefeild
  Richard 230
Wareing
  Basill 184
Warfeild
  (N) 117
Waring
  Humphrey 127
Warman
  Stephen 32
Warner
  Christopher 72
  Elisabeth 56
  George 69
  Thomas 56
Warren

Henry 232
Hum. 167, 180
Humphrey 70, 79,
  135, 172, 186,
  194, 195, 202
Humphry 53
Margarett 160
Thomas 58, 108,
  121, 190
Wasson
  John 63
Wast
  Peter 226
Waters
  Alex. 138
Waterton
  John 14, 27, 29,
    30, 49, 51, 62,
    70, 145, 155,
    169, 193, 200,
    207, 218, 227
Watkins
  (N) 77
  Francis 57, 145,
    153, 158
  John 77, 89
  Lydia 90, 100
  Thomas 90, 98, 100,
    120, 160
Watson
  Anthony 199, 211
  Jane 187
  John 30, 45
Watts
  Charles 222
  Eduard 222
  Emma 222
  Jane 95
  Joane 95, 126
  John 48
  Peter 31, 46, 49,
    59, 61, 130
  Robert 197
  William 27, 31, 32,
    40, 54, 106,
    221, 222
Wattson
  Anthony 219
  John 127, 154
Waugh
  John 170
Waughop
  Joane 30, 49
  John 30, 49

Wauhab
  Thomas 210
Waushop
  John 61
Way
  Richard 72
Weapon
  Thomas 147
Webb
  John 74, 111
  Richard 10, 31, 98
  widow 10
Webber
  Leon. 43
  Leonard 33
Weddill
  Roger 93
Wedge
  John 54, 69, 117,
    157, 168, 190
  Susanna 157, 168,
    190
Wedill
  Roger 225
Weecks
  Joseph 108
Weekes
  Joseph 1, 2, 3, 4,
    100, 132, 170
Weire
  John 92
  Major 80
Welch
  John 185
  William 31
Welles
  Tho. 33, 46
  Thomas 33, 46
Wells
  Col. 172, 211
  George 36, 80, 87,
    88, 92, 120,
    133, 142, 153,
    155, 163, 172,
    203, 219
  James 194
  John 141, 144, 152,
    210, 214, 217
  Martha 141, 144,
    214
  Thomas 33
  Tobias 11, 59
  William 73
Welsh

John 21, 53, 65,
  77, 91, 100,
  136, 140, 192,
  195, 197, 218,
  223, 230
Major 224
Mr. 77
Welshe
  John 77
West
  Peter 153
Westbury
  Margaret 29, 36
  William 29, 36, 51
Whale
  Charles 32
Wharfield
  Richard 61
Wharton
  Thomas 128, 145,
    160, 210
Wheeler
  Anne 164
  Elisabeth 5, 52
  James 5, 52, 166,
    175, 176, 180,
    199, 200, 203,
    206
  John 11, 21, 71,
    109, 145, 160,
    201, 210
  Major 192
Wheler
  James 224
Whethers
  Elisabeth 96, 100
  Samuell 90, 96
Whetstone
  Stephen 2, 6, 26
White
  Ambrose 154, 162
  Ambross 177
  Comfort 154, 162,
    177
  Elisabeth 72
  Gustavius 128
  Guy 6, 161
  John 8, 11, 36, 44,
    56, 123, 138
  Kazia 138
  Kezia 92
  Philis 128
  Rebecca 32
  Richard 188, 205

Samuell 31
Stephen 113, 121
Whithers
  Elisabeth 151
  Samuell 151
Whittington
  John 96
Whittinton
  John 139
Whittle
  Thomas 190
Whitton
  Barbara 169
  Richard 38
  Thomas 169
Wiborow
  John 218
Wickes
  (N) 178
  Joseph 26, 50, 141,
    144, 196
Wicks
  Joseph 76
Wigan
  William 43
Wiggun
  William 43
Wilcox
  Henry 69
Wilkinson
  Ann 201
  Elisabeth 199, 219
  John 201
  William 198, 199,
    219
Wilkisson
  Elisabeth 189
  William 189
William
  Morgan 124
Williams
  David 28, 30, 51,
    54, 87
  James 202, 216
  Jane 28, 30, 63,
    117, 119, 139,
    150, 154, 156
  Jeremiah 36, 44,
    52, 70
  John 187
  Joseph 221
  Mary 221
  Morgan 133, 146,
    157

Owen 124, 139
Ralph 37
Richard 4
Robert 193
Rowland 94, 154
William 20, 63,
  117, 119, 139,
  150, 154, 156,
  187
Willis
  John 104, 153, 168,
    182, 189, 190,
    199, 201, 221,
    223
Willmot
  John 38
Willoby
  William 135, 147
Willson
  Anne 131
  Richard 57
  Robert 57, 83, 101,
    166
  William 131, 133,
    159
Willymot
  John 179
Wilmer
  Simon 213
  Symon 93
Wilmott
  John 38, 153
Wilson
  Ann 138
  George 5
  Richard 57
  Robert 1, 81, 99
  Thomas 21, 55
  William 138
Winchester
  Isaac 2, 76, 87,
    91, 101, 108,
    133, 146, 157,
    170, 177, 197
  Isaack 118, 192
  John 2, 26, 36, 59,
    124, 133, 146,
    157, 170
Winckles
  Elisabeth 213
Wincles
  Elisabeth 150
Winclos
  widow 149

Winder
John 162
Windey
John 112
Window
Thomas 210
Wine
Francis 145, 159
Wingfield
Thomas 14
Winkcles
Edward 125
Elisabeth 125
Winkles
Edward 98
Winley
John 29
Richard 29, 51, 66
Winn
John 187
Winsmore
Robert 123
Winsore
Alexander 49
Wintcles
Elisabeth 74
Wintersell
William 115
Witham
John 3, 23
Withed
Mary 228
Withers
Samuell 205, 225, 229
Wittington
John 106
Witton
Barbara 164
Jane 176
John 176
Thomas 164
Wollman
Richard 74, 131
Wolman
Richard 58
Wood
John 19, 47, 51, 60, 191, 210, 227, 228
Thomas 60
Woodas
John 141
Woodfine

John 152, 158
Woodhous
John 150
Woodhouse
John 150
Woodward
Edeth 19, 28
John 78, 81, 90, 166
Woolcot
John 10
Woolcott
John 30
Woolf
Charles 112
Woolford
Roger 214
Woollford
Roger 9
Woollman
Richard 7, 125
Woolman
Alice 192, 214, 225
Mr. 149
Richard 93, 150, 192, 205, 214, 225
Woolverton
Robert 24
Woorkeman
Joane 108
Wooton
Symon 113, 157, 164, 179
Wootters
John 31
Wootton
Simon 4
Susanna 4
Worgan
William 147
Worgin
William 13, 19
Workeman
Anthony 108, 216
Workman
Anthony 50, 51, 206, 211
Joane 50
Worrall
Margarett 113, 135
Worrell
Robert 21
Wright

Abigall 107
Ant. 43
Anthony 43
Arthur 11, 107,
    146, 168
Auther 146
George 148
Ishmaell 179
John 26, 58, 105,
    143, 184
William 153, 228
Wroth
    James 223
Wyborow
    John 181, 197
Wyn
    John 117
Wynall
    John 182, 224
    Katherine 182
Wyndall
    Capt. 209
Wyne
    Elisabeth 189, 194
    Francis 70, 77,
        137, 138, 184,
        189, 194, 224
Wynes
    Samuell 194
Wynn
    Frances 213
    John 137, 154, 156,
        187
Wynnall
    John 212
    Katherine 224
Wynne
    (N) 208
    John 144, 150
    Thomas 18
Wynns
    John 34

Yate
    George 57, 81, 89,
        166
Yates
    George 101, 210
    John 16
    Sarah 214
Yeend
    Anne 42, 43, 45, 46
Yeo

Semelia 172
Yeoman
    Robert 35
Yorke's Hope 184
Yorke
    William 184, 207,
        218
Young
    Lawrence 151, 175
Younge
    George 75
    William 56

Index of Equity Cases

www.ingramcontent.com/pod-product-compliance
Lightning Source LLC
Chambersburg PA
CBHW060151280326
41932CB00012B/1721